(250) 564-4454

2005 EDITION

A GUIDE TO THE YOUTH CRIMINAL JUSTICE ACT

Lee Tustin, B.A., B.Ed., M.Ed.
Robert E. Lutes, Q.C.

LexisNexis®
Butterworths

A Guide to the Youth Criminal Justice Act, 2005 Edition

© LexisNexis Canada Inc. 2004
December 2004

All rights reserved. No part of this publication may be reproduced, stored in any material form (including photocopying or storing it in any medium by electronic means and whether or not transiently or incidentally to some other use of this publication) without the written permission of the copyright holder except in accordance with the provisions of the Copyright Act. Applications for the copyright holder's written permission to reproduce any part of this publication should be addressed to the publisher.

Warning: The doing of an unauthorized act in relation to a copyrighted work may result in both a civil claim for damages and criminal prosecution.

Members of the LexisNexis Group worldwide

Canada	LexisNexis Canada Inc, 123 Commerce Valley Dr E, MARKHAM, Ontario
Argentina	Abeledo Perrot, Jurisprudencia Argentina and Depalma, BUENOS AIRES
Australia	Butterworths, a Division of Reed International Books Australia Pty Ltd, CHATSWOOD, New South Wales
Austria	ARD Betriebsdienst and Verlag Orac, VIENNA
Chile	Publitecsa and Conosur Ltda, SANTIAGO DE CHILE
Czech Republic	Orac sro, PRAGUE
France	Éditions du Juris-Classeur SA, PARIS
Hong Kong	Butterworths Asia (Hong Kong), HONG KONG
Hungary	Hvg Orac, BUDAPEST
India	Butterworths India, NEW DELHI
Ireland	Butterworths (Ireland) Ltd, DUBLIN
Italy	Giuffré, MILAN
Malaysia	Malayan Law Journal Sdn Bhd, KUALA LUMPUR
New Zealand	Butterworths of New Zealand, WELLINGTON
Poland	Wydawnictwa Prawnicze PWN, WARSAW
Singapore	Butterworths Asia, SINGAPORE
South Africa	Butterworth Publishers (Pty) Ltd, DURBAN
Switzerland	Stämpfli Verlag AG, BERNE
United Kingdom	Butterworths Tolley, a Division of Reed Elsevier (UK), LONDON, WC2A
USA	LexisNexis, DAYTON, Ohio

Library and Archives Canada Cataloguing in Publication

Tustin, Lee
    A guide to the Youth Criminal Justice Act / Lee Tustin, Robert E. Lutes. — 2005 ed.

Includes text of Youth Criminal Justice Act.
Includes index.
ISBN 0-433-44810-5

1. Canada. Youth Criminal Justice Act. 2. Juvenile justice, Administration of — Canada. I. Lutes, Robert E. (Robert Edison), 1946- II. Title.

KE9445.A323T88 2004   345.71'08   C2004-906190-9
KF9780.ZA2T88 2004

Printed and bound in Canada.

DEDICATION

To my soul mate, Stephen, the only inspiration I ever need. And, to my two best friends, Erika and Jordan, who are always by my side.

Lee

In memory of my mother and mentor, Ruth Deware, who deserves the credit for any goodness I might bring to the table.

Bob

ABOUT THE AUTHORS

Lee Tustin, B.A., B.Ed., M.Ed., has an Ontario Teacher's Certificate and a graduate diploma in social work, law and administration. She has an extensive background in all of the areas that deal with youth in conflict. She is currently a Senior Policy Analyst for youth justice in Ontario. She is the author of a book on the *Young Offenders Act* entitled *Caught in the Act: A User's Guide to the Youth Justice System and Young Offenders Act*. She is also on the editorial board for the looseleaf service *Annotated Youth Criminal Justice Act Service* published by LexisNexis Canada.

Robert Edison Lutes, Q.C., received a B.Sc. from Mount Allison University in 1969, an LL.B. from the University of New Brunswick in 1973 and an LL.M. from Kings College at the University of London in 1974. After working in private practice from 1975 to 1980, Mr. Lutes joined the Province of Nova Scotia in 1980, and is presently a Senior Crown Attorney with the Public Prosecution Service for the Province. Since 1998, Mr. Lutes has had three secondments: Department of Justice Canada to assist with the *Youth Criminal Justice Act*; RCMP National Youth Strategy as a Youth Justice Training Specialist; and presently with the Learning and Development Human Resources Sector of the RCMP as a Justice Training Specialist.

PREFACE

This book was written for two reasons: first, to help the reader understand the *Youth Criminal Justice Act* by going one step further to demonstrate, where possible, how the Act might actually work; and, second, to empower the reader with the knowledge that will ensure this legislation gains public confidence.

The successful implementation of any legislation is strongly influenced by public perception as evidenced by the negative public reaction to the previous youth legislation, the *Young Offenders Act*. That Act was a progressive piece of legislation that was never implemented as intended, and, therefore, never really got a chance to gain public confidence. It was a complete shift in direction from the *Juvenile Delinquents Act*, and the public, the justice professionals and the media were ill-prepared. Most of the people working in the youth justice system knew only the part they played; few could actually tell a young person what might happen from "start to finish".

This book hopes to give enough information so the reader can speak informatively about what the youth justice system looks like under the *Youth Criminal Justice Act* beyond the application of the law. It is important for the public, media and professionals to be well-informed so the Act is supported rather than rejected due to ignorance.

As with any implementation of law, this legislation looks slightly different across jurisdictions partly due to the elective provisions. On April 1, 2003 this law came into force but implementation of the Act is an ongoing process. This book is intended to give the reader both a legal interpretation of the *Youth Criminal Justice Act* and an understanding of the intent of the lawmakers, as well as information on the programs and services that form part of the renewed youth justice system. The reader will find examples of current "best practices" developed under the *Young Offenders Act* and new practices developed under this Act. Reading the entire book will give the reader the best understanding of the intent of the *Youth Criminal Justice Act*, but each section can be read on its own as a quick reference.

The law is complex, as it is part of the general criminal law, but we should resist the temptation of saying that it is too complicated. This law will work if we allow it to; we should look for the positive aspects that support youth and help to make them contributing members of a more peaceful society.

Lee Tustin
Robert E. Lutes
September 2004

TABLE OF CONTENTS

	Page
About the Authors	v
Preface	vii
Table of Concordance	xv
Introduction	1
Youth Criminal Justice Act at a Glance	7

    1. Short Title 10
    2. Definitions 10
    3. Policy for Canada with respect to young persons 15

PART 1 EXTRAJUDICIAL MEASURES 17

    4. Declaration of principles 18
    5. Objectives 20
    6. Warnings, cautions and referrals 21
    7. Police cautions 22
    8. Crown cautions 24
    9. Evidence of measures is inadmissible 24
  10. Extrajudicial sanctions 25
  11. Notice to parent 28
  12. Victim's right to information 28

PART 2 ORGANIZATION OF YOUTH CRIMINAL JUSTICE SYSTEM 29

  13. Designation of youth justice court 29
  14. Exclusive jurisdiction of youth justice court 30
  15. Contempt against youth justice court 32
  16. Status of offender uncertain 33
  17. Youth justice court may make rules 33
  18. Youth justice committees 34
  19. Conferences may be convened 36
  20. Certain proceedings may be taken before justices 37
  21. Powers of clerks 38
  22. Powers, duties and functions of provincial directors 38

PART 3 JUDICIAL MEASURES 39

  23. Pre-charge screening 39
  24. Private prosecutions 40
  25. Right to counsel 40
  26. Notice in case of arrest or detention 43

Table of Contents

	Page
27. Order requiring attendance of parent	46
28. Application of Part XVI of *Criminal Code*	47
29. Detention as social measure prohibited	47
30. Designated place of temporary detention	49
31. Placement of young person in care of responsible person	51
32. Appearance before judge or justice	53
33. Application for release from or detention in custody.	55
34. Medical or psychological assessment	56
35. Referral to child welfare agency	60
36. When young person pleads guilty	61
37. Appeals	61

PART 4 SENTENCING 63

38. Purpose.	64
39. Committal to custody	66
40. Pre-sentence report	69
41. Recommendation of conference	72
42. Considerations as to youth sentence.	73
43. Additional youth sentences	83
44. Custodial portion if additional youth sentence	84
45. Supervision when additional youth sentence extends the period in custody	85
46. Exception when youth sentence in respect of earlier offence	86
47. Committal to custody deemed continuous	87
48. Reasons for the sentence	87
49. Warrant of committal	88
50. Application of Part XXIII of *Criminal Code*.	89
51. Mandatory prohibition order	89
52. Review of order made under section 51.	91
53. Funding for victims.	92
54. Where a fine or other payment is ordered	93
55. Conditions that must appear in orders	94
56. Communication of order	96
57. Transfer of youth sentence	97
58. Interprovincial arrangements	98
59. Review of youth sentences not involving custody	99
60. Provisions applicable to youth sentences on review.	101
61. Age for purpose of presumptive offences.	102
62. Imposition of adult sentence	103
63. Application by young person.	104
64. Application by Attorney General	104
65. Presumption does not apply	105
66. No election if youth sentence	106
67. Election – adult sentence	106
68. Proof of notice under subsection 64(4)	110
69. Paragraph (*a*) "presumptive offence" – included offences	111
70. Inquiry by court to young person	112

Table of Contents

Page

71. Hearing – adult sentences. ...113
72. Test – adult sentences ...113
73. Court must impose adult sentence ...114
74. Application of Parts XXIII and XXIV of *Criminal Code* ...115
75. Inquiry by the court to the young person ...115
76. Placement when subject to adult sentence ...117
77. Obligation to inform – parole. ...119
78. Release entitlement. ...119
79. If person convicted under another Act ...120
80. If person who is serving a sentence under another Act is sentenced to an adult sentence. ...121
81. Procedure for application or notice. ...121
82. Effect of absolute discharge or termination of youth sentence ...121

PART 5 CUSTODY AND SUPERVISION ...123

83. Purpose ...123
84. Young person to be held apart from adults. ...125
85. Levels of custody. ...126
86. Procedural safeguards ...128
87. Review ...128
88. Functions to be exercised by youth justice court ...130
89. Exception if young person is twenty years old or older ...130
90. Youth worker. ...131
91. Reintegration leave ...132
92. Transfer to adult facility. ...134
93. When young person reaches twenty years of age ...136
94. Annual review. ...137
95. Orders are youth sentences ...140
96. Recommendation of provincial director for conditional supervision of young person. ...140
97. Conditions to be included in custody and supervision order ...142
98. Application for continuation of custody. ...144
99. Report. ...146
100. Reasons. ...147
101. Review of youth justice court decision. ...148
102. Breach of conditions ...148
103. Review by youth justice court ...149
104. Continuation of custody. ...151
105. Conditional supervision ...153
106. Suspension of conditional supervision ...155
107. Apprehension. ...156
108. Review by provincial director. ...157
109. Review by youth justice court ...158

PART 6 PUBLICATION, RECORDS AND INFORMATION ...160

110. Identity of offender not to be published. ...161

		Page
111.	Identity of victim or witness not to be published	163
112.	Non-application.	164
113.	*Identification of Criminals Act* applies	164
114.	Youth justice court, review board and other courts	165
115.	Police records.	165
116.	Government records	166
117.	Exception – adult sentence.	167
118.	No access unless authorized	167
119.	Persons having access to records	168
120.	Access to R.C.M.P. records	173
121.	Deemed election.	175
122.	Disclosure of information and copies of record	176
123.	Where records may be made available	176
124.	Access to record by young person.	178
125.	Disclosure by peace officer during investigation	178
126.	Records in the custody, etc., of archivists	180
127.	Disclosure with court order	181
128.	Effect of end of access periods	182
129.	No subsequent disclosure	183

PART 7 GENERAL PROVISIONS 184

130.	Disqualification of judge	184
131.	Powers of substitute youth justice court judge	185
132.	Exclusion from hearing	185
133.	Transfer of charges	187
134.	Applications for forfeiture of recognizances	188
135.	Proceedings in case of default	188
136.	Inducing a young person, etc.	190
137.	Failure to comply with sentence or disposition	191
138.	Offences	191
139.	Offence and punishment	192
140.	Application of *Criminal Code*.	193
141.	Sections of *Criminal Code* applicable	193
142.	Part XXVII and summary conviction trial provisions of *Criminal Code* to apply	196
143.	Counts charged in information.	197
144.	Issue of subpoena	197
145.	Warrant.	197
146.	General law on admissibility of statements to apply.	198
147.	Statements not admissible against young person	200
148.	Testimony of a parent.	201
149.	Admissions	202
150.	Material evidence.	203
151.	Evidence of a child or young person	203
152.	Proof of service	203
153.	Seal not required.	204
154.	Forms.	204

Table of Contents

Page

155. Regulations 205
156. Agreements with provinces 205
157. Community-based programs 206

PART 8 TRANSITIONAL PROVISIONS 206

158. Prohibition on proceedings 206
159. Proceedings commenced under *Young Offenders Act* 207
160. Offences committed before this section in force 208
161. Applicable sentence 208
162. Proceedings commence with information 210
163. Application to delinquency and other offending behaviour 210
164. Agreements continue in force 210
165. Designation of youth justice court. 211

PART 9 CONSEQUENTIAL AMENDMENTS, REPEAL AND COMING INTO FORCE 213

SCHEDULE 228

APPENDICES 231

Index 255

TABLE OF CONCORDANCE

The Youth Criminal Justice Act **The Young Offenders Act**

Preamble
1. Short title — New
2. Definitions — New and incorporates[1] section 2 (deletes seven definitions and adds 17)
3. Policy for Canada with respect to young persons — New and incorporates section 3

Part 1 — Extrajudicial Measures
4. Declaration of principles — New
5. Objectives — New
6. Warning, cautions and referrals — New
7. Police cautions — New
8. Crown cautions — New
9. Evidence of measures is inadmissible — New
10. Extrajudicial Sanctions — New and incorporates section 4
11. Notice to parent — New
12. Victim's right to information — New

Part 2 — Organization of Youth Criminal Justice System
13. Designation of youth justice court — New and incorporates sections 19(4) and 5(5) (definitions of youth court and youth court judge from section 2)
14. Exclusion jurisdiction of youth justice court — New and incorporates section 5

---

[1] "Incorporates" means that part or parts of a section from the *Young Offenders Act* have been included in the new section of the *Youth Criminal Justice Act*. Many of the sections of the *Young Offenders Act* have been incorporated, most with changes, some minor and others major. It is necessary to read the sections together.

The Youth Criminal Justice Act | The Young Offenders Act

15.	Contempt against youth justice court	Section 47
16.	Status of offender uncertain	New
17.	Youth justice court may make rules	Section 68
18.	Youth justice committees	New and incorporates section 69
19.	Conferences may be convened	New
20.	Certain proceedings may be taken before justices	New and incorporates section 6
21.	Powers of clerks	Section 65
22.	Powers, duties and functions of provincial directors	Section 2.1

Part 3 — Judicial Measures

23.	Pre-charge screening	New
24.	Private prosecutions	New
25.	Right to counsel	New and incorporates section 11 with amendments (section 25(10) and (11) are new)
26.	Notice in case of arrest or detention	New and incorporates section 9 (section 26(12) is new)
27.	Order requiring attendance of parent	Section 10
28.	Application of Part XVI of the *Criminal Code*	New
29.	Detention as social measure prohibited	New and incorporates section 24(1.1)(*a*) (Section 29(2) is new)
30.	Designated place of temporary detention	New and incorporates section 7
31.	Placement of young person in care of responsible person	New and incorporates section 7.1 with amendments (section 31(2) is new)
32.	Appearance before judge or justice	New and incorporates section 12
33.	Application for release from or detention in custody	Section 8 (reference to Nunavut in section 33(6))
34.	Medical or psychological assessment	New and incorporates section 13

The Youth Criminal Justice Act	**The Young Offenders Act**
35. Referral to child welfare agency	New
36. When a young person pleads guilty	Section 19(1), 19(2)
37. Appeals	New and incorporates sections 10(4), 27, 47(6) (section 37(4) is new) (reference to Nunavut in section 37(9))

Part 4 — Sentencing

38. Purpose	New
39. Restriction on committal to custody	New and incorporates section 24
40. Pre-sentence report	New and incorporates section 14
41. Recommendation of conference	New
42. Considerations as to youth sentence	New and incorporates section 20
43. Additional youth sentences	New
44. Custodial portion if additional youth sentence	New
45. Supervision when additional youth sentence extends the period in custody	New
46. Exception when youth sentence in respect of earlier sentence	New
47. Committal to custody deemed continuous	New and incorporates section 24.4
48. Reasons for the sentence	New and incorporates section 20(6)
49. Warrant of committal	Sections 24.2(2), (3), (5)
50. Application of Part XXIII of *Criminal Code*	Section 20(8), (9) — subject to section 74
51. Mandatory prohibition order	New and incorporates most of section 20.1
52. Review of orders made under section 50	New and incorporates section 33
53. Funding for victims	New
54. Where a fine or other payment is ordered	Victim fine surcharge and section 21

Table of Concordance

The Youth Criminal Justice Act	The Young Offenders Act
55. Conditions that must appear in orders	New and incorporates section 23(1) and (2)
56. Communication of order	New and incorporates section 23(3) – (9)
57. Transfer of youth sentence	Section 25
58. Interprovincial arrangements	Section 25.1
59. Review of youth sentences not involving custody	New and incorporates section 32
60. Provisions applicable to youth sentences on review	New
61. Age for purpose of presumptive offence	New
62. Imposition of adult sentence	New
63. Application by young person	New
64. Application by Attorney General	New
65. Presumption does not apply	New
66. No election if youth sentence	New
67. Election — adult sentence	New
68. Proof of notice under section 64(4)	New
69. Paragraph (*a*) "presumptive offence" — included offences	New
70. Inquiry by court to young person	New
71. Hearing — adult sentences	New
72. Test — adult sentences	New (see section 16(1.1) of the *Young Offenders Act* for differences)
73. Court must impose adult sentence	New
74. Application of Parts XXIII and XXIV of *Criminal Code*	New
75. Inquiry by the court to the young person	New
76. Placement when subject to adult sentence	New and incorporates section 16.2
77. Obligation to inform — parole	New
78. Release entitlement	New

Table of Concordance

The Youth Criminal Justice Act		The Young Offenders Act
79.	If person convicted under another Act	New
80.	If person who is serving a sentence under another Act is sentenced to an adult sentence	New
81.	Procedure for application or notice	New
82.	Effect of absolute discharge or termination of youth sentence	New and incorporates section 36
Part 5 — Custody and Supervision		
83.	Purpose	New
84.	Young person to be held apart from adults	New and incorporates section 24.2(4)
85.	Levels of custody	New and incorporates parts of sections 24.1, 24.2
86.	Procedural safeguards	New
87.	Review	New and incorporates section 30
88.	Functions to be exercised by youth justice court	New
89.	Exception if young person is twenty years old or older	New
90.	Youth worker	New
91.	Reintegration leave	New and incorporates section 35
92.	Transfer to adult facility	New and incorporates section 24.5
93.	When young person reaches twenty years of age	New
94.	Annual review	New and incorporates section 28
95.	Orders are youth sentences	New and incorporates section 34(2)
96.	Recommendation of provincial director for conditional supervision of young person	New and incorporates section 29
97.	Conditions to be included in custody and supervision order	New section for new sentence and incorporates section 26.2

Table of Concordance

The Youth Criminal Justice Act		The Young Offenders Act
98.	Application for continuation of custody	New and incorporates parts of section 26.1(1) – (3)
99.	Report	New and incorporates parts of section 26.1(4) – 10
100.	Reasons	New and incorporates section 26.1(11)
101.	Review of youth justice court decision	New
102.	Breach of conditions	New
103.	Review by youth justice court	New and incorporates parts of section 26.6
104.	Continuation of custody	New and incorporates section 26.1
105.	Conditional supervision	New and incorporates section 26.2
106.	Suspension of conditional supervision	New and incorporates section 26.3
107.	Apprehension	New and incorporates section 26.4
108.	Review by provincial director	New and incorporates section 26.5
109.	Review by youth justice court	New and incorporates section 26.6
Part 6 — Publication, Records and Information		
110.	Identity of offender not to be published	New and incorporates parts of section 38
111.	Identity of victim or witness not to be published	New and incorporates parts of section 38
112.	Non-application	New
113.	*Identification of Criminals Act* applies	New and incorporates section 44
114.	Youth justice court, review board and other courts	New and incorporates section 40(1)
115.	Police records	New and incorporates sections 41, 42
116.	Government records	New and incorporates section 43
117.	Exception — adult sentence	New
118.	No access unless authorized	New and incorporates section 46(1) and (2)
119.	Persons having access to records	New and incorporates sections 44.1(1), (2), (2.1), (3), (4) and 45(1)

Table of Concordance

The Youth Criminal Justice Act	The Young Offenders Act
120. Access to R.C.M.P. records	New and incorporates section 45.03(2)
121. Deemed election	New and incorporates section 45(5)
122. Disclosure of information and copies of record	New
123. Where records may be made available	New and incorporates section 45.1
124. Access to record by young person	New
125. Disclosure by peace officer during investigation	New and incorporates sections 38(1.11), (1.13), (1.15) and 44.2
126. Records in the custody, *etc.*, of archivists	New and incorporates section 45.2
127. Disclosure with court order	Section 38(1.5-1.8)
128. Effect of end of access periods	New and incorporates section 45(2)
129. No subsequent disclosure	New and incorporates concept in section 38(1.14)
Part 7 — General Provisions	
130. Disqualification of judge	New and incorporates section 15
131. Powers of substitute youth justice court judge	Section 64
132. Exclusion from hearing	Section 39
133. Transfer of charges	Section 18
134. Applications for forfeiture of recognizances	Section 48
135. Proceedings in case of default	Section 49
136. Inducing a young person, *etc.*	New and incorporates section 50
137. Failure to comply with sentence or disposition	New and incorporates section 26
138. Offences	New and incorporates sections 38(2), (3) and 46(4)
139. Offence and punishment	New and incorporates sections 7.2, 36(4)
140. Application of *Criminal Code*	Section 51

Table of Concordance

The Youth Criminal Justice Act	The Young Offenders Act
141. Sections of *Criminal Code* applicable	New and incorporates section 13.2
142. Part XXVII and summary conviction trial provisions of *Criminal Code* to apply	New and incorporates section 52 (restructuring and addition of peace bonds)
143. Counts charged in information	New and incorporates section 53 with the words "or indictment" added
144. Issue of subpoena	Section 54
145. Warrant	Section 55
146. General law on admissibility of statements to apply	New and incorporates section 56
147. Statements not admissible against young person	Section 13.1 and additions for adult sentences
148. Testimony of parent	Section 57
149. Admissions	Section 58
150. Material evidence	Section 59
151. Evidence of a child or young person	Section 60
152. Proof of service	Section 62
153. Seal not required	Section 63
154. Forms	Section 66
155. Regulations	Section 67
156. Agreements with provinces	Section 70
157. Community-based programs	New
Part 8 — Transitional Provisions	See section 79
158. Prohibition on proceedings	New
159. Proceedings commenced under the *Young Offenders Act*	New
160. Offences committed before this section in force	New
161. Applicable sentence	New
162. Proceedings commence with information	New
163. Application to delinquency and other offending behaviour	New

Table of Concordance

The Youth Criminal Justice Act	**The Young Offenders Act**
164. Agreements continue in force	New
165. Designation of youth justice court	New

Part 9, Consequential Amendments, Repeal and Coming into Force, deals specifically with the transition to the *Youth Criminal Justice Act* and was not contained in the *Young Offenders Act*.

INTRODUCTION

Under the *Juvenile Delinquents Act*,[1] which was introduced in 1908 as Canada's first legislation to govern young persons in conflict with the law, the court played the role of a judicial parent in determining whether a young person should be deemed a delinquent. Children aged seven to 15 years old, or up to 17 by order of the Governor in Council, could be proceeded against under the *Juvenile Delinquents Act*. Young people were not given the benefit of legal representation, and the information brought before the court was often based on hearsay. Once the court deemed the youth to be a juvenile delinquent, the court could order the young person to a training school until the authorities felt the youth should be released. The state took over the role of parent and made all decisions regarding physical care, education and contact with family members. Future plans for the youth rested with the training school and the probation officer.

In 1984, Canada replaced the *Juvenile Delinquents Act* with the *Young Offenders Act*.[2] It was the beginning of a new approach, where youths were given the right to due process, and youths and their parents were expected to be accountable. It was a drastic change in the way youth justice had worked. The age in which a young person could be charged was raised from seven to a minimum of 12 and a maximum of 17. Each and every young person was represented in court by legal counsel, and the courts were expected to protect a young person's rights. The police had to follow the technical procedures of the Act to the letter when laying a charge, or the charge would not proceed.

The *Young Offenders Act* proved to be controversial to say the least. Some provinces, such as Ontario, were reluctant to increase the age of young offenders to 17. Sixteen- and 17-year-olds had always been considered adults and were treated as adults. So, when the *Young Offenders Act* came into force in April 1984, 16- and 17-year-olds in Ontario were still part of the adult system until 1985, when the federal government proclaimed the uniform maximum age provision of the *Young Offenders Act*, which required all provinces and territories to raise the maximum age of a youthful offender to 17. The result in Ontario was the implementation of the legislation in two phases, thus creating two separate systems divided by age. Ontario has since corrected this by moving all youth justice services and programs to a ministry for children and youths. Newfoundland and Labrador remains the only province to divide youths between two ministries, and their division is based on the sentence the youth receives, not on age. A young person receiving a custody sentence is dealt with by the correctional ministry that also provides services for adult offenders, and a young person with a community sentence is the responsibility of the social services ministry.

The *Young Offenders Act* failed to provide a clear legislative direction, and this eventually led to the inconsistent interpretation and implementation of the

---

[1] R.S.C. 1970, c. J-3.
[2] R.S.C. 1985, c. Y-1.

legislation. How the young offender system operated varied from province to province. Also, it was a complicated piece of legislation that was often misunderstood. Instead of promoting the use of diversionary programs to keep young people out of custody, the introduction of the *Young Offenders Act* increased the use of custody to the point where Canada had the highest rate of youth incarceration in the western world.

The media played an active role in undermining the intent of the *Young Offenders Act* and eroding public confidence in the legislation. In a high profile case 10 years after the Act had been in force, the media reported that the youth who had committed the violent murder could get a maximum of only three years in custody. Interestingly enough, the media failed to inform the public that the youth would be presumed to be dealt with in adult court and given an adult sentence that would, of course, exceed a three-year period. The misconceptions of the legislation were not limited to the media. There were many examples of people within the justice sector not familiar enough with the legislation even 17 years after it came into force, especially around the record provisions. Often, in the lobby of a youth court, the defence counsel could be heard reassuring a young person that his or her record would vanish once he or she turned 18 years of age.

Public criticism of the *Young Offenders Act* grew, and it was evident that the Act itself had contributed to the lack of confidence in the youth justice system. The federal government conducted an extensive review and consultation of the Act that spanned several years, citing best practices in implementing the *Young Offenders Act* throughout the nation. In 1998, the Department of Justice Canada introduced a Strategy for the Renewal of Youth Justice that spelled out the policy framework used in the consultations across Canada that developed the new *Youth Criminal Justice Act*[3] in March 1999.

The renewed youth justice system recognized the need for a broader, more inclusive approach to youth crime that integrates all of the areas that affect the lives of children. To have a youth justice system operating in isolation from child welfare, education, children's mental health, family and community does not give a youth support, nor does it mitigate a youth's risk to reoffend. It was also evident that a renewed youth justice system needed to make a distinction between violent and non-violent crime. Under the *Young Offenders Act*, youths were incarcerated at a higher rate than adults, and about 80 per cent of custodial sentences were for non-violent offences, of which 33 per cent were for administration of justice offences, *e.g.*, failure to comply with a disposition (Canadian Centre for Justice Statistics, 1998-99). Custody is the most intrusive intervention available to youth court and should be reserved only for serious and violent offenders; otherwise, by being incarcerated with more experienced, more antisocial peers, young people become better criminals. The *Youth Criminal Justice Act* provides a stronger emphasis for the use of measures outside of the formal court system and more stringent rules for the use of custody.

The introduction of the *Youth Criminal Justice Act* was in some ways an extension of the *Young Offenders Act*, as the *Youth Criminal Justice Act* builds on lessons learned and best practices from the *Young Offenders Act*. However,

---

[3] S.C. 2002, c. 1.

this legislation goes even further: it encourages the community and the victim to play a more active role in making a young person accountable for his or her criminal behaviour. Where possible, youths are to be dealt with outside of the more formal justice system, reserving the courts only for serious, violent and repeat offenders. This should ultimately have the effect of lowering custody rates for youth crime in Canada.

The *Youth Criminal Justice Act* goes beyond the *Young Offenders Act* and legislates the intent of the Act as well as the best practices learned. The principles in the *Youth Criminal Justice Act* are clearer and are inserted in the applicable sections throughout the Act rather than lumped altogether as they were in the *Young Offenders Act*. Protection of society is a key goal of the Act, and it is achieved by crime prevention, the application of meaningful consequences for youth crime and rehabilitation and reintegration of youths. There is greater emphasis on victim participation and repair to the victim and the community.

The definitions in this legislation have been expanded and include new definitions, such as extrajudicial measures, serious violent offence and expanded presumptive offences. The term "disposition" has been changed to "sentence"; a "pre-disposition report" has been changed to "pre-sentence report"; and "reintegration leave" has replaced the term "temporary release". The definitions of "open" and "secure" custody have been omitted from this legislation. Instead, there is a provision requiring at least two levels of custody to be distinguished by the degree of restraint of the young person.

The *Youth Criminal Justice Act* takes a sequential approach as each part demonstrates further penetration into the formal system. Part 1, extrajudicial measures, is introduced to legislate discretionary diversion outside of the formal justice system and is designed to provide a timely and effective response to offending behaviour, to encourage young people to acknowledge and repair the harm caused to the victim and the community, and to encourage families and victims to be involved in designing and implementing appropriate measures. Before any judicial proceedings begin, the Act states that police must consider taking no action, warn the young person, administer a caution or refer the young person to a program or agency in the community. Extrajudicial measures also introduce the ability to establish police and crown caution programs.

A youth's participation in these measures cannot be included as part of a young person's youth record. Extrajudicial sanctions are the next step in a graduated process if the offence is more serious, and a youth cannot be held accountable by a warning, caution or referral as a measure. Extrajudicial sanctions replace the alternative measures program under the *Young Offenders Act* and mark the beginning of a youth record that may later be referenced in court.

The *Youth Criminal Justice Act* encourages the use of youth justice committees in extrajudicial measures and as part of the formal system. It also introduces conferencing. Conferences can be convened to assist at various stages in the informal and formal proceedings, and the judiciary may cause a conference to be convened to give advice on sentencing.

The *Youth Criminal Justice Act* attempts to limit pre-trial detention by strengthening the provision that pre-trial detention is not to be used as a substitute for child protection, mental health or other social measures. The Act also requires the judge to inquire if there is a responsible person willing to care for the young person rather than detaining the youth. An additional provision in the *Youth Criminal Justice Act* is the authority for a judge to refer a young person to a child welfare agency for assessment at any stage in the proceedings to determine if the child is in need of child welfare services.

A number of significant changes were made with respect to youth sentencing. Unlike the *Young Offenders Act*, the *Youth Criminal Justice Act* contains specific purposes and principles. The purpose is to impose meaningful sanctions that promote rehabilitation and reintegration into society thereby contributing to the long-term protection of society. The principles address the proportionality of sentence based on the severity of the offence and should be the least restrictive sentence capable of achieving the purpose of the sentence, which is to rehabilitate and promote a sense of responsibility. Before imposing a custodial sentence, the court should be satisfied that all reasonable alternatives to custody have been considered and that there is no reasonable alternative capable of holding the youth accountable as set out in the purpose and principles of this Act.

The *Young Offenders Act* contained a provision for the provincial director to determine the level of custody; however, there were no safeguards for this process in that Act. The *Youth Criminal Justice Act* gives the provincial director the authority to determine the level of custody and includes an appeal process as well as procedural safeguards. There is also the option for provinces and territories to retain the judicial determination of custody, which all provinces and territories have so far elected to do.

All of the sentencing options available in the *Young Offenders Act* are contained in this legislation with the exception of custody. A custody sentence has been replaced by a custody and supervision order. Thus, every youth given a custody sentence is required to serve a period of community supervision following custody. This community supervision following custody poses difficulties in calculating multiple sentences; however, it can be beneficial in assisting young people in reintegrating to the community. The Act requires a youth worker to work with the young person to develop a reintegration plan when a young person is sentenced to a custody and supervision order.

A number of new sentence options, such as reprimand, intensive support and supervision order, deferred custody and supervision order, intermittent custody order, attendance order and intensive rehabilitation custody and supervision order, are introduced. And case law is quickly being established.

In order for a young person to be given an adult sentence under the *Young Offenders Act*, a transfer hearing had to take place before a finding of guilt. The *Youth Criminal Justice Act* requires the youth court to determine whether the young person is guilty of the offence and eliminates the transfer to adult court, giving the youth court the power to impose adult sentences in certain cases. Also, the age at which a young person is presumed to be given an adult sentence can be lowered from 16 to 14 years of age. Provisions are included to allow provinces to elect to set the age at 14, 15 or 16.

However, even before the Act came into force, it was challenged in the Quebec Court of Appeal. The Quebec government asked the court to decide if the new legislation violated the *Canadian Charter of Rights and Freedoms*. On March 31, 2003, the day before the Act came into force, the court ruled that two provisions of the *Youth Criminal Justice Act* violated section 7 of the Charter insofar as they place on the young person who has committed a presumptive offence the burden of proving the factors that justify imposing a youth sentence instead of an adult sentence. The court also ruled that the Charter is further violated by the presumption for publication for presumptive offences insofar as it requires the young person to justify maintaining the ban instead of placing the burden on the prosecutor to justify lifting the ban.

The presumption of an adult sentence was/is a critical provision of this legislation and upholding the Quebec Court of Appeal ruling will eliminate presumptive offences altogether from the legislation. Amendments to the affected sections are under consideration.

It is already evident that the success of this Act depends on jurisdictions developing and maintaining programs and services to support the key initiatives of this legislation, and on the knowledge and attitude of the people who are part of the system to foster an integrated approach to youth crime. Police, judges, justices of the peace, Crowns, lawyers, youth workers, probation officers and administrators all need to have an understanding of the purpose and objectives of this legislation — to give young people meaningful consequences that hold them accountable for their criminal behaviour and promote rehabilitation and reintegration. Interventions that address a youth's developmental issues and look to correct the offending behaviour are not only more meaningful to a young person, but also more meaningful to the victim, the family and the community. Professionals in the youth justice system need to have a range of community programs and services available from which to choose. They also need to be knowledgeable about them, to encourage the use of effective, meaningful alternatives to the formal system and to custody for non-violent youths.

Justice officials alone cannot renew the youth justice system. This legislation calls for the province, the community, the victim and the youth and his or her family to work collaboratively to protect society by providing meaningful consequences to criminal behaviour.

So far, media reaction to the new legislation has been mixed. There have been strong supporters that have seen the opportunities for community involvement and better accountability of young persons, and others who are anxious to quickly find fault and malign the Act.

Although the *Youth Criminal Justice Act* came into force on April 1, 2003, implementation of the Act will still continue over the next several years as more of the programs and services are developed and the principles and objectives of the Act are better realized by the judiciary, the justice professionals and the community.

As with any new legislation or programs, the effectiveness is based on the implementation. The number of young persons sentenced to custody has dropped significantly across the nation in the first years. This suggests that even at this early stage of implementation, the judicial system is respecting the principles of the Act.

Youth Criminal Justice Act at a Glance

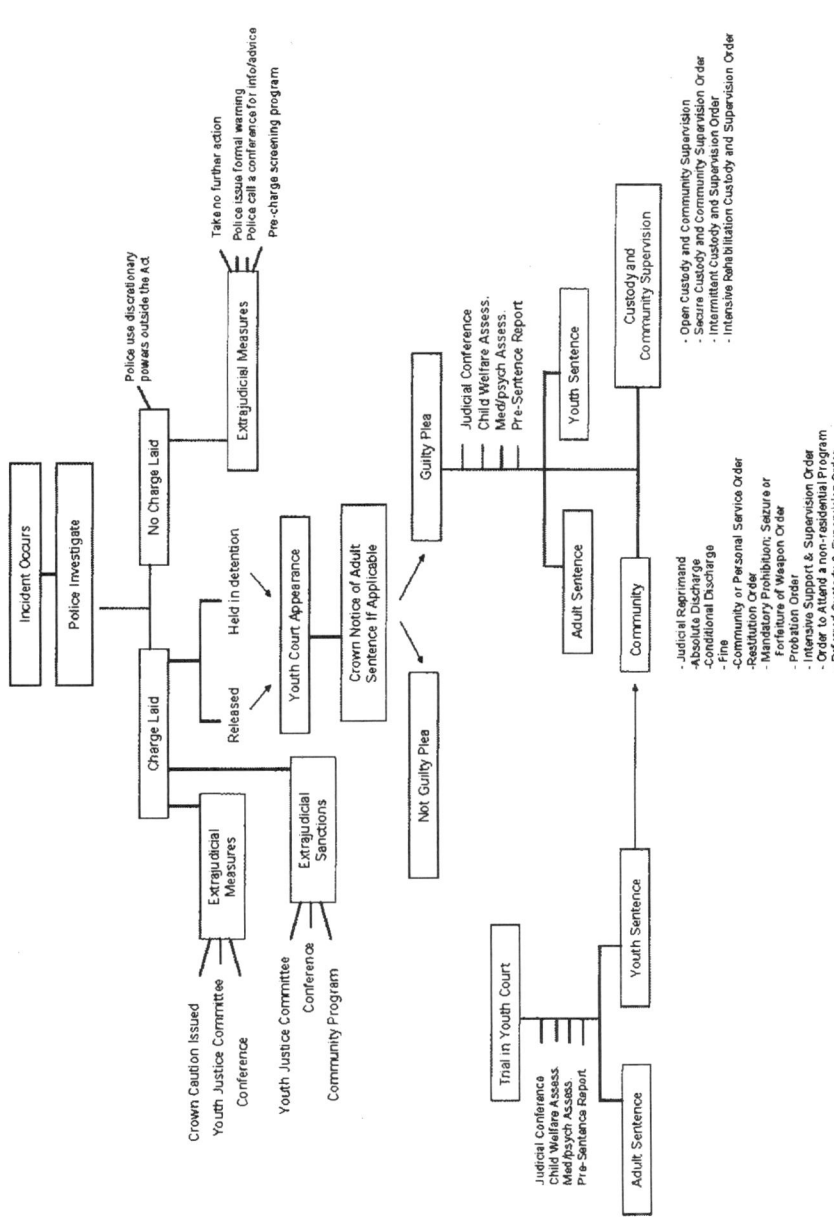

YOUTH CRIMINAL JUSTICE ACT

S.C. 2002, c. 1

(Assented to February 19, 2002)
(In force April 1, 2003)

Amendments: S.C. 2002, c. 7, s. 274; S.C. 2002, c. 13, s. 91; S.C. 2004, c. 11, ss. 48 and 49

Preamble

WHEREAS members of society share a responsibility to address the developmental challenges and the needs of young persons and to guide them into adulthood;

WHEREAS communities, families, parents and others concerned with the development of young persons should, through multi-disciplinary approaches, take reasonable steps to prevent youth crime by addressing its underlying causes, to respond to the needs of young persons, and to provide guidance and support to those at risk of committing crimes;

WHEREAS information about youth justice, youth crime and the effectiveness of measures taken to address youth crime should be publicly available;

WHEREAS Canada is a party to the United Nations Convention on the Rights of the Child and recognizes that young persons have rights and freedoms, including those stated in the *Canadian Charter of Rights and Freedoms* and the *Canadian Bill of Rights*, and have special guarantees of their rights and freedoms;

AND WHEREAS Canadian society should have a youth criminal justice system that commands respect, takes into account the interests of victims, fosters responsibility and ensures accountability through meaningful consequences and effective rehabilitation and reintegration, and that reserves its most serious intervention for the most serious crimes and reduces the over-reliance on incarceration for non-violent young persons;

NOW, THEREFORE, Her Majesty, by and with the advice and consent of the Senate and House of Commons of Canada, enacts as follows:

COMMENTARY

Legal Implications

The *Young Offenders Act* did not contain a preamble. This has been added to the *Youth Criminal Justice Act* to reinforce the values of the youth justice system — accountability, respect, responsibility and fairness.

Operational Implications

The preamble sets moral and legal standards for the protection and care of children in Canada as well as how they are to be treated by the youth justice system. It recognizes other legislation in place to protect young persons, such as the *Canadian Charter of Rights and Freedoms*. The preamble describes what a youth criminal justice system should look like and specifically addresses the problem of the overuse of custody, especially for non-violent young persons. It states that all available sanctions other than custody should be considered for all young persons.

SHORT TITLE

1. *Short title* — **This Act may be cited as the *Youth Criminal Justice Act*.**

COMMENTARY

Legal Implications

This section gives the name to this Act: the *Youth Criminal Justice Act*. The word "criminal" in the title of the Act conveys a more powerful piece of legislation than a youth justice act.

INTERPRETATION

2. (1) *Definitions* — **The definitions in this subsection apply in this Act.**

"adult" — "adult" means a person who is neither a young person nor a child.

"adult sentence" — "adult sentence", in the case of a young person who is found guilty of an offence, means any sentence that could be imposed on an adult who has been convicted of the same offence.

"Attorney General" — "Attorney General" means the Attorney General as defined in section 2 of the *Criminal Code*, read as if the reference in that definition to "proceedings" were a reference to "proceedings or extrajudicial measures", and includes an agent or delegate of the Attorney General.

"child" — "child" means a person who is or, in the absence of evidence to the contrary, appears to be less than twelve years old.

"conference" — "conference" means a group of persons who are convened to give advice in accordance with section 19.

"confirmed delivery service" — "confirmed delivery service" means certified or registered mail or any other method of service that provides proof of delivery.

"custodial portion" — "custodial portion", with respect to a youth sentence imposed on a young person under paragraph 42(2)(*n*), (*o*), (*q*) or (*r*), means the period of time, or the portion of the young person's youth sentence, that must be served in custody before he or she begins to serve the remainder under supervision in the community subject to conditions under paragraph 42(2)(*n*) or under conditional supervision under paragraph 42(2)(*o*), (*q*) or (*r*).

"disclosure" — "disclosure" means the communication of information other than by way of publication.

"extrajudicial measures" — "extrajudicial measures" means measures other than judicial proceedings under this Act used to deal with a young person alleged to have committed an offence and includes extrajudicial sanctions.

"extrajudicial sanction" — "extrajudicial sanction" means a sanction that is part of a program referred to in section 10.

"offence" — "offence" means an offence created by an Act of Parliament or by any regulation, rule, order, by-law or ordinance made under an Act of Parliament other than an ordinance of the Northwest Territories or a law of the Legislature of Yukon or the Legislature for Nunavut.

"parent" — "parent" includes, in respect of a young person, any person who is under a legal duty to provide for the young person or any person who has, in law or in fact, the custody or control of the young person, but does not include a person who has the custody or control of the young person by reason only of proceedings under this Act.

"pre-sentence report" — "pre-sentence report" means a report on the personal and family history and present environment of a young person made in accordance with section 40.

"presumptive offence" — "presumptive offence" means

(*a*) an offence committed, or alleged to have been committed, by a young person who has attained the age of fourteen years, or, in a province where the lieutenant governor in council has fixed an age greater than fourteen years under section 61, the age so fixed, under one of the following provisions of the *Criminal Code*:
  (i) section 231 or 235 (first degree murder or second degree murder within the meaning of section 231),
  (ii) section 239 (attempt to commit murder),
  (iii) section 232, 234 or 236 (manslaughter), or
  (iv) section 273 (aggravated sexual assault); or

(*b*) a serious violent offence for which an adult is liable to imprisonment for a term of more than two years committed, or alleged to have been committed, by a young person after the coming into force of section 62 (adult sentence) and after the young person has attained the age of fourteen years, or, in a province where the lieutenant governor in council has fixed an age greater than fourteen years under section 61, the age so fixed, if at the time of the commission or alleged commission of the offence at least two judicial determinations have been made under subsection 42(9), at different proceedings, that the young person has committed a serious violent offence.

"provincial director" — "provincial director" means a person, a group or class of persons or a body appointed or designated by or under an Act of the legislature of a province or by the lieutenant governor in council of a province or his or her delegate to perform in that province, either generally or in a specific case, any of the duties or functions of a provincial director under this Act.

"publication" — "publication" means the communication of information by making it known or accessible to the general public through any means, including print, radio or television broadcast, telecommunication or electronic means.

"record" — "record" includes any thing containing information, regardless of its physical form or characteristics, including microform, sound recording, videotape, machine-readable record, and any copy of any of those things, that is created or kept for the purposes of this Act or for the investigation of an offence that is or could be prosecuted under this Act.

"review board" — "review board" means a review board referred to in subsection 87(2).

"serious violent offence" — "serious violent offence" means an offence in the commission of which a young person causes or attempts to cause serious bodily harm.

"young person" — "young person" means a person who is or, in the absence of evidence to the contrary, appears to be twelve years old or older, but less than eighteen years old and, if the context requires, includes any person who is charged under this Act with having committed an offence while he or she was a young person or who is found guilty of an offence under this Act.

"youth custody facility" — "youth custody facility" means a facility designated under subsection 85(2) for the placement of young persons and, if so designated, includes a facility for the secure restraint of young persons, a community residential centre, a group home, a child care institution and a forest or wilderness camp.

"youth justice court" — "youth justice court" means a youth justice court referred to in section 13.

"youth justice court judge" — "youth justice court judge" means a youth justice court judge referred to in section 13.

"youth sentence" — "youth sentence" means a sentence imposed under section 42, 51 or 59 or any of sections 94 to 96 and includes a confirmation or a variation of that sentence.

"youth worker" — "youth worker" means any person appointed or designated, whether by title of youth worker or probation officer or by any other title, by or under an Act of the legislature of a province or by the lieutenant governor in council of a province or his or her delegate to perform in that province, either generally or in a specific case, any of the duties or functions of a youth worker under this Act.

(2) *Words and expressions* — Unless otherwise provided, words and expressions used in this Act have the same meaning as in the *Criminal Code*.

(3) *Descriptive cross-references* — If, in any provision of this Act, a reference to another provision of this Act or a provision of any other Act is followed by words in parentheses that are or purport to be descriptive of the subject-matter of the provision referred to, those words form no part of the provision in which they occur but are inserted for convenience of reference only.

[S.C. 2002, c. 7, s. 274]

COMMENTARY

Legal Implications

This section has 25 definitions of terms that are used throughout the Act. The *Young Offenders Act* contained only 15. This Act introduces a number of new definitions and amends some of the definitions used in the *Young Offenders Act*.

The following new definitions appear in the *Youth Criminal Justice Act*: adult sentence, Attorney General, conference, confirmed service delivery, custodial portion, disclosure, extrajudicial measures, extrajudicial sanction, pre-sentence report, presumptive offence, publication, record, serious violent offence, youth custodial facility, youth justice court, youth justice court judge and youth sentence.

The following definitions from the *Young Offenders Act* have been removed from the *Youth Criminal Justice Act*: alternative measures, disposition, ordinary court, predisposition report, progress report, youth court and youth court judge.

Operational Implications

These new and amended definitions mark a return to more adult language. The *Young Offenders Act* established definitions specific to youths whereas this Act has removed all of those references. For example, dispositions have been replaced by sentences and predisposition report is now a pre-sentence report. The definition of open and secure custody has been removed and replaced with a definition of a youth custody facility. There is also no reference in the Act to young offenders; instead the Act refers to young person(s).

Most of the new definitions are clear and straightforward; however, a few have already proven to be controversial. The definition for "conference" is very vague and only addresses the fact that a conference is a group of people who come together to give advice. What is not in the definition is what type of conference could, or should, be convened to get advice. A conference can be an informal discussion, a case management conference or a restorative conference. The definition is broad enough to include any type of conference.

The definition of "serious violent offence" is new, the nuances of which courts will decide as it is left to litigation, as section 42(9) provides for the youth justice court to make application for an offence to be designated as a serious violent offence.

Case law has already been established in *R. v. R.A.A.*, [2003] B.C.J. No. 1386 (Youth Ct.), where a young person was charged with incest committed against his sister who was one year younger. The court determined that the offence was not a serious violent offence as defined in this section because there was no attempt to cause serious bodily harm. The court considered incest an offence because of religious and social taboos against sexual intercourse between related people. Had they not been related there would have been no charge.

In an Ontario court, in *R. v. L.M.* (2003), 65 O.R. (3d) 158, [2003] O.J. No. 2212 (C.J.), Justice Beatty dismissed an application under section 42(9) because the offences had occurred prior to April 1, 2003, and the court ruled that endorsing the conviction as a serious violent offence would impose retroactive punishment on the young person, which would violate sections 7 and 11(*i*) of the Charter.

On the other hand, in *R. v. C.L.D.*, [2003] B.C.J. No. 1286 (Prov. Ct.), where the homeowner was shot and sustained severe injuries, the British Columbia Provincial Court designated an offence of break and enter as a serious violent offence due to the young person's age and the gravity of the offence notwithstanding that the offence had occurred before the *Youth Criminal Justice Act* came into force.

Another court in British Columbia, in *R. v. T.B.W.*, [2003] B.C.J. No. 1731 (Prov. Ct.), dismissed an application for a serious violent offence designation for assault with a weapon and carrying a concealed weapon. The court ruled that the underlying facts must support a finding of significant or serious harm. Serious violent offences usually involve either significant physical injury to the complainant or an attempt to cause serious harm.

A spin-off of the definition of "serious violent offence" is the courts' interpretation of "violent offence" as was demonstrated in the Alberta Court of Appeal case *R. v. C.D.* (2004), 184 C.C.C. (3d) 160, [2004] A.J. No. 179 (C.A.), where the court ruled that the meaning of "violent offence" is not simply an offence that is less serious than a serious violent offence. See also the Nova Scotia Court of Appeal case *R. v. T.M.D.* (2003), 181 C.C.C. (3d) 518, [2003] N.S.J. No. 488 (C.A.), where the definition of "serious violent offence" as defined in section 2 was the starting point for determining the meaning of "violent offence", as the court determined that "[c]ontextual integrity requires that 'violent offence' and 'serious violent offence' have connected meanings".

The definition of "presumptive offences" is also called into question based on the Quebec Court of Appeal ruling in *Reference Re: Bill C-7 Respecting the Criminal Justice System for Young Persons*, [2003] Q.J. No. 2850 (C.A.) (see section 62). The original intent was to create an automatic presumption for a young person to be given an adult sentence. Should this appeal remain unchallenged by other jurisdictions, the Act will no longer presume a youth to be sentenced as an adult; rather, the onus will be on the Attorney General to make application for the young person to be sentenced as an adult. Thus far, the Ontario Superior Court of Justice in the case of *R. v. D.B.*, [2004] O.J. No. 3823 (S.C.J.), endorsed the Quebec Court of Appeal decision.

DECLARATION OF PRINCIPLE

3. (1) *Policy for Canada with respect to young persons* — The following principles apply in this Act:

(*a*) the youth criminal justice system is intended to
  (i) prevent crime by addressing the circumstances underlying a young person's offending behaviour,
  (ii) rehabilitate young persons who commit offences and reintegrate them into society, and
  (iii) ensure that a young person is subject to meaningful consequences for his or her offence
  in order to promote the long-term protection of the public;

(*b*) the criminal justice system for young persons must be separate from that of adults and emphasize the following:
  (i) rehabilitation and reintegration,
  (ii) fair and proportionate accountability that is consistent with the greater dependency of young persons and their reduced level of maturity,
  (iii) enhanced procedural protection to ensure that young persons are treated fairly and that their rights, including their right to privacy, are protected,
  (iv) timely intervention that reinforces the link between the offending behaviour and its consequences, and
  (v) the promptness and speed with which persons responsible for enforcing this Act must act, given young persons' perception of time;

(*c*) within the limits of fair and proportionate accountability, the measures taken against young persons who commit offences should
  (i) reinforce respect for societal values,
  (ii) encourage the repair of harm done to victims and the community,
  (iii) be meaningful for the individual young person given his or her needs and level of development and, where appropriate, involve the parents, the extended family, the community and social or other agencies in the young person's rehabilitation and reintegration, and
  (iv) respect gender, ethnic, cultural and linguistic differences and respond to the needs of aboriginal young persons and of young persons with special requirements; and

(*d*) special considerations apply in respect of proceedings against young persons and, in particular,
  (i) young persons have rights and freedoms in their own right, such as a right to be heard in the course of and to participate in the processes, other than the decision to prosecute, that lead to decisions that affect them, and young persons have special guarantees of their rights and freedoms,

(ii) victims should be treated with courtesy, compassion and respect for their dignity and privacy and should suffer the minimum degree of inconvenience as a result of their involvement with the youth criminal justice system,
(iii) victims should be provided with information about the proceedings and given an opportunity to participate and be heard, and
(iv) parents should be informed of measures or proceedings involving their children and encouraged to support them in addressing their offending behaviour.

(2) *Act to be liberally construed* — This Act shall be liberally construed so as to ensure that young persons are dealt with in accordance with the principles set out in subsection (1).

COMMENTARY

Legal Implications

This is the general declaration of principle that applies to the whole of the Act. In other Parts of the Act, there are principles stated that apply specifically to the subject matter of that Part. The principles here have been stated differently, reordered and given priority. They apply throughout the Act and are to be read in conjunction with the other principles in the Act. It is necessary to read the principles closely and completely in order to fully appreciate the changes.

The principles of rehabilitation and reintegration of young persons is highlighted in a context of crime prevention. There is a focus on meaningful consequences in response to youth crime, with an underlying principle of proportionality. Under the *Young Offenders Act*, youths often received longer sentences than adults did for the same crime, and this is seen as being inappropriate. The *Youth Criminal Justice Act* recognizes the timeliness of interventions and the fact that youths are not adults, as well as a number of special considerations, such as the interests of victims and parents.

The Act also states a number of objectives, including respect for gender, ethnic origin, and cultural and linguistic differences. This section acknowledges the overrepresentation of aboriginal youth in custody and gives specific direction that the youth criminal system respond to the needs of aboriginal young persons.

In Newfoundland and Labrador Provincial Court in *R. v. D.L.C.*, [2003] N.J. No. 94 (Prov. Ct.), the court considered the wording "meaningful consequences" in this section and ruled that the words mandate a very individualistic judicial approach to sentencing. The circumstances of the young person must be the primary focus and the sentence must be fashioned with the personal circumstances of the specific young person in mind. The circumstances of the offence will normally be a secondary consideration, though not always so.

Operational Implications

Many of the themes contained in the *Young Offenders Act* have been carried over to this legislation, but have been stated with more clarity. The *Youth Criminal Justice Act* provides specific principles to guide police, prosecutors, judges and others at various stages of the process. This is important because these principles set the tone for how a young person should be treated by those working in the youth justice system. It has already been noted in Saskatchewan Provincial Youth Court, in *R. v. B.M.* (2003), 234 Sask. R. 244, [2003] S.J. No. 377 (Prov. Ct.), that the assembly line fashion in which youth matters are processed may be inconsistent with the guiding principles in this section of the Act. The *Young Offenders Act* was not clear about the goal of the youth justice system and was criticized for having inconsistent and competing principles. This new legislation states clearly that public protection is the primary purpose of the youth justice system, and this is best achieved through prevention, meaningful consequences and rehabilitation.

The principle of rehabilitation has already influenced many sentencing decisions. In *R. v. E.S.A.*, [2003] A.J. No. 571, 2003 ABPC 86, the judge felt that a non-custodial sentence would not ensure that the young person would receive the counselling and therapy necessary to rehabilitate him.

PART 1   EXTRAJUDICIAL MEASURES

INTRODUCTION

This part of the legislation can be credited for some of the early signals of anticipated changes to the youth justice system. Since the *Young Offenders Act* was implemented in Canada, statistics showed that too many youths in Canada went to court, and too many were sentenced to custody. Not all cases need to go to court, and, if a case does not go to court, it does not mean nothing has happened. The experience of those working with alternatives to court clearly indicates that court is not always necessary, not always beneficial, and may, in fact, be counterproductive. More than half of the cases that went to youth court were property crimes. Violent offences made up less than 20 per cent of the total charges across Canada.

There are appropriate and effective responses to youth crime not involving court that are beginning to be recognized as being as effective as court, and are likely more meaningful to the offender. Courts are busy places, and cases can be treated very quickly and routinely. A police officer intervening on a personal level and taking a young person to the police station for questioning, or home to talk with parents, may have a more significant impact on a youth than standing before an impersonal court several weeks or months after the offence occurred.

The continuation and expansion of these alternative approaches need to be supported by the youth justice system. Strengthening the front-end measures and building on good programs throughout the country will demonstrate for the youth justice system, and the public, the effectiveness of less formal responses to youth crime.

PRINCIPLES AND OBJECTIVES

4. *Declaration of principles* — **The following principles apply in this Part in addition to the principles set out in section 3:**

(*a*) extrajudicial measures are often the most appropriate and effective way to address youth crime;

(*b*) extrajudicial measures allow for effective and timely interventions focused on correcting offending behaviour;

(*c*) extrajudicial measures are presumed to be adequate to hold a young person accountable for his or her offending behaviour if the young person has committed a non-violent offence and has not previously been found guilty of an offence; and

(*d*) extrajudicial measures should be used if they are adequate to hold a young person accountable for his or her offending behaviour and, if the use of extrajudicial measures is consistent with the principles set out in this section, nothing in this Act precludes their use in respect of a young person who

  (i) has previously been dealt with by the use of extrajudicial measures, or

  (ii) has previously been found guilty of an offence.

COMMENTARY

Legal Implications

The declaration of principles in this part makes it clear that extrajudicial measures are an essential part of our response to youth crime and presumes that in many cases they are the most appropriate response to hold young persons accountable in an effective and timely manner. Extrajudicial measures are not an afterthought or an add-on to the judicial process. They are the first step to be considered before the formal court process is invoked.

Under the *Young Offenders Act*, the term used was "alternative measures", which implied that the primary response to youth crime was the court process, and alternative measures were only an alternative.

When warnings, cautions and referrals are used to hold a young person accountable for offending behaviour, they will not form part of the youth's record for court purposes. All measures, except extrajudicial sanctions, are considered inadmissible for the purpose of proving prior offending behaviour in any proceedings before a youth justice court. The provision of these measures is the responsibility of each jurisdiction, and they are not all mandatory to provide under the legislation.

Operational Implications

The introduction of extrajudicial measures in the legislation formalizes some of the current day-to-day practices that have proven to be appropriate and effective responses to youth crime and do not involve the use of the court. This section is based on best practices, commonly referred to as discretionary or diversion programs, already in use, formally and informally, throughout Canada and other countries. The *Youth Criminal Justice Act* provides greater authority to strengthen and formalize the use of these measures to hold a youth accountable for his or her offending behaviour. These front-end measures provide the ability to deal with youths in a more meaningful way than through the formal justice system and usually leave a young person with a stronger, more meaningful message.

This legislation goes much further than the *Young Offenders Act* did in trying to keep youths out of the formal justice system. Under the *Youth Criminal Justice Act*, it is now mandatory that police consider extrajudicial measures as a way to hold a youth accountable. Extrajudicial measures are not meant to be limited to first-time offenders. The eligibility of extrajudicial measures should be based on the offence, not the offender.

This concept is not always easily grasped by police officers who are diligently doing their job to ensure that young persons are taking the law seriously. The intent of the legislation is that the offence is what should be considered and if the young person can be held accountable by extrajudicial measures, then extrajudicial measures should be used.

It is really police and Crown Attorneys that initiate the use of extrajudicial measures at either the pre-charge or post-charge stage. The *Youth Criminal Justice Act* authorizes provinces and territories to use the following programs and services for extrajudical measures:

- taking no further action;
- informal police warnings;
- police cautions;
- police referrals to a program or agency in the community;
- Crown caution program;
- pre-charge screening program;
- youth justice committees;
- conferences.

The officer needs only to "consider" a warning, caution or referral. It may be that the officer decides to take the young person home and talk to the parents, or perhaps wait until Monday to proceed after being able to consult with others and look at referral options. Or, the officer may have considered a referral to a program but felt it was not appropriate to hold the young person accountable. Or, perhaps the police officer considered a referral to a program but there was no program available. In all of these situations the police officer will have satisfied the requirements of the legislation.

In order for any of these options to be effective, jurisdictions need to provide the programs and services as authorized under the legislation, and police and Crowns need to know they exist. Another key factor is the need for jurisdictions to communicate the benefits of extrajudicial measures to front-line police, Crowns and others that may be responsible for holding the youth accountable, and to encourage support for the use of extrajudicial measures. This option is more immediate, and the consequences may be tailored to the individual youth to strengthen his or her understanding of the impact of his or her criminal behaviour.

One issue that has been identified with these sections is the inability to track the number of times a youth participates in extrajudicial measures. Measures do not result in a finding of guilt and do not form part of a young person's record; therefore, measures cannot be entered onto the Canada-wide information system, the Canadian Police Information Centre (CPIC). Extrajudicial sanctions do require an admission of guilt but there is no finding of guilt; therefore they should not be entered onto CPIC as there is no appropriate screen to reflect this. Past experience with the alternative measures program showed that records of a youth's participation were not widely shared. If this continues to be the case with the use of extrajudicial measures, then it will be possible for a youth who moves from area to area to be eligible for extrajudicial measures several times for similar offences before it is realized that this has been a pattern of offences. This is not necessarily a bad thing as this Act is intended to be offence based. It is the severity of the offence that determines the consequence, and, generally, a young person who commits several offences that may be a pattern of offences, but are eligible for extrajudicial measures, will have escalating behaviour that will lead to more serious offences — and will get caught.

Professionals like police officers and Crown attorneys can usually predict which young persons will be longstanding members of the criminal justice system and at a very early stage are able to distinguish them from those who made a mistake that likely will not be repeated.

5. *Objectives* — Extrajudicial measures should be designed to

(*a*) provide an effective and timely response to offending behaviour outside the bounds of judicial measures;
(*b*) encourage young persons to acknowledge and repair the harm caused to the victim and the community;
(*c*) encourage families of young persons — including extended families where appropriate — and the community to become involved in the design and implementation of those measures;
(*d*) provide an opportunity for victims to participate in decisions related to the measures selected and to receive reparation; and
(*e*) respect the rights and freedoms of young persons and be proportionate to the seriousness of the offence.

COMMENTARY

Legal Implications

Timely response, acknowledgement of harm done, repairing the harm, participation of family, opportunity for victims to participate and respect for the rights of the young person are clearly set out as the objectives of extrajudicial measures. These objectives are included in this section in an effort to strengthen their use and effectiveness and to give guidance to those responsible for initiating extrajudicial measures.

Operational Implications

This section goes further than the *Young Offenders Act* to reinforce the notion of timeliness, which was only implied in that Act. A youth who commits an offence in June but does not appear in court until September may not even remember the circumstances of the offence after a long summer. The timeliness of the response is key to a youth's understanding of the impact and the consequences of his or her actions. Most youths aged 12-17 are still in the developmental stages of adolescence and have yet to grasp the full understanding of the consequences of their behaviour. This section also acknowledges that victims and communities are harmed by youth crime and, therefore, need to be part of the solution.

WARNINGS, CAUTIONS AND REFERRALS

6. (1) *Warnings, cautions and referrals* **— A police officer shall, before starting judicial proceedings or taking any other measures under this Act against a young person alleged to have committed an offence, consider whether it would be sufficient, having regard to the principles set out in section 4, to take no further action, warn the young person, administer a caution, if a program has been established under section 7, or, with the consent of the young person, refer the young person to a program or agency in the community that may assist the young person not to commit offences.**

(2) *Saving* **— The failure of a police officer to consider the options set out in subsection (1) does not invalidate any subsequent charges against the young person for the offence.**

COMMENTARY

Legal Implications

These sections legislate options from which the police may choose: take no further action, warn the young person, administer a caution or refer the young person to a program or agency in the community. The intent is to stimulate the development of nationwide options for police in order to promote effective and speedy responses to youth crime and to leave formal court time for the more serious offences. The impact of police work cannot be overstated, as the police are the frontline professionals who make the first decisions on how to respond to the inappropriate conduct of a young person. The police may choose from a number of options when deciding how to respond to each case. The least intrusive option is to do nothing further than appear on the scene, interview the persons involved and provide direction. Or police may decide to take additional steps, which are the focus of the next few sections.

There is a need for governments and communities to look at options that can be used by police when considering the best approach to take with a young person. Ultimately the police will exercise their discretion but the more options available in the community the more likely the objectives of the legislation will be met. Police need as many "off-ramps" to the formal justice system as possible to adequately deal with young people and hold them accountable outside of the justice system. Early interventions can save valuable resources in the formal justice system and specifically address the ability to prevent youth crime by addressing its underlying causes as set out in the preamble of this Act.

Operational Implications

The *Young Offenders Act* did not specifically address the role of police other than setting out procedures in areas such as laying charges and taking young offender statements. This section legislates a stronger role for police outside of the formal court system. Many of these options existed informally under the *Young Offenders Act*, but this new legislation requires that these options be considered prior to a youth penetrating the formal youth justice system.

The role of police is key to the success of extrajudicial measures. The police officer still retains his or her discretion to take no further action than appear on the scene, or to take a youth home and speak to a parent. Any further action taken by the police is designed to be progressively more onerous, based on the nature and circumstances of the offence.

One of the key messages and policies underlying the *Youth Criminal Justice Act* is the diversion of youth from the formal court system. In order to fulfill this objective, alternatives to court were included in sections 6 and 10. In addition there were limitations placed on police discretion in that police are required to consider the options set out in section 6 (extrajudicial measures) before commencing formal proceedings.

In order for police to make the most effective use of these options, the support and cooperation of other partners in the criminal justice system is required. The police caution program requires the support of the Attorney General in order for a formally recognized program to be established. This is not to say that police cannot create options of informal and formal warnings. The reality however is that the program will be more widely used if it is recognized and endorsed by the Attorney General to whom Crown attorneys are accountable.

Another area where the police require support is in the case of referrals. When police consider making a referral, it is essential that there be community options and that police are aware of the options for referral in their community. This takes some effort on the part of police to seek out programs, and also requires support from the community to make the police and others aware of the programs available and to continually monitor to ascertain any other programs that might be needed to assist police in this process.

The key to these non-court options working effectively to hold young people accountable is the knowledge and desire of the police to make it work and the cooperation the police receive from governments and community partners. The *Youth Criminal Justice Act* calls for full community/agency support to be most effective.

7. *Police cautions* **— The Attorney General, or any other minister designated by the lieutenant governor of a province, may establish a**

program authorizing the police to administer cautions to young persons instead of starting judicial proceedings under this Act.

COMMENTARY

Legal Implications

This section authorizes the establishment of the police caution program. For this option to be successful, it must be perceived by the public as an effective and efficient tool for the police. Police cautions can have the potential to strengthen the response to youth crime and to regain public confidence.

Not all provinces and territories developed a police caution program when the Act was implemented. Ideally this program will be piloted and evaluated for future implementation as it has been a successful program in Saint John, New Brunswick for several years.

A police caution program could give this section national consistency and be of great assistance to police.

Operational Implications

Police warnings are intended to be less formal and to be used as the first step before more formal police cautions. The caution is the next level of formality and is more structured than the warning. A caution may involve the young person and his or her parent(s) attending at the police station to meet with a police officer to discuss the offending behaviour. The next progression into a more formal process would be participation in a Crown caution program, where the Crown Attorney rather than the police issues a caution.

Establishing formal warning or caution programs is optional under this legislation; therefore, this option is not available in all provinces and territories. Provinces and territories all have their own protocols and procedures on the use of warnings and cautions (see Appendices, Form 1.1). The fact that the jurisdiction must authorize caution programs sets these programs apart from lesser interventions, and provides for program consistency within the jurisdiction. Manitoba has a provincewide police cautioning program, and Saskatchewan's program is under development. The National Youth Strategy for the RCMP has developed for general distribution a "Discussion Paper Police Cautioning Under Section 7 of the YCJA" to assist communities in implementing a police caution program.

Police are also authorized to refer a youth to an existing community program, such as a shoplift program, a school mediation program or an anger management program operated by a local agency. A police officer has the discretion to decide whether a particular program is the most effective response to the actions of the young person. One of the difficulties this section has already demonstrated is that oftentimes police officers are not aware of, or familiar with, the community programs/services available for referral. Some jurisdictions have begun to develop a compendium of programs and services available for young persons. The question that is always asked is: "What do I do with Johnny at 10 p.m. on Friday night?" The officer needs only to "consider" a warning, caution or referral. It may be that the officer decides to take the young person home and talk to the parents, or perhaps wait until Monday to proceed after being able to consult with others and to look at referral options.

Hopefully these provisions in the legislation will lead to further development of community programs as police officers begin to identify the need for more specialized program options. This presents communities with an opportunity to come together and discuss the options that may be available to the police as an alternative to taking more formal action and supports the shared responsibility as directed in the preamble of the Act.

8. *Crown cautions* — The Attorney General may establish a program authorizing prosecutors to administer cautions to young persons instead of starting or continuing judicial proceedings under this Act.

COMMENTARY

Legal Implications

The Crown caution provides another option in responding to youth crime outside of the court process (see sample caution form in Appendices, Form 1.2). The more options available, the more likely it is that the most appropriate response will be used to achieve the best outcome. Alberta has used Crown cautions as an effective tool to deal with less serious cases outside of the formal court system for several years. Nevertheless, there appears to be hesitation to put this program in place nationally. Yet, as is the case for a police caution program, a Crown caution could provide national consistency and support the objectives of the legislation.

Operational Implications

It is not mandatory for jurisdictions to provide this option; however, some jurisdictions have already seen the benefits of establishing a Crown caution program. Manitoba has a Crown caution program provincewide, as does Quebec. It is hoped that more jurisdictions will choose to use this option, as it will lead to more uniformity in our response to youth crime across Canada.

9. *Evidence of measures is inadmissible* — Evidence that a young person has received a warning, caution or referral mentioned in section 6, 7 or 8 or that a police officer has taken no further action in respect of an offence, and evidence of the offence, is inadmissible for the purpose of proving prior offending behaviour in any proceedings before a youth justice court in respect of the young person.

COMMENTARY

Legal Implications

This section prohibits the subsequent use of previous warnings, cautions, referrals and police interventions where no further action was taken. This prohibition exists because there are no protections to ensure proof of the young person's involvement. There is no information (the document that lays the charge) sworn, no requirement that the Attorney General confirm that there is sufficient evidence to proceed to court and no requirement that the young person accept responsibility or admit involvement in the alleged criminal activity. Recognition is also given to the principle that youths should not be burdened with a record of all previous bad decisions.

Operational Implications

The legislation does not specifically require it, but a police officer should use these discretionary measures only if there is enough evidence to proceed with a charge, otherwise it leads to "net widening". Some of the issues that have already surfaced in this section revolve around victim disclosure. Since these measures do not form part of a young person's record, police have vague direction regarding what information can/should be provided to victims. Tracking the use of measures is also an issue (see the discussion under Operational Implications under section 4).

EXTRAJUDICIAL SANCTIONS

10. (1) *Extrajudicial sanctions* — **An extrajudicial sanction may be used to deal with a young person alleged to have committed an offence only if the young person cannot be adequately dealt with by a warning, caution or referral mentioned in section 6, 7 or 8 because of the seriousness of the offence, the nature and number of previous offences committed by the young person or any other aggravating circumstances.**

(2) *Conditions* — An extrajudicial sanction may be used only if

(a) it is part of a program of sanctions that may be authorized by the Attorney General or authorized by a person, or a member of a class of persons, designated by the lieutenant governor in council of the province;
(b) the person who is considering whether to use the extrajudicial sanction is satisfied that it would be appropriate, having regard to the needs of the young person and the interests of society;
(c) the young person, having been informed of the extrajudicial sanction, fully and freely consents to be subject to it;
(d) the young person has, before consenting to be subject to the extrajudicial sanction, been advised of his or her right to be represented by counsel and been given a reasonable opportunity to consult with counsel;

(e) the young person accepts responsibility for the act or omission that forms the basis of the offence that he or she is alleged to have committed;
(f) there is, in the opinion of the Attorney General, sufficient evidence to proceed with the prosecution of the offence; and
(g) the prosecution of the offence is not in any way barred at law.

(3) *Restriction on use* — An extrajudicial sanction may not be used in respect of a young person who

(a) denies participation or involvement in the commission of the offence; or
(b) expresses the wish to have the charge dealt with by a youth justice court.

(4) *Admissions not admissible in evidence* — Any admission, confession or statement accepting responsibility for a given act or omission that is made by a young person as a condition of being dealt with by extrajudicial measures is inadmissible in evidence against any young person in civil or criminal proceedings.

(5) *No bar to judicial proceedings* — The use of an extrajudicial sanction in respect of a young person alleged to have committed an offence is not a bar to judicial proceedings under this Act, but if a charge is laid against the young person in respect of the offence,

(a) the youth justice court shall dismiss the charge if it is satisfied on a balance of probabilities that the young person has totally complied with the terms and conditions of the extrajudicial sanction; and
(b) the youth justice court may dismiss the charge if it is satisfied on a balance of probabilities that the young person has partially complied with the terms and conditions of the extrajudicial sanction and if, in the opinion of the court, prosecution of the charge would be unfair having regard to the circumstances and the young person's performance with respect to the extrajudicial sanction.

(6) *Laying of information, etc.* — Subject to subsection (5) and section 24 (private prosecutions only with consent of Attorney General), nothing in this section shall be construed as preventing any person from laying an information or indictment, obtaining the issue or confirmation of any process or proceeding with the prosecution of any offence in accordance with law.

COMMENTARY

Legal Implications

The process is similar to alternative measures under the *Young Offenders Act*, although it is anticipated that as the Act matures criteria for a referral will be expanded in jurisdictions to include more serious offences. This legislation clarifies the intent of the *Young Offenders Act* and spells out options such as the use of youth justice committees for extrajudicial sanctions. The fact that a young person has received an extrajudicial sanction may, for a limited time, be referred to in court (see section 119(2)). The reason for this is that the protections that have been built into extrajudicial sanctions of admission of guilt, the right to counsel, confirmation that there is sufficient evidence to proceed and that the case is not barred at law do not apply. Without these safeguards, it is not appropriate to refer to a previous warning, or caution, and imply that an offence had been committed; therefore, the fact that a young person has received a warning or caution cannot be referred to in court proceedings.

Operational Implications

Extrajudicial sanctions under the Act replace and build on alternative measures under the *Young Offenders Act*. The name has been changed to remove the inference that court is always the best option and that sometimes an alternative is appropriate. Extrajudicial sanctions can be thought of as part two of extrajudicial measures. Usually a youth dealt with by extrajudicial sanctions has already been charged and it marks the beginning of a youth court record. Also, a youth must accept responsibility for the offence in order to participate in extrajudicial sanctions.

As made evident by the alternative measures program authorized under the *Young Offenders Act*, there are many different approaches and programs developed as extrajudicial sanctions across Canada. As the use of extrajudicial sanctions increases, it will foster the development of new approaches that will lead to more active participation by the community in response to youth crime. Part of the strength of this option is the involvement of all interested parties: the victim (if he or she chooses), parents, extended family, persons with a special interest and the community.

Extrajudicial sanctions can be applied at the pre-charge or post-charge stage in the proceedings. Sanctions can be anything from apologies to the victim to community service work or restitution for damages. This approach allows for creative, individual responses to a youth's offending behaviour. Because extrajudicial sanctions are unique to the youth and the circumstances, this option can have a more powerful impact on a youthful offender and provide a better opportunity to repair the harm done to the victim and the community. Typically, although not always a requirement, sanctions would involve the youth's parent(s), the victim and the community at some stage in the process. A designate of the provincial director would meet with the youth and the parent, as well as the victim, to discuss the circumstances of the offence and to agree on the sanctions (see Appendices, Form 1.4). A youth justice committee could also be involved in the extrajudicial sanctions agreement.

11. *Notice to parent* — **If a young person is dealt with by an extrajudicial sanction, the person who administers the program under which the sanction is used shall inform a parent of the young person of the sanction.**

COMMENTARY

Legal Implications

This section is new and is a stronger legal requirement than that provided by the *Young Offenders Act* for notice to be given to a parent if a young person is dealt with by way of extrajudicial sanctions (see Appendices, Form 1.4).

Operational Implications

This section begins to address formal court procedures. It supports research that recognizes that parents are part of the solution and often offer the best hope of the young person getting back on track; therefore, formal notice to the parent is essential.

12. *Victim's right to information* — **If a young person is dealt with by an extrajudicial sanction, a police officer, the Attorney General, the provincial director or any organization established by a province to provide assistance to victims shall, on request, inform the victim of the identity of the young person and how the offence has been dealt with.**

COMMENTARY

Legal Implications

Section 44.1(5) of the *Young Offenders Act* authorized the disclosure of information to a victim when a youth was dealt with by alternative measures. This legislation requires the police, the Attorney General or the provincial director, on the request of the victim, to actually identify the youth and inform the victim of how the youth was dealt with.

Operational Implications

This section gives the victim the right to be told the identity of the young person and how the offence was dealt with. If the police continue to be in contact with the victim they can provide this information. Although in many cases the police will not be aware of how the offence was dealt with, victims need to know where to go to, and who to go to, to get information.

Victims have a key role to play in the criminal justice system, with one of the goals being the restoring of their dignity and integrity. This Act seeks to increase victim participation at all stages of the process. Where appropriate, victims should also have the opportunity to convey their feelings to the young person.

It is far more powerful to have the victim tell the offender how the offence has affected his or her life rather than have a third party description of the victim's impact. Victims were not automatically part of the process in the *Young Offenders Act*. Usually, the police would take a victim impact statement, but the victim would unlikely be part of the proceedings. One of the key issues in this section and other sections providing disclosure to victims is where and how victims receive this information. Procedures and protocols are starting to fall into place in some jurisdictions to assist victims so they know where to go to get the information, and to support police, courts, and probation officers in disclosing the appropriate information. Usually the Crown Attorney's office will have information of how an offence was dealt with by extrajudicial sanctions, and in most situations a probation officer can also make that information available to victims.

PART 2 ORGANIZATION OF YOUTH CRIMINAL JUSTICE SYSTEM

INTRODUCTION

The youth justice system is separate from the adult system, with separate courts, judges and rules. Many of the offences and rules in the *Criminal Code*, which apply to adults, also apply to youths but only as they are modified by this legislation. Part 2 of the *Youth Criminal Justice Act* requires separate courts and judges to be established for youths, and provides the power to make rules to govern the operation of these courts.

Youth justice courts and youth justice court judges are given the power to deal exclusively with cases involving youths. There are general powers conferred on courts, and sections that attempt to clarify specific situations that come before courts. These situations include peace bonds and cases where the age of the person is uncertain.

In addition to judges, there are sections that give powers to others who are known to play a role in the daily operation of the youth justice system — justices of the peace, clerks of the court and provincial directors. There is also an expanded description of the role of youth justice committees.

Also included is conferencing, a restorative process that involves communities and other interested parties and which is introduced and officially recognized as a part of the youth justice system. Police, for example, can convene a conference to help determine whether an extrajudicial measure or an extrajudical sanction is the most appropriate police response.

YOUTH JUSTICE COURT

13. (1) *Designation of youth justice court* **— A youth justice court is any court that may be established or designated by or under an Act of the**

legislature of a province, or designated by the Governor in Council or the lieutenant governor in council of a province, as a youth justice court for the purposes of this Act, and a youth justice court judge is a person who may be appointed or designated as a judge of the youth justice court or a judge sitting in a court established or designated as a youth justice court.

(2) *Deemed youth justice court* — When a young person elects to be tried by a judge without a jury, the judge shall be a judge as defined in section 552 of the *Criminal Code*, or if it is an offence set out in section 469 of that Act, the judge shall be a judge of the superior court of criminal jurisdiction in the province in which the election is made. In either case, the judge is deemed to be a youth justice court judge and the court is deemed to be a youth justice court for the purpose of the proceeding.

(3) *Deemed youth justice court* — When a young person elects or is deemed to have elected to be tried by a court composed of a judge and jury, the superior court of criminal jurisdiction in the province in which the election is made or deemed to have been made is deemed to be a youth justice court for the purpose of the proceeding, and the superior court judge is deemed to be a youth justice court judge.

(4) *Court of record* — A youth justice court is a court of record.

COMMENTARY

Legal Implications

This section is technical, and is key to the procedural operation of the Act. Provision is made for each province or territory to establish, or designate, youth justice courts and youth justice court judges.

When a case is to be heard by a court composed of a judge and jury, or by a judge without a jury, it must be heard by an appropriate court as defined in the *Criminal Code*. Superior courts will hear all jury cases. A superior court that hears cases involving young persons is deemed to be a youth justice court for that purpose only and not as a whole. The choices a young person has for trial are set out in section 67, and this section must be read with section 67 in order to fully understand the limitations of the superior court deemed to be a youth justice court.

14. (1) *Exclusive jurisdiction of youth justice court* — Despite any other Act of Parliament but subject to the *Contraventions Act* and the *National Defence Act*, a youth justice court has exclusive jurisdiction in respect of any offence alleged to have been committed by a person while he or she was a young person, and that person shall be dealt with as provided in this Act.

(2) *Orders* — A youth justice court has jurisdiction to make orders against a young person under sections 810 (recognizance — fear of injury or damage), 810.01 (recognizance — fear of criminal organization offence)

and 810.2 (recognizance — fear of serious personal injury offence) of the *Criminal Code*. If the young person fails or refuses to enter into a recognizance referred to in any of those sections, the court may impose any one of the sanctions set out in subsection 42(2) (youth sentences) except that, in the case of an order under paragraph 42(2)(*n*) (custody and supervision order), it shall not exceed thirty days.

(3) *Prosecution prohibited* — Unless the Attorney General and the young person agree, no extrajudicial measures shall be taken or judicial proceedings commenced under this Act in respect of an offence after the end of the time limit set out in any other Act of Parliament or any regulation made under it for the institution of proceedings in respect of that offence.

(4) *Continuation of proceedings* — Extrajudicial measures taken or judicial proceedings commenced under this Act against a young person may be continued under this Act after the person attains the age of eighteen years.

(5) *Young persons over the age of eighteen years* — This Act applies to persons eighteen years old or older who are alleged to have committed an offence while a young person.

(6) *Powers of youth justice court judge* — For the purpose of carrying out the provisions of this Act, a youth justice court judge is a justice and a provincial court judge and has the jurisdiction and powers of a summary conviction court under the *Criminal Code*.

(7) *Powers of a judge of a superior court* — A judge of a superior court of criminal jurisdiction, when deemed to be a youth justice court judge for the purpose of a proceeding, retains the jurisdiction and powers of a superior court of criminal jurisdiction.

COMMENTARY

Legal Implications

This section also contains technical provisions that are key to the operation of the courts.

The fundamental principle is that the youth justice court has the exclusive right to hear cases dealing with young persons. This is the reason that a superior court is deemed to be a youth justice court with limited powers for certain purposes but not as a whole when it hears a case.

A clarification of the powers of youth justice courts is the power to hear applications for peace bonds. Peace bonds are issued to prevent contact, or to prevent certain activities, in an attempt to avoid criminal activity by the use of a court order. In the *Young Offenders Act*, peace bonds were not specifically listed in the powers of the court, which left some courts questioning the court's authority to deal with peace bond applications. There is nothing in this section that requires a peace bond application to be made under section 525 of the *Criminal Code*. This provision makes it clear that youth justice courts have this power.

15. (1) *Contempt against youth justice court* — **Every youth justice court has the same power, jurisdiction and authority to deal with and impose punish-ment for contempt against the court as may be exercised by the superior court of criminal jurisdiction of the province in which the court is situated.**

(2) *Jurisdiction of youth justice court* — **A youth justice court has jurisdiction in respect of every contempt of court committed by a young person against the youth justice court whether or not committed in the face of the court, and every contempt of court committed by a young person against any other court otherwise than in the face of that court.**

(3) *Concurrent jurisdiction of youth justice court* — **A youth justice court has jurisdiction in respect of every contempt of court committed by a young person against any other court in the face of that court and every contempt of court committed by an adult against the youth justice court in the face of the youth justice court, but nothing in this subsection affects the power, jurisdiction or authority of any other court to deal with or impose punishment for contempt of court.**

(4) *Youth sentence – contempt* — **When a youth justice court or any other court finds a young person guilty of contempt of court, it may impose as a youth sentence any one of the sanctions set out in subsection 42(2) (youth sentences), or any number of them that are not inconsistent with each other, but no other sentence.**

(5) *Section 708 of Criminal Code applies in respect of adults* — **Section 708 (contempt) of the** *Criminal Code* **applies in respect of proceedings under this section in youth justice court against adults, with any modifications that the circumstances require.**

COMMENTARY

Legal Implications

Contempt of court is not a new section. Although it is not a common occurrence, it is necessary for the court to have the power to punish a person for not doing what the court has ordered during the hearing. Contempt of court is a very powerful tool that allows the court to keep control of proceedings.

Operational Implications

Unfortunately contempt of court may also be used to coerce justice officials into doing the bidding of the court in areas of professional discretion that are not legislated. For example, a youth justice court wanted to charge a children's aid society worker with contempt of court when the worker indicated her role was not to sit in youth court all day in the event that the court may want to make a referral for a child welfare assessment under section 35.

16. *Status of offender uncertain* — **When a person is alleged to have committed an offence during a period that includes the date on which the person attains the age of eighteen years, the youth justice court has jurisdiction in respect of the offence and shall, after putting the person to their election under section 67 (adult sentence) if applicable, and on finding the person guilty of the offence,**

> (*a*) **if it has been proven that the offence was committed before the person attained the age of eighteen years, impose a sentence under this Act;**
>
> (*b*) **if it has been proven that the offence was committed after the person attained the age of eighteen years, impose any sentence that could be imposed under the *Criminal Code* or any other Act of Parliament on an adult who has been convicted of the same offence; and**
>
> (*c*) **if it has not been proven that the offence was committed after the person attained the age of eighteen years, impose a sentence under this Act.**

COMMENTARY

Legal Implications

This section has a very limited and special purpose. Youth justice courts are the only courts that can hear cases dealing with young persons, and sometimes it is not clear whether the person was a young person or an adult at the time the offence occurred.

This provision gives the youth justice court the power to hear cases when it is not certain if the person was a young person or an adult, and prevents these cases from falling between the technical cracks in the legal system. Under the *Young Offenders Act*, the youth court had the exclusive jurisdiction to handle cases involving young persons, but no power to handle cases involving adults; thus, when the age of the person was uncertain, it was possible that no court had jurisdiction over the offence. This section is intended to resolve that problem. See the case of *R. v. A.M.*, [2004] A.J. No. 67, 2004 ABPC 10, where this section was applied.

17. (1) *Youth justice court may make rules* — **The youth justice court for a province may, subject to the approval of the lieutenant governor in council of the province, establish rules of court not inconsistent with this Act or any other Act of Parliament or with any regulations made under section 155 regulating proceedings within the jurisdiction of the youth justice court.**

(2) *Rules of court* — Rules under subsection (1) may be made

(a) generally to regulate the duties of the officers of the youth justice court and any other matter considered expedient to attain the ends of justice and carry into effect the provisions of this Act;
(b) subject to any regulations made under paragraph 155(b), to regulate the practice and procedure in the youth justice court; and
(c) to prescribe forms to be used in the youth justice court if they are not otherwise provided for by or under this Act.

(3) *Publication of rules* — Rules of court that are made under the authority of this section shall be published in the appropriate provincial gazette.

COMMENTARY

Legal Implications

Courts have procedures and rules that control proceedings before them for the purpose of keeping order and to assist lawyers and those who appear before the courts to be clear of what is expected of them so that they may be properly prepared.

This section gives youth justice courts the power to make these rules. Any rules that are made must be published and be available to the public. The publication of the rules is part of honouring the principle that courts be open to the public.

YOUTH JUSTICE COMMITTEES

18. (1) *Youth justice committees* — The Attorney General of Canada or a province or any other minister that the lieutenant governor in council of the province may designate may establish one or more committees of citizens, to be known as youth justice committees, to assist in any aspect of the administration of this Act or in any programs or services for young persons.

(2) *Role of committee* — The functions of a youth justice committee may include the following:

(a) in the case of a young person alleged to have committed an offence,
  (i) giving advice on the appropriate extrajudicial measure to be used in respect of the young person,
  (ii) supporting any victim of the alleged offence by soliciting his or her concerns and facilitating the reconciliation of the victim and the young person,
  (iii) ensuring that community support is available to the young person by arranging for the use of services from within the

community, and enlisting members of the community to provide short-term mentoring and supervision, and

(iv) when the young person is also being dealt with by a child protection agency or a community group, helping to coordinate the interaction of the agency or group with the youth criminal justice system;

(b) advising the federal and provincial governments on whether the provisions of this Act that grant rights to young persons, or provide for the protection of young persons, are being complied with;

(c) advising the federal and provincial governments on policies and procedures related to the youth criminal justice system;

(d) providing information to the public in respect of this Act and the youth criminal justice system;

(e) acting as a conference; and

(f) any other functions assigned by the person who establishes the committee.

COMMENTARY

Legal Implications

Youth justice committees were authorized under section 69 of the *Young Offenders Act*, but were not mandatory for jurisdictions to provide. Several provinces and territories did establish youth justice committees under the *Young Offenders Act*. In this new legislation, youth justice committees are still optional, but there is further support for the use of youth justice committees and a detailed description of their functions. The role of communities, parents, victims and other people affected by an offence are recognized as important to the appropriate response to youth crime.

Operational Implications

Youth justice committees need to have the support of both the community and the formal justice system. These committees represent a unique approach that gives recognition to a broad community response to youth crime that reflects the needs of the community, the victim and the offender. Each jurisdiction, or, in many cases, the community, determines the types of cases that will go before a youth justice committee and at what stage in the proceedings. There is also a wide variance in the role and functions of youth justice committees from province to province. At the pre-charge stage, a police officer may refer a youth to a youth justice committee. At the post-charge stage, the Crown, the provincial director or the court may make the referral. There is no legislative restriction on the number or types of offences that may be referred to a youth justice committee. Provinces and territories make their own rules around eligible offences. The majority of the youth justice committees usually deal with first-time offenders with less serious offences. However, there are also communities that use youth justice committees for more serious offences that often result in bringing the young person back into the community and restoring the harm to the community. There is some variation across the country in all aspects of how youth justice committees operate, as is the case with many parts of this legislation.

Many jurisdictions such as Alberta and Saskatchewan have developed sophisticated networks of youth justice committees with provincial standards and protocols to deal with a range of offences.

CONFERENCES

19. (1) *Conferences may be convened* — A youth justice court judge, the provincial director, a police officer, a justice of the peace, a prosecutor or a youth worker may convene or cause to be convened a conference for the purpose of making a decision required to be made under this Act.

(2) *Mandate of a conference* — The mandate of a conference may be, among other things, to give advice on appropriate extrajudicial measures, conditions for judicial interim release, sentences, including the review of sentences, and reintegration plans.

(3) *Rules for conferences* — The Attorney General or any other minister designated by the lieutenant governor in council of a province may establish rules for the convening and conducting of conferences other than conferences convened or caused to be convened by a youth justice court judge or a justice of the peace.

(4) *Rules to apply* — In provinces where rules are established under subsection (3), the conferences to which those rules apply must be convened and conducted in accordance with those rules.

COMMENTARY

Legal Implications

Although there are many types of conferences that have been used at varying stages in youth justice across Canada, this is the first time the use of conferences has been entrenched in legislation. The objective is to encourage more input from interested parties and people affected by the misconduct of the youth.

Some jurisdictions have developed rules for the convening and conducting of conferences. Although the Act does not permit jurisdictions to make rules for judiciary conferences under section 41, some jurisdictions have been successful in presenting rules to judges as suggested guidelines.

Operational Implications

A conference can be as simple as the police officer meeting with school officials to determine if a charge should be laid, or the best approach to provide meaningful consequences for a youth's offending behaviour. On the other end of the scale, a Crown Attorney or provincial director could call medical, psychiatric and psychological professionals together for input on a youth's behaviour. Or, a conference can be a restorative conference for serious or less serious offences that seeks to repair harm to the community. The intent is for any person who has the responsibility to make a decision in the justice system to be able to turn to others for input. The legislation also allows for youth justice committees to act as a conference (section 18(2)(*e*)) and for judges to use conferences (section 41) to assist with recommendations for sentencing.

There is no legislative restriction on the scope of a conference, and each jurisdiction can set limitations through policies and procedures for all conferences other than those convened by the judiciary. Legislating conferencing has brought mixed reactions. Jurisdictions can agree that conferencing is an effective tool that can greatly benefit youth justice; however, with so many models with varying degrees of intensity, there is the potential to make conferencing a less effective and more expensive tool unless proper policies and procedures are in place. The legislation is not prescriptive regarding the number of persons requested to attend a conference, or the type of conference. The best approach is to establish protocols to clarify the rules in each jurisdiction to make conferences meaningful and effective. Thus far, conferences under this section are not being overly utilized in Canada.

Police officers and Crown attorneys are the most likely to convene conferences under section 19 of the Act. Conferences will enable them to bring together people who are significant in the young person's life to get enough information to decide what should be the next steps in the process and what will hold the young person accountable.

JUSTICES OF THE PEACE

20. (1) *Certain proceedings may be taken before justices* **— Any proceeding that may be carried out before a justice under the *Criminal Code*, other than a plea, a trial or an adjudication, may be carried out before a justice in respect of an offence alleged to have been committed by a young person, and any process that may be issued by a justice under the *Criminal Code* may be issued by a justice in respect of an offence alleged to have been committed by a young person.**

(2) *Orders under section 810 of Criminal Code* **— A justice has jurisdiction to make an order under section 810 (recognizance — fear of injury or damage) of the *Criminal Code* in respect of a young person. If the young person fails or refuses to enter into a recognizance referred to in that section, the justice shall refer the matter to a youth justice court.**

COMMENTARY

Legal Implications

As in the *Young Offenders Act*, justices of the peace have an important role in the criminal justice system. This section has incorporated all of section 6 from the *Young Offenders Act* and added a new subsection (2) in which a justice of the peace can make a recognizance order under the *Criminal Code* and can refer the young person to a youth justice court for failing or refusing to enter into a recognizance. This section sets out some of the differences between the youth and adult systems as to how justices of the peace are to conduct their business. There are some limitations placed on the powers of justices from those they have with adults. This is an added protection for young persons.

It is noteworthy that the *Youth Criminal Justice Act*, as did the *Young Offenders Act*, states "other than a plea, a trial or an adjudication" when referring to proceedings that may be carried out by a justice. An Order in Council or other jurisdictional document will set out the powers and limitations a justice of the peace can exercise in addition to this section.

CLERKS OF THE COURT

21. *Powers of clerks* — In addition to any powers conferred on a clerk of a court by the *Criminal Code*, a clerk of the youth justice court may exercise the powers ordinarily exercised by a clerk of a court, and, in particular, may

(a) **administer oaths or solemn affirmations in all matters relating to the business of the youth justice court; and**
(b) **in the absence of a youth justice court judge, exercise all the powers of a youth justice court judge relating to adjournment.**

COMMENTARY

Legal Implications

Clerks of a court also have traditional powers that they exercise in adult courts, and this section clarifies their role in the youth justice court.

PROVINCIAL DIRECTORS

22. *Powers, duties and functions of provincial directors* — The provincial director may authorize any person to exercise the powers or perform the duties or functions of the provincial director under this Act, in which case the powers, duties or functions are deemed to have been exercised or performed by the provincial director.

COMMENTARY

Legal Implications

The role of provincial director has expanded under this Act. There are many duties and functions that a provincial director can, and may be required to, exercise, and this section allows those duties and functions to be carried out by anyone authorized to do so by the provincial director. For example, section 42(2)(c) of the legislation states that in sentencing a young person to a conditional discharge, the youth justice court may require the young person to report to, and be supervised by, the provincial director. This section, which deals with the powers and duties of the provincial director, allows the provincial director to delegate the duty of supervising a conditional discharge sentence to a probation officer.

Operational Implications

This section allows the provincial director to delegate some of the approximately 108 duties and functions required under the Act. Probation officers or facility supervisors are often designated as provincial directors for the purpose of case management decisions, or placement or movement of youths.

PART 3 JUDICIAL MEASURES

INTRODUCTION

The criminal law is complex, and detailed legal rules are required so that procedures before court will be orderly and fair to the accused, victims, witnesses and the officers of the court.

The sections that follow in Part 3 are detailed legal rules that are of great interest and well known to many of the lawyers and other court officials who work in the youth justice system, but may generally be of little interest to the general public.

CONSENT TO PROSECUTE

23. (1) *Pre-charge screening* **— The Attorney General may establish a program of pre-charge screening that sets out the circumstances in which the consent of the Attorney General must be obtained before a young person is charged with an offence.**

(2) *Pre-charge screening program* **— Any program of pre-charge screening of young persons that is established under an Act of the legislature of a province or by a directive of a provincial government, and that is in place before the coming into force of this section, is deemed to be a program of pre-charge screening for the purposes of subsection (1).**

COMMENTARY

Legal Implications

This is a new section that authorizes the Attorney General to establish a pre-charge screening program.

New Brunswick, Quebec and British Columbia provide pre-charge screening programs, and there are several pilot programs across Canada that are currently being evaluated. The provinces that have the program have indicated that it reduces the number of cases that go to court; however, in some of the other jurisdictions, the police see Crown approval of charges as an infringement on police discretion.

One of the strengths of a pre-charge screening program is that it allows the Crown to raise options with the police without having to ask the court for an adjournment or a stay of proceedings. It provides a better, more timely opportunity to discuss a decision before it becomes public through the formal charging process.

Operational Implications

Pre-charge screening was a concept under the *Young Offenders Act* that was formally used in three Canadian provinces, and informally in several other areas. It has proven to be successful in reducing the number of cases that proceed to the formal court system. By legislating this concept, it is anticipated that other jurisdictions will develop a pre-charge screening program. The program involves a Crown Attorney reviewing the charge recommended by the police and approving proceeding to court, or suggesting alternatives to youth court. This requires the Crown attorneys and defence counsel to be aware of, and familiar with, community-based programs that may be appropriate alternatives to the formal court system.

24. *Private prosecutions* **— No prosecutions may be conducted by a prosecutor other than the Attorney General without the consent of the Attorney General.**

COMMENTARY

Legal Implications

This is a new section that prohibits the commencement of criminal court proceedings against young persons without the consent of the Attorney General. It is possible for members of the public to commence proceedings against an adult, for an assault charge, for example, without involving the police or the Crown Attorney's office. This is not possible where young persons are involved.

RIGHT TO COUNSEL

25. (1) *Right to counsel* **— A young person has the right to retain and instruct counsel without delay, and to exercise that right personally, at any stage of proceedings against the young person and before and during any consideration of whether, instead of starting or continuing judicial proceedings against the young person under this Act, to use an extrajudicial sanction to deal with the young person.**

(2) *Arresting officer to advise young person of right to counsel* **— Every young person who is arrested or detained shall, on being arrested or detained, be advised without delay by the arresting officer or the officer in**

charge, as the case may be, of the right to retain and instruct counsel, and be given an opportunity to obtain counsel.

(3) *Justice, youth justice court or review board to advise young person of right to counsel* — When a young person is not represented by counsel

- (*a*) at a hearing at which it will be determined whether to release the young person or detain the young person in custody prior to sentencing,
- (*b*) at a hearing held under section 71 (hearing — adult sentences),
- (*c*) at trial,
- (*d*) at any proceedings held under subsection 98(3) (continuation of custody), 103(1) (review by youth justice court), 104(1) (continuation of custody), 105(1) (conditional supervision) or 109(1) (review of decision),
- (*e*) at a review of a youth sentence held before a youth justice court under this Act, or
- (*f*) at a review of the level of custody under section 87,

the justice or youth justice court before which the hearing, trial or review is held, or the review board before which the review is held, shall advise the young person of the right to retain and instruct counsel and shall give the young person a reasonable opportunity to obtain counsel.

(4) *Trial, hearing or review before youth justice court or review board* — When a young person at trial or at a hearing or review referred to in subsection (3) wishes to obtain counsel but is unable to do so, the youth justice court before which the hearing, trial or review is held or the review board before which the review is held

- (*a*) shall, if there is a legal aid program or an assistance program available in the province where the hearing, trial or review is held, refer the young person to that program for the appointment of counsel; or
- (*b*) if no legal aid program or assistance program is available or the young person is unable to obtain counsel through the program, may, and on the request of the young person shall, direct that the young person be represented by counsel.

(5) *Appointment of counsel* — When a direction is made under paragraph (4)(*b*) in respect of a young person, the Attorney General shall appoint counsel, or cause counsel to be appointed, to represent the young person.

(6) *Release hearing before justice* — When a young person, at a hearing referred to in paragraph (3)(*a*) that is held before a justice who is not a youth justice court judge, wishes to obtain counsel but is unable to do so, the justice shall

(a) if there is a legal aid program or an assistance program available in the province where the hearing is held,
   (i) refer the young person to that program for the appointment of counsel, or
   (ii) refer the matter to a youth justice court to be dealt with in accordance with paragraph (4)(a) or (b); or
(b) if no legal aid program or assistance program is available or the young person is unable to obtain counsel through the program, refer the matter without delay to a youth justice court to be dealt with in accordance with paragraph (4)(b).

(7) *Young person may be assisted by adult* — When a young person is not represented by counsel at trial or at a hearing or review referred to in subsection (3), the justice before whom or the youth justice court or review board before which the proceedings are held may, on the request of the young person, allow the young person to be assisted by an adult whom the justice, court or review board considers to be suitable.

(8) *Counsel independent of parents* — If it appears to a youth justice court judge or a justice that the interests of a young person and the interests of a parent are in conflict or that it would be in the best interests of the young person to be represented by his or her own counsel, the judge or justice shall ensure that the young person is represented by counsel independent of the parent.

(9) *Statement of right to counsel* — A statement that a young person has the right to be represented by counsel shall be included in

(a) any appearance notice or summons issued to the young person;
(b) any warrant to arrest the young person;
(c) any promise to appear given by the young person;
(d) any undertaking or recognizance entered into before an officer in charge by the young person;
(e) any notice given to the young person in relation to any proceedings held under subsection 98(3) (continuation of custody), 103(1) (review by youth justice court), 104(1) (continuation of custody), 105(1) (conditional supervision) or 109(1) (review of decision); or
(f) any notice of a review of a youth sentence given to the young person.

(10) *Recovery of costs of counsel* — Nothing in this Act prevents the lieutenant governor in council of a province or his or her delegate from establishing a program to authorize the recovery of the costs of a young person's counsel from the young person or the parents of the young person. The costs may be recovered only after the proceedings are completed and the time allowed for the taking of an appeal has expired or, if an appeal is taken, all proceedings in respect of the appeal have been completed.

(11) *Exception for persons over the age of twenty* — Subsections (4) to (9) do not apply to a person who is alleged to have committed an offence while a young person, if the person has attained the age of twenty years at the time of his or her first appearance before a youth justice court in respect of the offence; however, this does not restrict any rights that a person has under the law applicable to adults.

COMMENTARY

Legal Implications

The right to counsel, or the right to have a lawyer, is one of the fundamental concepts of youth justice law and one of the areas where youths have rights in addition to those that adults have. It is this section that sets out the rules for young persons obtaining legal representation. This section gives the *Youth Criminal Justice Act* the authority to order the Attorney General to appoint a lawyer to represent a young person, as was the case under the *Young Offenders Act*.

An amendment to this section is being proposed by provinces and territories, as the word "obtain" in section 25(2) does not appear to reflect the intention of section 25(1), which is to retain and instruct counsel. The two subsections need to be connected.

Operational Implications

This section deals with a young person's right to counsel and provides all of the rights that were given under the *Young Offenders Act*. The Act also includes a provision that recognizes the right of jurisdictions to look to the parents of a young person to recover the costs of legal counsel. Generally, it is considered to be costly to recover the costs of legal fees, so most jurisdictions will likely not have a cost recovery program in place. Whether to establish a cost recovery program or not is the decision of each jurisdiction and is not mandatory, and can be implemented at any time. Jurisdictions have rules for the operation of legal aid, and this includes rules regarding access to a lawyer. For the most part, young persons in conflict with the law have access to free legal counsel for serious offences in all parts of Canada. This legislation retains the court's ability to direct that the youth be represented by counsel before proceeding.

NOTICES TO PARENTS

26. (1) *Notice in case of arrest or detention* — Subject to subsection (4), if a young person is arrested and detained in custody pending his or her appearance in court, the officer in charge at the time the young person is detained shall, as soon as possible, give or cause to be given to a parent of the young person, orally or in writing, notice of the arrest stating the place of detention and the reason for the arrest.

(2) *Notice in other cases* — Subject to subsection (4), if a summons or an appearance notice is issued in respect of a young person, the person who issued the summons or appearance notice, or, if a young person is released on giving a promise to appear or entering into an undertaking or recognizance, the officer in charge, shall, as soon as possible, give or cause to be given to a parent of the young person notice in writing of the summons, appearance notice, promise to appear, undertaking or recognizance.

(3) *Notice to parent in case of ticket* — Subject to subsection (4), a person who serves a ticket under the *Contraventions Act* on a young person, other than a ticket served for a contravention relating to parking a vehicle, shall, as soon as possible, give or cause to be given notice in writing of the ticket to a parent of the young person.

(4) *Notice to relative or other adult* — If the whereabouts of the parents of a young person are not known or it appears that no parent is available, a notice under this section may be given to an adult relative of the young person who is known to the young person and is likely to assist the young person or, if no such adult relative is available, to any other adult who is known to the young person and is likely to assist the young person and who the person giving the notice considers appropriate.

(5) *Notice on direction of youth justice court judge or justice* — If doubt exists as to the person to whom a notice under this section should be given, a youth justice court judge or, if a youth justice court judge is, having regard to the circumstances, not reasonably available, a justice may give directions as to the person to whom the notice should be given, and a notice given in accordance with those directions is sufficient notice for the purposes of this section.

(6) *Contents of notice* — Any notice under this section shall, in addition to any other requirements under this section, include

    (a) the name of the young person in respect of whom it is given;
    (b) the charge against the young person and, except in the case of a notice of a ticket served under the *Contraventions Act*, the time and place of appearance; and
    (c) a statement that the young person has the right to be represented by counsel.

(7) *Notice of ticket under Contraventions Act* — A notice under subsection (3) shall include a copy of the ticket.

(8) *Service of notice* — Subject to subsections (10) and (11), a notice under this section that is given in writing may be served personally or be sent by confirmed delivery service.

(9) *Proceedings not invalid* — Subject to subsections (10) and (11), failure to give a notice in accordance with this section does not affect the validity of proceedings under this Act.

(10) *Exception* — Failure to give a notice under subsection (2) in accordance with this section in any case renders invalid any subsequent proceedings under this Act relating to the case unless

   (a) a parent of the young person attends court with the young person; or
   (b) a youth justice court judge or a justice before whom proceedings are held against the young person
      (i) adjourns the proceedings and orders that the notice be given in the manner and to the persons that the judge or justice directs, or
      (ii) dispenses with the notice if the judge or justice is of the opinion that, having regard to the circumstances, the notice may be dispensed with.

(11) *Where notice is not served* — Where there has been a failure to give a notice under subsection (1) or (3) in accordance with this section and none of the persons to whom the notice may be given attends court with the young person, a youth justice court judge or a justice before whom proceedings are held against the young person may

   (a) adjourn the proceedings and order that the notice be given in the manner and to the persons that the judge or justice directs; or
   (b) dispense with the notice if the judge or justice is of the opinion that, having regard to the circumstances, the notice may be dispensed with.

(12) *Exception for persons over the age of twenty* — This section does not apply to a person who is alleged to have committed an offence while a young person, if the person has attained the age of twenty years at the time of his or her first appearance before a youth justice court in respect of the offence.

COMMENTARY

Legal Implications

Parents play a very important part in successfully changing the direction of youth justice law in Canada. There are many sections of the *Youth Criminal Justice Act* which specifically mention parents. This one makes provision for parents receiving notice in the event a young person is arrested or detained, or in the event other steps are taken that would bring a young person into the justice system. One provision not included in the *Young Offenders Act* is the provision that no notice is required if the person was 20 years of age at the time of the first court appearance.

Operational Implications

Early indications of the impact of implementation of this legislation indicate that confirmed service delivery as per section 26(8) is proving to be costly in some jurisdictions. It is recommended that this be amended to return to section 9(7) of the *Young Offenders Act*, where the requirement was ordinary mail.

27. (1) *Order requiring attendance of parent* **— If a parent does not attend proceedings held before a youth justice court in respect of a young person, the court may, if in its opinion the presence of the parent is necessary or in the best interests of the young person, by order in writing require the parent to attend at any stage of the proceedings.**

(2) *No order in ticket proceedings* **— Subsection (1) does not apply in proceedings commenced by filing a ticket under the *Contraventions Act*.**

(3) *Service of order* **— A copy of the order shall be served by a peace officer or by a person designated by a youth justice court by delivering it personally to the parent to whom it is directed, unless the youth justice court authorizes service by confirmed delivery service.**

(4) *Failure to attend* **— A parent who is ordered to attend a youth justice court under subsection (1) and who fails without reasonable excuse, the proof of which lies on the parent, to comply with the order**

- **(*a*) is guilty of contempt of court;**
- **(*b*) may be dealt with summarily by the court; and**
- **(*c*) is liable to the punishment provided for in the *Criminal Code* for a summary conviction offence.**

(5) *Warrant to arrest parent* **— If a parent who is ordered to attend a youth justice court under subsection (1) does not attend when required by the order or fails to remain in attendance as required and it is proved that a copy of the order was served on the parent, a youth justice court may issue a warrant to compel the attendance of the parent.**

COMMENTARY

Legal Implications

The ideal in the renewed youth justice system is for parents to attend court and support the young person; however, in the case where the parents do not attend, the youth justice courts have the authority to issue a court order for the parents to attend court. The courts also have the authority to force parents to attend court, for example, by issuing a warrant for the arrest of the parent(s). If a parent is ordered to attend court, but fails, the parent may be held in contempt of court.

DETENTION BEFORE SENTENCING

28. *Application of Part XVI of Criminal Code* — Except to the extent that they are inconsistent with or excluded by this Act, the provisions of Part XVI (compelling appearance of an accused and interim release) of the *Criminal Code* apply to the detention and release of young persons under this Act.

COMMENTARY

Legal Implications

The next few sections of the Act deal with judicial interim release, or bail as it is more commonly known. This section sets out the general rule that bail provisions of the *Criminal Code* apply to youths, with the exception of some special provisions set out in the *Youth Criminal Justice Act* that are specific to youths.

29. (1) *Detention as social measure prohibited* — A youth justice court judge or a justice shall not detain a young person in custody prior to being sentenced as a substitute for appropriate child protection, mental health or other social measures.

(2) *Detention presumed unnecessary* — In considering whether the detention of a young person is necessary for the protection or safety of the public under paragraph 515(10)(*b*) (substantial likelihood — commit an offence or interfere with the administration of justice) of the *Criminal Code*, a youth justice court or a justice shall presume that detention is not necessary under that paragraph if the young person could not, on being found guilty, be committed to custody on the grounds set out in paragraphs 39(1)(*a*) to (*c*) (restrictions on committal to custody).

COMMENTARY

Legal Implications

This partially new section strengthens the message from the *Young Offenders Act* that incarceration should not be used for any reason other than criminal law purposes. The general rule set out in this section states that detaining a youth in custody is not to be used as a substitute for child protection, mental health or other social measures.

Operational Implications

This more effective section signals an important policy direction for youth justice as it sets the tone for offence-based rather than client-based legislation, meaning that it is the nature of the offence that should determine the system response, including the consequences. This notion has been reinforced in *R. v.*

D.A.I., [2003] B.C.J. No. 1065 (Prov. Ct.), where the court ruled that judicial interim release with strict terms was granted to a youth charged with possession of a stolen vehicle and failure to remain at the scene of an accident and several counts of breach of probation but only one conviction. The youth had made all court appearances in the past and the court ruled there was no "pattern" of committing indictable offences and therefore no basis upon which to find that detention was necessary to ensure court appearance.

The inappropriate use of detention is well documented. It has been common practice to incarcerate a youth because his or her behaviour is out of control at home or at school, or because social service systems have failed. Detaining a youth in custody is very serious and should not be viewed as a way to access other services such as child welfare or children's mental health programs.

Case law was established on June 12, 2003 by the British Columbia Youth Court in *R. v. A.S.D.*, [2003] B.C.J. No. 1831 (Youth Ct.), when the court denied bail to a 14-year-old young person with no previous record who was virtually uncontrollable in her foster care and group homes. She displayed assaultive, disobedient and disruptive behaviour, and she had problems with substance abuse. She did not obey existing bail orders, in particular with respect to reporting and curfew conditions, nor did she keep the peace and be of good behaviour. In the months prior to the hearing, the police had dealt almost daily with the youth in trying to control her behaviour. At the group home, there appeared to have been daily problems with no discernible improvement in the youth's behaviour.

In denying bail to the young person, the youth court judge reasoned that failure to comply with non-custodial sentences must be interpreted in this context to include not only charges of breach of probation, but also convictions or allegations of failing to comply with a judicial interim release condition that had not yet come to court, where the Crown shows a *prima facie* case against the accused. The youth court judge remarked that some intermediate level of care between the youth's current foster home and a youth detention facility was necessary in the province, but felt that despite that theoretical need, in the case of this youth, the youth detention facility was appropriate. The youth court judge concluded that denying bail to the young person would not be an improper substitute for appropriate child protection or other social measures since the youth's repeated failures to respect bail conditions raised concerns regarding the administration of justice. Without detention, the young person was likely to continue to be in almost daily breach of her bail provisions. Furthermore, failure to obey her bail conditions would likely lead to more substantial breaches of the law. The youth court judge said that the youth was someone who would likely get into more serious situations until efforts at rehabilitation had some chance of success. Denying bail was likely the only way to achieve any compliance by the youth with her bail conditions.

One month later, on July 9, 2003, in British Columbia Provincial Court in *R. v. J.R.M.*, [2003] B.C.J. No. 1720 (Prov. Ct.), the Crown sought detention of a young person on the secondary ground, that the accused would, if released from custody, commit a criminal offence or interfere with the administration of justice. The offence occurred at the youth's group home, where he began to throw dishes, smash walls and break glass. The youth had been diagnosed with schizophrenia and had either discontinued or been erratic in taking his antipsychotic medication. The youth court judge noted that one of the changes under the *Youth Criminal Justice Act* was that there was a presumption that there ought not to be a detention order unless certain circumstances existed. Also, section 29(1) specified that detention should not be used as a substitute for appropriate child protection, mental health or other social measures. The court concluded that the Act precluded detaining the youth notwithstanding the concerns of the Crown, the doctors and perhaps the court. Under the *Young Offenders Act*, the youth could perhaps have been detained, but the *Youth Criminal Justice Act* contemplated an alternative measure where there were mental health issues. The *Youth Criminal Justice Act* required mental health issues to be dealt with by someone other than the courts. The youth court judge concluded that since the young person could not be committed to custody for this offence, the youth could not be detained until trial. The outstanding concerns regarding the youth would have to be addressed by placing the young person on terms for release.

Some jurisdictions have initiated bail supervisions programs, or judicial interim release programs, to provide the courts with alternatives to detention. These programs provide intense community supervision that satisfy the court that not detaining the youth will not jeopardize the protection or safety of the public.

Places of temporary detention differ across jurisdictions. Some areas detain youths in smaller children's residences designated as detention/custody, while others use larger institution-like settings for detention. There are no provisions set out in this Act for the physical setting of detention or custody other than it must be separate and apart from adult offenders.

30. (1) *Designated place of temporary detention* — **Subject to subsection (7), a young person who is arrested and detained prior to being sentenced, or who is detained in accordance with a warrant issued under subsection 59(6) (compelling appearance for review of sentence), shall be detained in any place of temporary detention that may be designated by the lieutenant governor in council of the province or his or her delegate or in a place within a class of places so designated.**

(2) *Exception* — **A young person who is detained in a place of temporary detention under subsection (1) may, in the course of being transferred from that place to the court or from the court to that place, be held under the supervision and control of a peace officer.**

(3) *Detention separate from adults* — **A young person referred to in subsection (1) shall be held separate and apart from any adult who is detained or held in custody unless a youth justice court judge or a justice is satisfied that, having regard to the best interests of the young person,**

> **(*a*) the young person cannot, having regard to his or her own safety or the safety of others, be detained in a place of detention for young persons; or**

(b) no place of detention for young persons is available within a reasonable distance.

(4) *Transfer to adult facility* — When a young person is detained under subsection (1), the youth justice court may, on application of the provincial director made at any time after the young person attains the age of eighteen years, after giving the young person an opportunity to be heard, authorize the provincial director to direct, despite subsection (3), that the young person be temporarily detained in a provincial correctional facility for adults, if the court considers it to be in the best interests of the young person or in the public interest.

(5) *When young person is twenty years old or older* — When a young person is twenty years old or older at the time his or her temporary detention under subsection (1) begins, the young person shall, despite subsection (3), be temporarily detained in a provincial correctional facility for adults.

(6) *Transfer by provincial director* — A young person who is detained in custody under subsection (1) may, during the period of detention, be transferred by the provincial director from one place of temporary detention to another.

(7) *Exception relating to temporary detention* — Subsections (1) and (3) do not apply in respect of any temporary restraint of a young person under the supervision and control of a peace officer after arrest, but a young person who is so restrained shall be transferred to a place of temporary detention referred to in subsection (1) as soon as is practicable, and in no case later than the first reasonable opportunity after the appearance of the young person before a youth justice court judge or a justice under section 503 of the *Criminal Code*.

(8) *Authorization of provincial authority for detention* — In any province for which the lieutenant governor in council has designated a person or a group of persons whose authorization is required, either in all circumstances or in circumstances specified by the lieutenant governor in council, before a young person who has been arrested may be detained in accordance with this section, no young person shall be so detained unless the authorization is obtained.

(9) *Determination by provincial authority of place of detention* — In any province for which the lieutenant governor in council has designated a person or a group of persons who may determine the place where a young person who has been arrested may be detained in accordance with this section, no young person may be so detained in a place other than the one so determined.

COMMENTARY

Legal Implications

This section deals with the placement of young persons detained in custody before trial. This section requires young persons, as a rule, to be held separate from adults. This rule is based on the offender's age. Once a young person reaches the age of 18, the need to be kept separate from adults becomes optional. There are rules in this section that deal with young persons who reach 18 or 20 years of age being transferred to an adult facility.

There is also provision for designating someone to decide whether to keep a youth in detention rather than release the young person into the community, and where he or she is to be held if the designated persons decide to keep the youth in detention.

31. (1) *Placement of young person in care of responsible person* **— A young person who has been arrested may be placed in the care of a responsible person instead of being detained in custody if a youth justice court or a justice is satisfied that**

- (*a*) **the young person would, but for this subsection, be detained in custody under section 515 (judicial interim release) of the** *Criminal Code***;**
- (*b*) **the person is willing and able to take care of and exercise control over the young person; and**
- (*c*) **the young person is willing to be placed in the care of that person.**

(2) *Inquiry as to availability of a responsible person* **— If a young person would, in the absence of a responsible person, be detained in custody, the youth justice court or the justice shall inquire as to the availability of a responsible person and whether the young person is willing to be placed in that person's care.**

(3) *Condition of placement* **— A young person shall not be placed in the care of a person under subsection (1) unless**

- (*a*) **that person undertakes in writing to take care of and to be responsible for the attendance of the young person in court when required and to comply with any other conditions that the youth justice court judge or the justice may specify; and**
- (*b*) **the young person undertakes in writing to comply with the arrangement and to comply with any other conditions that the youth justice court judge or the justice may specify.**

(4) *Removing young person from care* **— A young person, a person in whose care a young person has been placed or any other person may, by application in writing to a youth justice court judge or a justice, apply for an order under subsection (5) if**

(*a*) the person in whose care the young person has been placed is no longer willing or able to take care of or exercise control over the young person; or

(*b*) it is, for any other reason, no longer appropriate that the young person remain in the care of the person with whom he or she has been placed.

(5) *Order* — When a youth justice court judge or a justice is satisfied that a young person should not remain in the custody of the person in whose care he or she was placed under subsection (1), the judge or justice shall

(*a*) make an order relieving the person and the young person of the obligations undertaken under subsection (3); and

(*b*) issue a warrant for the arrest of the young person.

(6) *Effect of arrest* — If a young person is arrested in accordance with a warrant issued under paragraph (5)(*b*), the young person shall be taken before a youth justice court judge or a justice without delay and dealt with under this section and sections 28 to 30.

COMMENTARY

Legal Implications

This section provides for a young person, who would otherwise be sent to detention, to be released to the care of a responsible person. This is another provision of the *Youth Criminal Justice Act* that will help keep youths out of custody. To strengthen this concept and to ensure that a responsible person is sought out, the youth justice court is obliged to inquire if there is a responsible person to whom the young person can be released. There are rules for the placement of a young person with a responsible person and for the suspension of that placement if necessary.

If a youth justice court judge determines that a young person could be detained in custody pre-trial then the judge is required to make an inquiry to see if there is a "responsible person" to whom a young person can be released. This implies that the police, Crown or some other person needs to make this inquiry in order to advise the court. Ultimately the decision is that of the court. Even though this provision is directed to a bail situation, if in fact a person is found who will support and perhaps house a young person, the bail hearing may even be avoided.

Operational Implications

This section is an improvement over that in the *Young Offenders Act*, as it forces the court to go one step further before denying bail and placing a young person into detention. The court is now required to make an inquiry to see if there is a responsible person to whose care the young person can be released.

The youth court must determine whether the responsible person is indeed responsible, which is not always an easy task. Even the court can be fooled. There have been situations under the *Young Offenders Act* where a young person was released to a responsible pimp, to an uncle who operates a crack house and to various other sundry characters. Unfortunately, the Act does not set out of whom the inquiry regarding the responsible person is to be made. It does however require that the responsible person commit in writing to be responsible to care for the youth, ensure the youth's court appearance and any conditions the youth must abide by. The young person must put his or her willingness to comply in writing. Confusion has already surfaced regarding this section as youth courts attempt to order community agencies and children's aid societies to be responsible persons under the Act.

This section should be clarified to provide for the inquiry to be made of the young person or of the young person's counsel. The timing of the inquiry also needs to be addressed in the legislation.

Tracking the number of youths in pre-trial detention over the next few years will be important to see if this provision has had its intended effect — to reduce the number of youths in pre-trial detention.

APPEARANCE

32. (1) *Appearance before judge or justice* **— A young person against whom an information or indictment is laid must first appear before a youth justice court judge or a justice, and the judge or justice shall**

- (*a*) cause the information or indictment to be read to the young person;
- (*b*) if the young person is not represented by counsel, inform the young person of the right to retain and instruct counsel;
- (*c*) if notified under subsection 64(2) (intention to seek adult sentence) or if section 16 (status of accused uncertain) applies, inform the young person that the youth justice court might, if the young person is found guilty, order that an adult sentence be imposed; and
- (*d*) if the young person is charged with having committed an offence set out in paragraph (*a*) of the definition "presumptive offence" in subsection 2(1), inform the young person in the following words of the consequences of being charged with such an offence:
    > An adult sentence will be imposed if you are found guilty unless the court orders that you are not liable to an adult sentence and that a youth sentence must be imposed.

(2) *Waiver* **— A young person may waive the requirements of subsection (1) if the young person is represented by counsel and counsel advises the court that the young person has been informed of that provision.**

(3) *Young person not represented by counsel* **— When a young person is not represented by counsel, the youth justice court, before accepting a plea, shall**

(a) satisfy itself that the young person understands the charge;
(b) if the young person is liable to an adult sentence, explain to the young person the consequences of being liable to an adult sentence and the procedure by which the young person may apply for an order that a youth sentence be imposed; and
(c) explain that the young person may plead guilty or not guilty to the charge or, if subsection 67(1) (election of court for trial — adult sentence) or (3) (election of court for trial in Nunavut — adult sentence) applies, explain that the young person may elect to be tried by a youth justice court judge without a jury and without having a preliminary inquiry, or to have a preliminary inquiry and be tried by a judge without a jury, or to have a preliminary inquiry and be tried by a court composed of a judge and jury and, in either of the latter two cases, a preliminary inquiry will only be conducted if requested by the young person or the prosecutor.

(4) *If youth justice court not satisfied* — If the youth justice court is not satisfied that a young person understands the charge, the court shall, unless the young person must be put to his or her election under subsection 67(1) (election of court for trial — adult sentence) or, with respect to Nunavut, subsection 67(3) (election of court for trial in Nunavut — adult sentence), enter a plea of not guilty on behalf of the young person and proceed with the trial in accordance with subsection 36(2) (young person pleads not guilty).

(5) *If youth justice court not satisfied* — If the youth justice court is not satisfied that a young person understands the matters set out in subsection (3), the court shall direct that the young person be represented by counsel.

[S.C. 2002, c. 13, s. 91]

COMMENTARY

Legal Implications

This section sets out the rules to be followed the first time a young person appears in the youth justice court. The purpose behind these rules is to satisfy the need for the youth to clearly understand what is happening in court as well as the consequences of what lies ahead. The youth justice court has the obligation to be sure that the young person understands and, in the event the young person does not have a lawyer and the court feels one is needed, the court will direct that a lawyer be provided. This protects the rights of the young person and ensures legal counsel where needed.

Should the Quebec Court of Appeal ruling in *Reference re: Bill C-7 Respecting the Criminal Justice System for Young Persons*, [2003] Q.J. No. 2850 (C.A.), be upheld this section will need to be amended to reflect the fact that the presumption of an adult offence does not apply and the burden is no longer on the young person.

RELEASE FROM OR DETENTION IN CUSTODY

33. (1) *Application for release from or detention in custody* — If an order is made under section 515 (judicial interim release) of the *Criminal Code* in respect of a young person by a justice who is not a youth justice court judge, an application may, at any time after the order is made, be made to a youth justice court for the release from or detention in custody of the young person, as the case may be, and the youth justice court shall hear the matter as an original application.

(2) *Notice to prosecutor* — An application under subsection (1) for release from custody shall not be heard unless the young person has given the prosecutor at least two clear days notice in writing of the application.

(3) *Notice to young person* — An application under subsection (1) for detention in custody shall not be heard unless the prosecutor has given the young person at least two clear days notice in writing of the application.

(4) *Waiver of notice* — The requirement for notice under subsection (2) or (3) may be waived by the prosecutor or by the young person or his or her counsel, as the case may be.

(5) *Application for review under section 520 or 521 of Criminal Code* — An application under section 520 or 521 of the *Criminal Code* for a review of an order made in respect of a young person by a youth justice court judge who is a judge of a superior court shall be made to a judge of the court of appeal.

(6) *Nunavut* — Despite subsection (5), an application under section 520 or 521 of the *Criminal Code* for a review of an order made in respect of a young person by a youth justice court judge who is a judge of the Nunavut Court of Justice shall be made to a judge of that court.

(7) *No review* — No application may be made under section 520 or 521 of the *Criminal Code* for a review of an order made in respect of a young person by a justice who is not a youth justice court judge.

(8) *Interim release by youth justice court judge only* — If a young person against whom proceedings have been taken under this Act is charged with an offence referred to in section 522 of the *Criminal Code*, a youth justice court judge, but no other court, judge or justice, may release the young person from custody under that section.

(9) *Review by court of appeal* — A decision made by a youth justice court judge under subsection (8) may be reviewed in accordance with section 680 of the *Criminal Code* and that section applies, with any modifications that the circumstances require, to any decision so made.

COMMENTARY

Legal Implications

One of the problems with this section is that the hearing can be reviewed *de novo* by a provincial court, but release variations can be granted only by a superior court. This section should provide for reviews of release orders in provincial court.

Operational Implications

This section, like in the *Young Offenders Act*, provides for a review of the original decision to release or detain a young person following a hearing (a show cause hearing). It is common practice for a young person who was detained by the youth justice court, or a justice of the peace, to return to the court for a review of the detainment. Only those youths who are considered at risk of flight, are repeat offenders or are considered high-risk offenders, where it is necessary to protect the public, or to maintain the confidence of the administration of justice, should remain in detention until sentencing.

MEDICAL AND PSYCHOLOGICAL REPORTS

34. (1) *Medical or psychological assessment* — **A youth justice court may, at any stage of proceedings against a young person, by order require that the young person be assessed by a qualified person who is required to report the results in writing to the court,**

- (*a*) **with the consent of the young person and the prosecutor; or**
- (*b*) **on its own motion or on application of the young person or the prosecutor, if the court believes a medical, psychological or psychiatric report in respect of the young person is necessary for a purpose mentioned in paragraphs (2)(*a*) to (*g*) and**
  - (i) **the court has reasonable grounds to believe that the young person may be suffering from a physical or mental illness or disorder, a psychological disorder, an emotional disturbance, a learning disability or a mental disability,**
  - (ii) **the young person's history indicates a pattern of repeated findings of guilt under this Act or the** *Young Offenders Act,* **chapter Y-1 of the Revised Statutes of Canada, 1985, or**
  - (iii) **the young person is alleged to have committed a serious violent offence.**

(2) *Purpose of assessment* — **A youth justice court may make an order under subsection (1) in respect of a young person for the purpose of**

- (*a*) **considering an application under section 33 (release from or detention in custody);**
- (*b*) **making its decision on an application heard under section 71 (hearing — adult sentences);**

(c) making or reviewing a youth sentence;
   (d) considering an application under subsection 104(1) (continuation of custody);
   (e) setting conditions under subsection 105(1) (conditional supervision);
   (f) making an order under subsection 109(2) (conditional supervision); or
   (g) authorizing disclosure under subsection 127(1) (information about a young person).

(3) *Custody for assessment* — Subject to subsections (4) and (6), for the purpose of an assessment under this section, a youth justice court may remand a young person to any custody that it directs for a period not exceeding thirty days.

(4) *Presumption against custodial remand* — A young person shall not be remanded in custody in accordance with an order made under subsection (1) unless

   (a) the youth justice court is satisfied that
      (i) on the evidence custody is necessary to conduct an assessment of the young person, or
      (ii) on the evidence of a qualified person detention of the young person in custody is desirable to conduct the assessment of the young person, and the young person consents to custody; or
   (b) the young person is required to be detained in custody in respect of any other matter or by virtue of any provision of the *Criminal Code*.

(5) *Report of qualified person in writing* — For the purposes of paragraph (4)(a), if the prosecutor and the young person agree, evidence of a qualified person may be received in the form of a report in writing.

(6) *Application to vary assessment order if circumstances change* — A youth justice court may, at any time while an order made under subsection (1) is in force, on cause being shown, vary the terms and conditions specified in the order in any manner that the court considers appropriate in the circumstances.

(7) *Disclosure of report* — When a youth justice court receives a report made in respect of a young person under subsection (1),

   (a) the court shall, subject to subsection (9), cause a copy of the report to be given to
      (i) the young person,
      (ii) any parent of the young person who is in attendance at the proceedings against the young person,
      (iii) any counsel representing the young person, and
      (iv) the prosecutor; and
   (b) the court may cause a copy of the report to be given to

(i) a parent of the young person who is not in attendance at the proceedings if the parent is, in the opinion of the court, taking an active interest in the proceedings, or

(ii) despite subsection 119(6) (restrictions respecting access to certain records), the provincial director, or the director of the provincial correctional facility for adults or the penitentiary at which the young person is serving a youth sentence, if, in the opinion of the court, withholding the report would jeopardize the safety of any person.

(8) *Cross-examination* — When a report is made in respect of a young person under subsection (1), the young person, his or her counsel or the adult assisting the young person under subsection 25(7) and the prosecutor shall, subject to subsection (9), on application to the youth justice court, be given an opportunity to cross-examine the person who made the report.

(9) *Non-disclosure in certain cases* — A youth justice court shall withhold all or part of a report made in respect of a young person under subsection (1) from a private prosecutor, if disclosure of the report or part, in the opinion of the court, is not necessary for the prosecution of the case and might be prejudicial to the young person.

(10) *Non-disclosure in certain cases* — A youth justice court shall withhold all or part of a report made in respect of a young person under subsection (1) from the young person, the young person's parents or a private prosecutor if the court is satisfied, on the basis of the report or evidence given in the absence of the young person, parents or private prosecutor by the person who made the report, that disclosure of the report or part would seriously impair the treatment or recovery of the young person, or would be likely to endanger the life or safety of, or result in serious psychological harm to, another person.

(11) *Exception – interests of justice* — Despite subsection (10), the youth justice court may release all or part of the report to the young person, the young person's parents or the private prosecutor if the court is of the opinion that the interests of justice make disclosure essential.

(12) *Report to be part of record* — A report made under subsection (1) forms part of the record of the case in respect of which it was requested.

(13) *Disclosure by qualified person* — Despite any other provision of this Act, a qualified person who is of the opinion that a young person held in detention or committed to custody is likely to endanger his or her own life or safety or to endanger the life of, or cause bodily harm to, another person may immediately so advise any person who has the care and custody of the young person whether or not the same information is contained in a report made under subsection (1).

(14) *Definition of "qualified person"* — In this section, "qualified person" means a person duly qualified by provincial law to practice medicine or psychiatry or to carry out psychological examinations or assessments, as the circumstances require, or, if no such law exists, a person who is, in the opinion of the youth justice court, so qualified, and includes a person or a member of a class of persons designated by the lieutenant governor in council of a province or his or her delegate.

COMMENTARY

Legal Implications

The youth justice court has the authority to order a medical, psychological or psychiatric assessment at any stage of the proceedings. This is an important provision in order to safeguard the rights of a young person and to provide the youth justice court with the guidance of medical and/or mental health professionals on the status of a young person. The youth court may order a youth to be detained in custody for a maximum of 30 days if it is evident that detainment is necessary in order to prepare the assessment. There are no restrictions on where, or who, the youth justice court can order to prepare a report.

Operational Implications

Under the *Young Offenders Act*, these assessments were known as pre-disposition assessments and used primarily for the purpose of sentencing. The use of these assessments has been expanded to include pre-trial detention hearings, and they can be ordered by the court at any time, even when the court is not considering a custody sentence. An assessment, commonly known as PSA, is used to identify both the historical and current mental health issues of the young person and his or her environment, and to make recommendations to the court, if appropriate, for medical/psychological/psychiatric treatment plans. There is a presumption that all of these assessments will be done in the community, not in a custodial setting. The assessment may have a variety of purposes, including developing a plan to address the youth's needs within the community. Section 34(6) authorizes the youth justice court to vary the order for remand and allow the 30-day maximum to be extended for completion of an assessment. Section 34(7) should be clarified to ensure that the provincial director is authorized in all circumstances to be provided with a copy of the report. The circumstances in this section are too narrow and these assessments are essential to case management and reintegration planning. Psychological/behavioural issues contained in a report such as this are critical to direct the program and the treatment to facilitate the successful reintegration and rehabilitation of young persons.

The youth justice court can also deny a request for a section 34 assessment as was done by the British Columbia Provincial Court in *R. v. D.G.*, [2004] B.C.J. No. 1295, 2004 BCPC 182, when the Crown sought a psychological assessment on the ground that the young person had committed a serious violent offence, yet the Crown was not seeking a serious violent determination. The youth court judge declined to order the assessment on the grounds that he could not conclude that the requirements of section 34 had been met without evidence that the offences constituted serious violent offences as defined in the Act.

The youth justice court may also order an assessment under section 141 of the *Criminal Code* to make a determination if a young person is unfit to stand trial or under section 672.11 of the *Criminal Code* to assess whether a young person can be found not criminally responsible.

REFERRAL TO CHILD WELFARE AGENCY

35. *Referral to child welfare agency* — **In addition to any order that it is authorized to make, a youth justice court may, at any stage of proceedings against a young person, refer the young person to a child welfare agency for assessment to determine whether the young person is in need of child welfare services.**

COMMENTARY

Legal Implications

Judges often hear evidence that may lead the court to believe that a young person is in need of child welfare services. This new section allows a youth justice court judge to refer the youth to a child welfare agency at any stage in the proceedings if the court believes the youth may be in need of child welfare services. This is meant to assist judges in what the court may see as an obligation to make a report. It is hoped that this will assist a young person in gaining access to services they may require. The referral, which is authorized, is separate from criminal proceedings before the youth court, and it is anticipated that it will have no impact on the proceedings. This is not a court order. It is a referral and there is no provision in the legislation for a report back to the court. Provincial child welfare legislation must be the determining factor in this section.

Operational Implications

While one can recognize the intent of this new section, the language is vague, leaving much open to interpretation. Regulations or clarification are definitely required for this section. The section authorizes the court to refer a youth to a child welfare agency, but does not indicate whether this agency is an agency authorized by the province. It is also unclear on the kind of assessment the court may request. If it is an assessment to determine that the youth is a child in need of protection, it may interfere with provincial legislation.

All jurisdictions have provincial legislation that governs the child welfare system. In the provinces of Ontario and Nova Scotia, for example, this section could challenge the provincial obligation to provide child welfare services to youths over the age of 16. Even if the court refers a youth 16 or 17 years of age to a child welfare agency for an assessment, he or she would probably not be eligible for child welfare services based on the provincial legislation. This could create the perception of a two-tier service system for young persons.

ADJUDICATION

36. (1) *When young person pleads guilty* — **If a young person pleads guilty to an offence charged against the young person and the youth justice court is satisfied that the facts support the charge, the court shall find the young person guilty of the offence.**

(2) *When young person pleads not guilty* — **If a young person charged with an offence pleads not guilty to the offence or pleads guilty but the youth justice court is not satisfied that the facts support the charge, the court shall proceed with the trial and shall, after considering the matter, find the young person guilty or not guilty or make an order dismissing the charge, as the case may be.**

COMMENTARY

Legal Implications

This section gives direction to the court on the options available when a young person enters a plea of guilty, or not guilty. For example, if a young person pleads guilty, and the court is satisfied that the facts support the charge, the court shall find the young person guilty of the offence.

APPEALS

37. (1) *Appeals* — **An appeal in respect of an indictable offence or an offence that the Attorney General elects to proceed with as an indictable offence lies under this Act in accordance with Part XXI (appeals — indictable offences) of the *Criminal Code*, which Part applies with any modifications that the circumstances require.**

(2) *Appeals for contempt of court* — **A finding of guilt under section 15 for contempt of court or a sentence imposed in respect of the finding may be appealed as if the finding were a conviction or the sentence were a sentence in a prosecution by indictment.**

(3) *Appeal* — **Section 10 of the *Criminal Code* applies if a person is convicted of contempt of court under subsection 27(4) (failure of parent to attend court).**

(4) *Appeals to be heard together* — **A judicial determination under subsection 42(9) (judicial determination of serious violent offence), or an order under subsection 72(1) (court order — adult or youth sentence), 75(3) (ban on publication) or 76(1) (placement when subject to adult sentence), may be appealed as part of the sentence and, unless the court to which the**

appeal is taken otherwise orders, if more than one of these is appealed they must be part of the same appeal proceeding.

(5) *Appeals for summary conviction offences* — An appeal in respect of an offence punishable on summary conviction or an offence that the Attorney General elects to proceed with as an offence punishable on summary conviction lies under this Act in accordance with Part XXVII (summary conviction offences) of the *Criminal Code*, which Part applies with any modifications that the circumstances require.

(6) *Appeals where offences are tried jointly* — An appeal in respect of one or more indictable offences and one or more summary conviction offences that are tried jointly or in respect of which youth sentences are jointly imposed lies under this Act in accordance with Part XXI (appeals — indictable offences) of the *Criminal Code*, which Part applies with any modifications that the circumstances require.

(7) *Deemed election* — For the purpose of appeals under this Act, if no election is made in respect of an offence that may be prosecuted by indictment or proceeded with by way of summary conviction, the Attorney General is deemed to have elected to proceed with the offence as an offence punishable on summary conviction.

(8) *If the youth justice court is a superior court* — In any province where the youth justice court is a superior court, an appeal under subsection (5) shall be made to the court of appeal of the province.

(9) *Nunavut* — Despite subsection (8), if the Nunavut Court of Justice is acting as a youth justice court, an appeal under subsection (5) shall be made to a judge of the Nunavut Court of Appeal, and an appeal of that judge's decision shall be made to the Nunavut Court of Appeal in accordance with section 839 of the *Criminal Code*.

(10) *Appeal to the Supreme Court of Canada* — No appeal lies under subsection (1) from a judgment of the court of appeal in respect of a finding of guilt or an order dismissing an information or indictment to the Supreme Court of Canada unless leave to appeal is granted by the Supreme Court of Canada.

(11) *No appeal from youth sentence on review* — No appeal lies from a youth sentence under section 59 or any of sections 94 to 96.

COMMENTARY

Legal Implications

This section retains seven subsections from the appeals section of the *Young Offenders Act* as well as two subsections on contempt of court from other parts of the *Young Offenders Act*, and places them in the appeals section of this Act.

There are also two new subsections: one that refers to Nunavut and one that makes appeal procedures less complicated by combining a number of decisions related to adult sentences under the heading of sentence. Should the Quebec Court of Appeal ruling eliminating the presumption of an adult offence be upheld, subsection (4) of this section will require an amendment.

Operational Implications:

Should a young person incur further charges that lead to a custody sentence while awaiting an appeal, section 44 provisions for merging custody sentences can result in the original sentence under appeal already having expired by the time it is heard due to the merging of sentences.

PART 4   SENTENCING

INTRODUCTION

This part of the legislation provides more sentence options than the *Young Offenders Act*, eliminates a custody sentence and introduces a custody and supervision sentence that includes a mandatory period of community supervision following all committals to custody. Part 4, which sets out provisions that seek to address the overuse of custody, includes new sentencing principles and stronger restrictions on the use of custody. The term "disposition" from the *Young Offenders Act* is replaced with the term "sentence" to be consistent with adult terminology.

However, in *R. v. R.P.B.*, [2003] A.J. No. 925 (Prov. Ct.), the Alberta Provincial Court reviewed the use of the word "dispositions" in sections 82, 137 and 161 of the *Youth Criminal Justice Act* and found it to be consistent with the conclusion that sentences in section 39 include "dispositions" under the *Young Offenders Act*.

A number of new sentences have been introduced in the *Youth Criminal Justice Act* to give judges more options which should lead to more youths being appropriately sentenced to community programs. The only option under the *Young Offenders Act* would have been a custody sentence. While it is mandatory for jurisdictions to provide most of the new sentences, there are also optional sentences that can be ordered by the youth justice court only if the province or territory has the sentence program in place.

The following new sentences must be made available in each jurisdiction:

- judicial reprimand;
- community supervision following all custody; and
- deferred custody and supervision order.

Three additional sentencing options can be ordered provided the provincial director has determined that a program to enforce the order is available in the jurisdiction. These options include:

- an intensive support and supervision order;
- an order to attend a non-residential program for a specified period of time; and
- intensive rehabilitation custody and supervision order, subject to the approval of the provincial director.

There are detailed rules for sentences for the most serious offences, and for exceptional cases where a young person may seek an adult sentence. The legislation provides the youth justice system with the capability to deal with all cases, no matter how complex or serious.

Sentence administration is always complicated, but the detailed rules in this Act clarify many of the sentencing and correctional issues. There are a number of rules in Part 4 to provide guidance and national consistency and to ensure that due process procedures are followed. Despite all of the rules, sentence calculation is proving to be a challenge, especially when sentences are combined and multiple sentences are involved.

PURPOSE AND PRINCIPLES

38. (1) *Purpose* — **The purpose of sentencing under section 42 (youth sentences) is to hold a young person accountable for an offence through the imposition of just sanctions that have meaningful consequences for the young person and that promote his or her rehabilitation and reintegration into society, thereby contributing to the long-term protection of the public.**

(2) *Sentencing principles* — **A youth justice court that imposes a youth sentence on a young person shall determine the sentence in accordance with the principles set out in section 3 and the following principles:**

  (*a*) **the sentence must not result in a punishment that is greater than the punishment that would be appropriate for an adult who has been convicted of the same offence committed in similar circumstances;**

  (*b*) **the sentence must be similar to the sentences imposed in the region on similar young persons found guilty of the same offence committed in similar circumstances;**

  (*c*) **the sentence must be proportionate to the seriousness of the offence and the degree of responsibility of the young person for that offence;**

  (*d*) **all available sanctions other than custody that are reasonable in the circumstances should be considered for all young persons, with particular attention to the circumstances of aboriginal young persons; and**

  (*e*) **subject to paragraph (*c*), the sentence must**
    (i) **be the least restrictive sentence that is capable of achieving the purpose set out in subsection (1),**
    (ii) **be the one that is most likely to rehabilitate the young person and reintegrate him or her into society, and**
    (iii) **promote a sense of responsibility in the young person, and an acknowledgement of the harm done to victims and the community.**

(3) *Factors to be considered* — **In determining a youth sentence, the youth justice court shall take into account**

   (*a*) the degree of participation by the young person in the commission of the offence;
   (*b*) the harm done to victims and whether it was intentional or reasonably foreseeable;
   (*c*) any reparation made by the young person to the victim or the community;
   (*d*) the time spent in detention by the young person as a result of the offence;
   (*e*) the previous findings of guilt of the young person; and
   (*f*) any other aggravating and mitigating circumstances related to the young person or the offence that are relevant to the purpose and principles set out in this section.

COMMENTARY

Legal Implications

This is a new section that is intended to bring more balance and consistency to sentencing youths in Canada and, at the same time, attempt to correct the fact that, generally, youths have been sentenced more harshly than adults. The purpose and principles of sentencing a youth, in addition to the general principles as described earlier in section 3, are set out in this section. There is also a list of factors the court must consider before imposing a sentence. The idea is that custody should be used only for the most serious and repeat offenders. The principle of general deterrence contained in the *Young Offenders Act* has been purposely removed from this legislation, as research has shown that general deterrence is ineffective for adults, and especially ineffective where youths are concerned.

Operational Implications

The declaration of principles under the *Young Offenders Act* were all contained in the same section, that is, section 3. This meant flipping the pages from the sentencing sections to the section on principles when determining a youth sentence. The *Youth Criminal Justice Act* provides more effective principles than did the *Young Offenders Act*, and places them in each section, making it easier to understand their applicability. The principles and factors to consider in the Act, along with section 39, restrict the imposition of custody to a very limited number of situations. Youth court judges have been given added responsibility in the sentencing principles in the *Youth Criminal Justice Act*. In particular, the principles require that the sentence imposed be similar to the sentences imposed in the region on similar young persons found guilty of the same offence.

In *R. v. D.L.C.*, [2003] N.J. No. 94 (Prov. Ct.), the Newfoundland and Labrador Provincial Court defined "region" as the province, and recognized that there may be regional differences within the province that must be taken into account. One principle states that a young person must not receive a sentence greater than an adult would. This is a clarification and strengthening of a principle under the *Young Offenders Act*. These principles differ somewhat from those in the *Young Offenders Act*, and require court officials to be familiar with regional sentencing practices and non-custodial alternatives as well as the range of adult sentences for the same offence.

39. (1) *Committal to custody* — **A youth justice court shall not commit a young person to custody under section 42 (youth sentences) unless**

- (*a*) **the young person has committed a violent offence;**
- (*b*) **the young person has failed to comply with non-custodial sentences;**
- (*c*) **the young person has committed an indictable offence for which an adult would be liable to imprisonment for a term of more than two years and has a history that indicates a pattern of findings of guilt under this Act or the** *Young Offenders Act***, chapter Y-1 of the Revised Statutes of Canada, 1985; or**
- (*d*) **in exceptional cases where the young person has committed an indictable offence, the aggravating circumstances of the offence are such that the imposition of a non-custodial sentence would be inconsistent with the purpose and principles set out in section 38.**

(2) *Alternatives to custody* — **If any of paragraphs (1)(*a*) to (*c*) apply, a youth justice court must not impose a custodial sentence under section 42 (youth sentences) unless the court has considered all alternatives to custody raised at the sentencing hearing that are reasonable in the circumstances, and determined that there is not a reasonable alternative, or combination of alternatives, that is in accordance with the purpose and principles set out in section 38.**

(3) *Factors to be considered* — **In determining whether there is a reasonable alternative to custody, a youth justice court shall consider submissions relating to**

- (*a*) **the alternatives to custody that are available;**
- (*b*) **the likelihood that the young person will comply with a non-custodial sentence, taking into account his or her compliance with previous non-custodial sentences; and**
- (*c*) **the alternatives to custody that have been used in respect of young persons for similar offences committed in similar circumstances.**

(4) *Imposition of same sentence* — **The previous imposition of a particular non-custodial sentence on a young person does not preclude a youth justice court from imposing the same or any other non-custodial sentence for another offence.**

(5) *Custody as social measure prohibited* — A youth justice court shall not use custody as a substitute for appropriate child protection, mental health or other social measures.

(6) *Pre-sentence report* — Before imposing a custodial sentence under section 42 (youth sentences), a youth justice court shall consider a pre-sentence report and any sentencing proposal made by the young person or his or her counsel.

(7) *Report dispensed with* — A youth justice court may, with the consent of the prosecutor and the young person or his or her counsel, dispense with a pre-sentence report if the court is satisfied that the report is not necessary.

(8) *Length of custody* — In determining the length of a youth sentence that includes a custodial portion, a youth justice court shall be guided by the purpose and principles set out in section 38, and shall not take into consideration the fact that the supervision portion of the sentence may not be served in custody and that the sentence may be reviewed by the court under section 94.

(9) *Reasons* — If a youth justice court imposes a youth sentence that includes a custodial portion, the court shall state the reasons why it has determined that a non-custodial sentence is not adequate to achieve the purpose set out in subsection 38(1), including, if applicable, the reasons why the case is an exceptional case under paragraph (1)(*d*).

COMMENTARY

Legal Implications

This new section seeks to address one of the underlying principles of reducing the number of youths in custody in Canada by placing limitations on courts when sentencing a youth to custody. The general rule is that a youth justice court must not impose a custody sentence unless the court has considered all alternatives to custody at the time of sentencing. Custody is to be used only if a young person has been found guilty of a violent offence, fails to comply with previous sentences or has a history of offences, or in exceptional cases where a non-custodial sentence would be inconsistent with the principle of the Act. What is not clear is does the failure "to comply with non-custodial sentences" refer to a breach of different court orders, or can two breaches of the same court order qualify? If the intent of this paragraph is to reinforce the principle that non-custodial sentences should be used before using custody, a young person would not need to have two separate non-custodial sentences, as two breaches of any sentence would suffice even if they both arise from the same sentence.

The Alberta Provincial Court in *R. v. R.P.B.*, [2003] A.J. No. 925 (Prov. Ct.), and the Newfoundland and Labrador Provincial Court in *R. v. D.L.C.*, [2003] N.J. No. 94 (Prov. Ct.), both ruled that prior dispositions under the *Young*

Offenders Act were included within the phrase "non-custodial sentences" in this section of the *Youth Criminal Justice Act*.

The Manitoba Provincial Court reviewed section 39(1)(*c*) in *R. v. S.B.*, [2003] M.J. No. 491 (Prov. Ct.). The youth justice court found that a "term of more than two years" refers to the penalty that an adult could receive, not the penalty that an adult would receive. Thus, the reference is to the maximum penalty that an adult could face and not the penalty that an adult would receive.

In addition the court looked at the meaning of "pattern of findings of guilt". The youth justice court found that these words refer to the number of charges and not the number of court appearances.

Therefore, it is possible for a young person to have a pattern of findings of guilt if there are a number of charges that arise out of the same court proceeding. In this case the pattern of findings of guilt arose from being sentenced on a single court date.

Yet, the Ontario Court of Justice in *R. v. A.W*, [2004] O.J. No. 2593 (C.J.), ruled that although section 39(1)(*c*) incorporated by reference dispositions under the *Young Offenders Act*, but section 39(1)(*b*) made no such reference, and although the youth court judge agreed this omission was likely the result of sloppy drafting, the court was bound by the rules of statutory interpretation to exclude dispositions under the *Young Offenders Act* and treat a young offender with a lengthy record under the *Young Offenders Act* as a first-time offender for the purposes of section 39(1)(*b*).

Operational Implications

This new section is instrumental in ensuring that young people get the opportunity to benefit from appropriate community alternatives. Under the *Young Offenders Act*, there were few rules to safeguard against a youth's circumstances influencing the decision for a custody sentence. For example, some youth court judges routinely ordered a youth found guilty of assault into custody, even when the assault was less serious and the youth was a first-time offender. It is now necessary for the youth court judge to examine these sentencing rules for each case. This should result in fewer youths being sentenced to custody. What is not clear in this section is the definition of "violent offence". Section 2 contains a definition of "serious violent offence" but not of "violent offence".

Judging from case law already established with respect to sentencing, youth court judges are not just relying on submissions by Crowns and defence lawyers, but are seriously and meticulously considering the principles and factors in the Act. Section 39(4) specifically states the imposition of a non-custodial sentence does not preclude the youth justice court from imposing the same or any other non-custodial sentence for another offence. There is a strong emphasis on rehabilitating a young person in youth justice court rulings. Thus far, early indications are that custody rates have dropped across the country, yet it is premature to state it is solely the result of the Act and the new sentencing provisions.

PRE-SENTENCE REPORT

40. (1) *Pre-sentence report* — Before imposing sentence on a young person found guilty of an offence, a youth justice court

  (*a*) shall, if it is required under this Act to consider a pre-sentence report before making an order or a sentence in respect of a young person, and
  (*b*) may, if it considers it advisable, require the provincial director to cause to be prepared a pre-sentence report in respect of the young person and to submit the report to the court.

(2) *Contents of report* — A pre-sentence report made in respect of a young person shall, subject to subsection (3), be in writing and shall include the following, to the extent that it is relevant to the purpose and principles of sentencing set out in section 38 and to the restrictions on custody set out in section 39:

  (*a*) the results of an interview with the young person and, if reasonably possible, the parents of the young person and, if appropriate and reasonably possible, members of the young person's extended family;
  (*b*) the results of an interview with the victim in the case, if applicable and reasonably possible;
  (*c*) the recommendations resulting from any conference referred to in section 41;
  (*d*) any information that is applicable to the case, including
   (i) the age, maturity, character, behaviour and attitude of the young person and his or her willingness to make amends,
   (ii) any plans put forward by the young person to change his or her conduct or to participate in activities or undertake measures to improve himself or herself,
   (iii) subject to subsection 119(2) (period of access to records), the history of previous findings of delinquency under the *Juvenile Delinquents Act*, chapter J-3 of the Revised Statutes of Canada, 1970, or previous findings of guilt for offences under the *Young Offenders Act*, chapter Y-1 of the Revised Statutes of Canada, 1985, or under this or any other Act of Parliament or any regulation made under it, the history of community or other services rendered to the young person with respect to those findings and the response of the young person to previous sentences or dispositions and to services rendered to him or her,
   (iv) subject to subsection 119(2) (period of access to records), the history of alternative measures under the *Young Offenders Act*, chapter Y-1 of the Revised Statutes of Canada, 1985, or extrajudicial sanctions used to deal with the young person and the response of the young person to those measures or sanctions,

(v) the availability and appropriateness of community services and facilities for young persons and the willingness of the young person to avail himself or herself of those services or facilities,
(vi) the relationship between the young person and the young person's parents and the degree of control and influence of the parents over the young person and, if appropriate and reasonably possible, the relationship between the young person and the young person's extended family and the degree of control and influence of the young person's extended family over the young person, and
(vii) the school attendance and performance record and the employment record of the young person;
(e) any information that may assist the court in determining under subsection 39(2) whether there is an alternative to custody; and
(f) any information that the provincial director considers relevant, including any recommendation that the provincial director considers appropriate.

(3) *Oral report with leave* — If a pre-sentence report cannot reasonably be committed to writing, it may, with leave of the youth justice court, be submitted orally in court.

(4) *Report forms part of record* — A pre-sentence report shall form part of the record of the case in respect of which it was requested.

(5) *Copies of pre-sentence report* — If a pre-sentence report made in respect of a young person is submitted to a youth justice court in writing, the court

(a) shall, subject to subsection (7), cause a copy of the report to be given to
(i) the young person,
(ii) any parent of the young person who is in attendance at the proceedings against the young person,
(iii) any counsel representing the young person, and
(iv) the prosecutor; and
(b) may cause a copy of the report to be given to a parent of the young person who is not in attendance at the proceedings if the parent is, in the opinion of the court, taking an active interest in the proceedings.

(6) *Cross-examination* — If a pre-sentence report made in respect of a young person is submitted to a youth justice court, the young person, his or her counsel or the adult assisting the young person under subsection 25(7) and the prosecutor shall, subject to subsection (7), on application to the court, be given the opportunity to cross-examine the person who made the report.

(7) *Report may be withheld from private prosecutor* — If a pre-sentence report made in respect of a young person is submitted to a youth justice court, the court may, when the prosecutor is a private prosecutor and disclosure of all or part of the report to the prosecutor might, in the opinion of the court, be prejudicial to the young person and is not, in the opinion of the court, necessary for the prosecution of the case against the young person,

(a) withhold the report or part from the prosecutor, if the report is submitted in writing; or
(b) exclude the prosecutor from the court during the submission of the report or part, if the report is submitted orally in court.

(8) *Report disclosed to other persons* — If a pre-sentence report made in respect of a young person is submitted to a youth justice court, the court

(a) shall, on request, cause a copy or a transcript of the report to be supplied to
  (i) any court that is dealing with matters relating to the young person, and
  (ii) any youth worker to whom the young person's case has been assigned; and
(b) may, on request, cause a copy or a transcript of all or part of the report to be supplied to any person not otherwise authorized under this section to receive a copy or a transcript of the report if, in the opinion of the court, the person has a valid interest in the proceedings.

(9) *Disclosure by the provincial director* — A provincial director who submits a pre-sentence report made in respect of a young person to a youth justice court may make all or part of the report available to any person in whose custody or under whose supervision the young person is placed or to any other person who is directly assisting in the care or treatment of the young person.

(10) *Inadmissibility of statements* — No statement made by a young person in the course of the preparation of a pre-sentence report in respect of the young person is admissible in evidence against any young person in civil or criminal proceedings except those under section 42 (youth sentences), 59 (review of non-custodial sentence) or 71 (hearing — adult sentences) or any of sections 94 to 96 (reviews and other proceedings related to custodial sentences).

COMMENTARY

Legal Implications

The adult term "pre-sentence report", or PSR, has replaced the term "pre-disposition report" used in the *Young Offenders Act*. The rules for the preparation, content, distribution and use of the pre-sentence report set out in this section remain the same as in the *Young Offenders Act*.

Operational Implications

Generally, the preparation of a pre-sentence report is delegated by the provincial director to the probation officer, and, in most jurisdictions, the PSR includes sentencing recommendations. The *Youth Criminal Justice Act* requires the pre-sentence report to address the restriction on the use of custody (section 39) in relation to the youth and to explore the viability of any available community alternatives to custody.

When a community-based sentence is recommended, the report should describe in detail the proposed living arrangements, educational program and other necessary programs and supervision plans to address both the youth's level of risk to reoffend and his or her individual needs. If a custody sentence is recommended, the report should indicate why a community-based sentence would not be appropriate to hold the young person accountable. A pre-sentence report may be submitted orally, with leave of the court; however, a written pre-sentence report is a more useful tool for sentencing, as it is more accurate and comprehensive and provides the youth with an accompanying document to ensure that his or her individual needs are met by those in the youth justice system. A written pre-sentence report provides a documented history of the circumstance of the offence(s), the impact on the victim(s) and information about the youth's family, school and social development which is essential to ensure that the youth has continued access to services that address his or her risks and needs throughout the length of the sentence. In addition to the rules set out in the *Youth Criminal Justice Act*, most jurisdictions also have policies and guidelines to assist in the preparation of the reports.

YOUTH SENTENCES

41. *Recommendation of conference* **— When a youth justice court finds a young person guilty of an offence, the court may convene or cause to be convened a conference under section 19 for recommendations to the court on an appropriate youth sentence.**

COMMENTARY

Legal Implications

After a finding of guilt, the youth court judge may ask that a conference be convened to give the judge further insight into the circumstances of the young person and to provide advice on the most appropriate sentence to hold the young person accountable for his or her actions.

Operational Implications

This is a new and possibly controversial approach in youth justice legislation that has not yet proven to be popular with the judiciary. The wording of the legislation is vague; therefore, it leaves this section open to individual interpretation. This section allows a judge, at any stage in the proceedings, to call a conference to give advice to the court. Some jurisdictions have developed a conference model with policies and guidelines to support the court-ordered conference process to ensure continuity across the jurisdiction. It needs to be clear that it is only advice on sentencing that a conference may give to the court and who should participate in this process. The legislation is silent on the youth's right to legal representation at this conference. The legislation does not prohibit the judiciary from convening a conference on any offence no matter how serious the offence may be.

Numerous forms of conferences already exist ranging from an informal discussion with selected individuals to a more formal family group conference model with a paid mediator. There can be costs associated with conferences, and policies and guidelines need to identify responsibility for any costs. Members of the judiciary have already expressed varying interpretations on the procedural aspects of conferencing. The legislation permits the judge to convene, or cause to be convened, a conference but gives no authority to require any specific individuals to attend. There is also no direction regarding organizing conferences. The legislation does not authorize probation officers or provincial directors to coordinate conferences; however, in some jurisdictions probation officers have taken on that role, while others have community agencies or paid conference coordinators.

42. (1) *Considerations as to youth sentence* — A youth justice court shall, before imposing a youth sentence, consider any recommendations submitted under section 41, any pre-sentence report, any representations made by the parties to the proceedings or their counsel or agents and by the parents of the young person, and any other relevant information before the court.

COMMENTARY

Legal Implications

This key section of the *Youth Criminal Justice Act* provides a list of all of the sentences contained in the *Young Offenders Act* as well as new mandatory and optional sentences that a judge may impose upon a young person under this legislation.

The section sets out conditions under which particular sentences, such as deferred custody and supervision orders, and intensive rehabilitation custody and supervision orders can occur. It also sets out rules for sentence duration. The youth justice court also has the authority to make a judicial determination that an offence is a serious violent offence in this legislation.

There are 18 possible sentences that range from a judicial reprimand to an intensive rehabilitative custody and supervision order. All of the sentences available under the *Young Offenders Act* have been retained, and six new sentence options have been added:

- judicial reprimand;
- intensive support and supervision order;
- an order to attend a non-residential program for a specified period of time;
- community supervision following all custody;
- deferred custody and supervision order; and
- intensive rehabilitation custody and supervision order.

The possible length of sentences range from an absolute discharge for the less serious offences, up to a maximum of 10 years for the most serious offence — first degree murder.

This section deals only with youth sentences, but the possibility of a young person receiving an adult sentence in exceptional circumstances is still available and is dealt with later in the Act.

(2) *Youth sentence* — When a youth justice court finds a young person guilty of an offence and is imposing a youth sentence, the court shall, subject to this section, impose any one of the following sanctions or any number of them that are not inconsistent with each other and, if the offence is first degree murder or second degree murder within the meaning of section 231 of the *Criminal Code*, the court shall impose a sanction set out in paragraph (*q*) or subparagraph (*r*)(ii) or (iii) and may impose any other of the sanctions set out in this subsection that the court considers appropriate:

(*a*) reprimand the young person;

(*b*) by order direct that the young person be discharged absolutely, if the court considers it to be in the best interests of the young person and not contrary to the public interest;

(*c*) by order direct that the young person be discharged on any conditions that the court considers appropriate and may require the young person to report to and be supervised by the provincial director;

(*d*) impose on the young person a fine not exceeding $1,000 to be paid at the time and on the terms that the court may fix;

(*e*) order the young person to pay to any other person at the times and on the terms that the court may fix an amount by way of compensation for loss of or damage to property or for loss of income or support, or an amount for, in the Province of Quebec, pre-trial pecuniary loss or, in any other province, special damages, for personal injury arising from the commission of the offence if the value is readily ascertainable, but no order shall be made for other damages in the Province of Quebec or for general damages in any other province;

(*f*) order the young person to make restitution to any other person of any property obtained by the young person as a result of the commission of the offence within the time that the court may fix, if the property is owned by the other person or was, at the time of the offence, in his or her lawful possession;

(g) if property obtained as a result of the commission of the offence has been sold to an innocent purchaser, where restitution of the property to its owner or any other person has been made or ordered, order the young person to pay the purchaser, at the time and on the terms that the court may fix, an amount not exceeding the amount paid by the purchaser for the property;

(h) subject to section 54, order the young person to compensate any person in kind or by way of personal services at the time and on the terms that the court may fix for any loss, damage or injury suffered by that person in respect of which an order may be made under paragraph (e) or (g);

(i) subject to section 54, order the young person to perform a community service at the time and on the terms that the court may fix, and to report to and be supervised by the provincial director or a person designated by the youth justice court;

(j) subject to section 51 (mandatory prohibition order), make any order of prohibition, seizure or forfeiture that may be imposed under any Act of Parliament or any regulation made under it if an accused is found guilty or convicted of that offence, other than an order under section 161 of the *Criminal Code*;

(k) place the young person on probation in accordance with sections 55 and 56 (conditions and other matters related to probation orders) for a specified period not exceeding two years;

(l) subject to subsection (3) (agreement of provincial director), order the young person into an intensive support and supervision program approved by the provincial director;

(m) subject to subsection (3) (agreement of provincial director) and section 54, order the young person to attend a non-residential program approved by the provincial director, at the times and on the terms that the court may fix, for a maximum of two hundred and forty hours, over a period not exceeding six months;

(n) make a custody and supervision order with respect to the young person, ordering that a period be served in custody and that a second period — which is one half as long as the first — be served, subject to sections 97 (conditions to be included) and 98 (continuation of custody), under supervision in the community subject to conditions, the total of the periods not to exceed two years from the date of the coming into force of the order or, if the young person is found guilty of an offence for which the punishment provided by the *Criminal Code* or any other Act of Parliament is imprisonment for life, three years from the date of coming into force of the order;

(o) in the case of an offence set out in subparagraph (a)(ii), (iii) or (iv) of the definition "presumptive offence" in subsection 2(1), make a custody and supervision order in respect of the young person for a specified period not exceeding three years from the date of committal that orders the young person to be committed into a continuous period of custody for the first portion of the sentence and, subject to subsection 104(1) (continuation of custody), to serve the remainder of the sentence under conditional supervision in the community in accordance with section 105;

(p) subject to subsection (5), make a deferred custody and supervision order that is for a specified period not exceeding six months, subject to the conditions set out in subsection 105(2), and to any conditions set out in subsection 105(3) that the court considers appropriate;

(q) order the young person to serve a sentence not to exceed
- (i) in the case of first degree murder, ten years comprised of
  - (A) a committal to custody, to be served continuously, for a period that must not, subject to subsection 104(1) (continuation of custody), exceed six years from the date of committal, and
  - (B) a placement under conditional supervision to be served in the community in accordance with section 105, and
- (ii) in the case of second degree murder, seven years comprised of
  - (A) a committal to custody, to be served continuously, for a period that must not, subject to subsection 104(1) (continuation of custody), exceed four years from the date of committal, and
  - (B) a placement under conditional supervision to be served in the community in accordance with section 105;

(r) subject to subsection (7), make an intensive rehabilitative custody and supervision order in respect of the young person
- (i) that is for a specified period that must not exceed
  - (A) two years from the date of committal, or
  - (B) if the young person is found guilty of an offence for which the punishment provided by the *Criminal Code* or any other Act of Parliament is imprisonment for life, three years from the date of committal,

  and that orders the young person to be committed into a continuous period of intensive rehabilitative custody for the first portion of the sentence and, subject to subsection 104(1) (continuation of custody), to serve the remainder under conditional supervision in the community in accordance with section 105,
- (ii) that is for a specified period that must not exceed, in the case of first degree murder, ten years from the date of committal, comprising
  - (A) a committal to intensive rehabilitative custody, to be served continuously, for a period that must not exceed six years from the date of committal, and
  - (B) subject to subsection 104(1) (continuation of custody), a placement under conditional supervision to be served in the community in accordance with section 105, and

(iii) that is for a specified period that must not exceed, in the case of second degree murder, seven years from the date of committal, comprising
- (A) a committal to intensive rehabilitative custody, to be served continuously, for a period that must not exceed four years from the date of committal, and
- (B) subject to subsection 104(1) (continuation of custody), a placement under conditional supervision to be served in the community in accordance with section 105; and

(s) impose on the young person any other reasonable and ancillary conditions that the court considers advisable and in the best interests of the young person and the public.

(3) *Agreement of provincial director* — A youth justice court may make an order under paragraph (2)(*l*) or (*m*) only if the provincial director has determined that a program to enforce the order is available.

(4) *Youth justice court statement* — When the youth justice court makes a custody and supervision order with respect to a young person under paragraph (2)(*n*), the court shall state the following with respect to that order:

You are ordered to serve (*state the number of days or months to be served*) in custody, to be followed by (*state one-half of the number of days or months stated above*) to be served under supervision in the community subject to conditions.

If you breach any of the conditions while you are under supervision in the community, you may be brought back into custody and required to serve the rest of the second period in custody as well.

You should also be aware that, under other provisions of the *Youth Criminal Justice Act*, a court could require you to serve the second period in custody as well.

The periods in custody and under supervision in the community may be changed if you are or become subject to another sentence.

(5) *Deferred custody and supervision order* — The court may make a deferred custody and supervision order under paragraph (2)(*p*) if

(a) the young person is found guilty of an offence that is not a serious violent offence; and
(b) it is consistent with the purpose and principles set out in section 38 and the restrictions on custody set out in section 39.

(6) *Application of sections 106 to 109* — Sections 106 to 109 (suspension of conditional supervision) apply to a breach of a deferred custody and supervision order made under paragraph (2)(*p*) as if the breach were a

breach of an order for conditional supervision made under subsection 105(1) and, for the purposes of sections 106 to 109, supervision under a deferred custody and supervision order is deemed to be conditional supervision.

(7) *Intensive rehabilitative custody and supervision order* — A youth justice court may make an intensive rehabilitative custody and supervision order under paragraph (2)(*r*) in respect of a young person only if

- (*a*) either
    - (i) the young person has been found guilty of an offence under one of the following provisions of the *Criminal Code*, namely, section 231 or 235 (first degree murder or second degree murder within the meaning of section 231), section 239 (attempt to commit murder), section 232, 234 or 236 (manslaughter) or section 273 (aggravated sexual assault), or
    - (ii) the young person has been found guilty of a serious violent offence for which an adult is liable to imprisonment for a term of more than two years, and the young person had previously been found guilty at least twice of a serious violent offence;
- (*b*) the young person is suffering from a mental illness or disorder, a psychological disorder or an emotional disturbance;
- (*c*) a plan of treatment and intensive supervision has been developed for the young person, and there are reasonable grounds to believe that the plan might reduce the risk of the young person repeating the offence or committing a serious violent offence; and
- (*d*) the provincial director has determined that an intensive rehabilitative custody and supervision program is available and that the young person's participation in the program is appropriate.

(8) *Safeguard of rights* — Nothing in this section abrogates or derogates from the rights of a young person regarding consent to physical or mental health treatment or care.

(9) *Determination by court* — On application of the Attorney General after a young person is found guilty of an offence, and after giving both parties an opportunity to be heard, the youth justice court may make a judicial determination that the offence is a serious violent offence and endorse the information or indictment accordingly.

(10) *Appeals* — For the purposes of an appeal in accordance with section 37, a determination under subsection (9) is part of the sentence.

(11) *Inconsistency* — An order may not be made under paragraphs (2)(*k*) to (*m*) in respect of an offence for which a conditional discharge has been granted under paragraph (2)(*c*).

(12) *Coming into force of youth sentence* — A youth sentence or any part of it comes into force on the date on which it is imposed or on any later date that the youth justice court specifies.

(13) *Consecutive youth sentences* — Subject to subsections (15) and (16), a youth justice court that sentences a young person may direct that a sentence imposed on the young person under paragraph (2)(*n*), (*o*), (*q*) or (*r*) be served consecutively if the young person

- (*a*) is sentenced while under sentence for an offence under any of those paragraphs; or
- (*b*) is found guilty of more than one offence under any of those paragraphs.

(14) *Duration of youth sentence for a single offence* — No youth sentence, other than an order made under paragraph (2)(*j*), (*n*), (*o*), (*q*) or (*r*), shall continue in force for more than two years. If the youth sentence comprises more than one sanction imposed at the same time in respect of the same offence, the combined duration of the sanctions shall not exceed two years, unless the sentence includes a sanction under paragraph (2)(*j*), (*n*), (*o*), (*q*) or (*r*) that exceeds two years.

(15) *Duration of youth sentence for different offences* — Subject to subsection (16), if more than one youth sentence is imposed under this section in respect of a young person with respect to different offences, the continuous combined duration of those youth sentences shall not exceed three years, except if one of the offences is first degree murder or second degree murder within the meaning of section 231 of the *Criminal Code*, in which case the continuous combined duration of those youth sentences shall not exceed ten years in the case of first degree murder, or seven years in the case of second degree murder.

(16) *Duration of youth sentences made at different times* — If a youth sentence is imposed in respect of an offence committed by a young person after the commencement of, but before the completion of, any youth sentences imposed on the young person,

- (*a*) the duration of the sentence imposed in respect of the subsequent offence shall be determined in accordance with subsections (14) and (15);
- (*b*) the sentence may be served consecutively to the sentences imposed in respect of the previous offences; and
- (*c*) the combined duration of all the sentences may exceed three years and, if the offence is, or one of the previous offences was,
  - (i) first degree murder within the meaning of section 231 of the *Criminal Code*, the continuous combined duration of the youth sentences may exceed ten years, or

(ii) **second degree murder within the meaning of section 231 of the *Criminal Code*, the continuous combined duration of the youth sentences may exceed seven years.**

(17) *Sentence continues when adult* — **Subject to sections 89, 92 and 93 (provisions related to placement in adult facilities) of this Act and section 743.5 (transfer of jurisdiction) of the *Criminal Code*, a youth sentence imposed on a young person continues in effect in accordance with its terms after the young person becomes an adult.**

COMMENTARY

Operational Impacts

The addition of new sentences gives the courts a wide range of options to address the individual needs and circumstances of each young person.

(a) *Reprimand* — This is a new sentencing option commonly referred to as a judicial tongue-lashing. This sentence may be appropriate for a youth whose personal circumstances have changed significantly and who made reparation since being found guilty of a serious offence. Another example of a case where a reprimand may be used is one where the evidence brought forward in court does not paint as bleak a picture as was thought at the time the decision was made to proceed to court. Justice Lynch of the Nova Scotia Supreme Court in *R. v. K.D.* (2003), 214 N.S.R. (2d) 100, [2003] N.S.J. No. 165 (S.C.), discussed the purpose and principles of sentencing in relation to the facts of the case. She rejected the sentences proposed by the Crown and in the pre-sentence report, and described why she did not agree with the recommendation of community service work and a period of probation. She indicated that it is not the job of sentencing to achieve what is being recommended in the pre-sentence report, but clarified that the Department of Community Services and the Department of Health should be dealing with the issues. A reprimand may also be an appropriate sentence for those charges that ought never to have been heard by the youth justice court.

(b) *Absolute discharge* — This was a sentence option under the *Young Offenders Act*. It allows the court to discharge the youth without any conditions, and is usually used for offences where the court is satisfied that nothing further is required or in cases where circumstances have changed significantly since the offence occurred.

(c) *Conditional discharge* — This was a sentence option under the *Young Offenders Act*, but it has been modified to address the difficulties in administering this sentence. Under the *Young Offenders Act*, there was no instruction regarding the supervision or monitoring of a youth's conditions. New wording in the Act indicates that this sentence may require the youth to report to, and be supervised by, the provincial director. The provincial director can then delegate the function of supervision to a probation officer as per section 2(1) of this Act. This

sentence provides a discharge once the youth has fulfilled the court-imposed conditions.
(d) *Fine* — There is a fine of up to $1,000. This has not been changed from the *Young Offenders Act*.
(e) *Compensation order* — This was available in the *Young Offenders Act*; however, a new provision has been added to expand compensation to pre-trial pecuniary loss in the Province of Quebec.
(f) *Restitution order* — There has been no change from the *Young Offenders Act*.
(g) *Restitution to purchaser of property obtained by the commission of an offence* — There has been no change from the *Young Offenders Act*.
(h) *Personal service order* — There has been no change from the *Young Offenders Act*.
(i) *Community service order* — This was an option under the *Young Offenders Act*, but it has been modified to address the difficulties in administering this sentence when it is not attached to a probation order. Under the *Young Offenders Act*, there was no instruction regarding the supervision or monitoring of a youth's conditions. New wording indicates that this sentence requires the youth to report to, and be supervised by, the provincial director or a person designated by the youth justice court. As in the case of a conditional discharge, the provincial director can delegate the function of supervision to a probation officer as per section 2(1) of this Act.
(j) *Prohibition order* — The *Young Offenders Act* contained a mandatory prohibition order as well. When a youth is found guilty of certain offences involving firearms and weapons (sections 109 and 110 of the *Criminal Code*), the youth justice court is required to impose a prohibition order.
(k) *Probation order* — The only change from the *Young Offenders Act* has been the listing of additional conditions of probation in this legislation.
(l) *Intensive support and supervision order (ISSP)* — This is a new sentence option. This sentence, which is a community-based alternative to a custodial sentence, provides more supervision than a probation order and can be imposed only upon the agreement of the provincial director. It is not mandatory to provide this sentence, as it requires the jurisdiction to have an intensive support and supervision program in place. Many jurisdictions do provide this program, while others are still in the development stage.
(m) *Non-residential order* — This is a new option. The young person may be sentenced to attend a non-residential community program, also referred to as an attendance program, at the times and terms fixed by the court, subject to the approval of the provincial director. The sentence is a maximum of 240 hours over a period not exceeding six months. Under the *Young Offenders Act*, an attendance order was often included as one of the terms of a probation order where available. It is not mandatory for jurisdictions to provide an attendance program; therefore, the sentence may not be available in every community. Programs vary according to community and individual needs. They

may be provided during the day, after school, in the evenings or on weekends.

(n) *Custody and supervision order* — This new provision in the *Youth Criminal Justice Act* is one of the most significant changes from the *Young Offenders Act*. This new order requires that when the court imposes a custody order, it must be followed by a period of community supervision half as long as the custody order. Thus, if the court imposes a six-month custody order, the order would be followed by three months of community supervision. Section 97 gives the court the authority to set mandatory conditions for the community supervision portion of this sentence. The maximum length of this order includes both the custody and community supervision portions and remains the same as in the *Young Offenders Act* — two years from the date of committal, or three years if the offence is one in which life imprisonment could be imposed under the *Criminal Code*. This gives the perception that this new mandatory sentence has reduced the maximum time a youth may be sentenced to custody. However, section 98 allows for an application to be made to the court for a youth to remain in custody for the entire sentence if there are compelling reasons for keeping the young person in custody.

(o) *Custody and supervision order for presumptive offences* — There has been a slight change from the *Young Offenders Act*. This is a sentence for presumptive offences other than murder, and it is a maximum of three years in length. Section 105 requires that a youth who has been given this sentence be brought back to the youth court at least one month before the expiry of the custodial portion of the sentence in order for the court to set the conditions of the youth's community supervision. An application can also be made under section 104(1) to have a young person remain in custody for a period not exceeding the remainder of the youth sentence if there is reason to believe that the young person is likely to commit an offence causing the death of, or serious harm to, another person before the expiry of the youth sentence. Should the presumptive offence category be repealed or amended as a result of the Quebec Court of Appeal ruling in *Reference re: Bill C-7 Respecting the Criminal Justice System for Young Persons*, [2003] Q.J. No. 2850 (C.A.), this sentence is subject to technical changes.

(p) *Deferred custody and supervision order* — This is a new order. The youth justice court may make an order for a youth to be placed in custody, then defer the custody portion and set conditions on which the youth is to be supervised in the community. Mandatory community supervision conditions are contained in section 105(2), while other conditions the court may impose are set out in section 105(3). The deferred custody and supervision order may not exceed six months.

This sentence, which is gaining popularity with the judiciary, is often followed by a probation order. The British Columbia Youth Court in *R. v. J.R.R.*, [2003] B.C.J. No. 3007 (Youth Ct.), ruled that a concurrent deferred custody and supervision order and probation order violates section 42(2), which prohibits inconsistent sentences, while section

56(5) does not preclude imposing a probation order consecutive to a deferred custody and supervision order, as the deferred custody and supervision order is included in 56(5)(*b*), and section 42(12) allows the youth court to specify the date the order comes into force.

(q) *Sentence for first and second degree murder* — This was available in the *Young Offenders Act*. The sentence for first degree murder remains a maximum of 10 years, with the custody portion not to exceed six years, and the conditional supervision to include the mandatory community supervision conditions contained in section 105(2). The sentence for second degree murder is a maximum of seven years, with custody to be no more than four years, and conditional supervision to follow the provisions as set out in section 105(2). In both cases, an application may be made under section 104(1) to have a young person remain in custody for a period not exceeding the remainder of the youth sentence if there is reason to believe that the young person is likely to commit an offence causing the death of, or serious harm to, another person before the expiry of the youth sentence.

(r) *Intensive rehabilitative custody and supervision order* — This is a new order. This sentence is intended to be a treatment sentence and is restricted to a young person who has been found guilty of first degree murder, second degree murder, attempt to commit murder, manslaughter or aggravated sexual assault, or who has committed three serious violent offences and is suffering from a mental, psychological or emotional disorder. The court may impose this sentence only if the provincial director has determined that an intensive rehabilitative custody and supervision program is available and that the youth's participation is appropriate. Also, a treatment plan that the young person agrees to participate in, including a plan for the intensive community supervision of the youth, must be presented to the youth court. The criteria for a young person to be eligible for this sentence is so restrictive that only a handful of young persons have had this sentence imposed.

(s) *Impose any other conditions that the court considers advisable and in the best interest of the young person and the public* — There has been no change from the *Young Offenders Act*.

43. *Additional youth sentences* — **Subject to subsection 42(15) (duration of youth sentences), if a young person who is subject to a custodial sentence imposed under paragraph 42(2)(*n*), (*o*), (*q*) or (*r*) that has not expired receives an additional youth sentence under one of those paragraphs, the young person is, for the purposes of the** *Corrections and Conditional Release Act,* **the** *Criminal Code,* **the** *Prisons and Reformatories Act* **and this Act, deemed to have been sentenced to one youth sentence commencing at the beginning of the first of those youth sentences to be served and ending on the expiry of the last of them to be served.**

COMMENTARY

Legal Implications

This section says that additional youth sentences will become one sentence and other acts of parliament will apply to help calculate the combined sentence. When more than one sentence is imposed on the same day, the custody and community portions are merged to form one period of custody beginning on the date of the sentence and ending on the expiry date of the longest sentence.

44. *Custodial portion if additional youth sentence* **— Subject to subsection 42(15) (duration of youth sentences) and section 46 (exception when youth sentence in respect of earlier offence), if an additional youth sentence under paragraph 42(2)(*n*), (*o*), (*q*) or (*r*) is imposed on a young person on whom a youth sentence had already been imposed under one of those paragraphs that has not expired and the expiry date of the youth sentence that includes the additional youth sentence, as determined in accordance with section 43, is later than the expiry date of the youth sentence that the young person was serving before the additional youth sentence was imposed, the custodial portion of the young person's youth sentence is, from the date the additional sentence is imposed, the total of**

- (*a*) **the unexpired portion of the custodial portion of the youth sentence before the additional youth sentence was imposed, and**
- (*b*) **the relevant period set out in subparagraph (i), (ii) or (iii):**
   - (i) **if the additional youth sentence is imposed under paragraph 42(2)(*n*), the period that is two thirds of the period that constitutes the difference between the expiry of the youth sentence as determined in accordance with section 43 and the expiry of the youth sentence that the young person was serving before the additional youth sentence was imposed,**
   - (ii) **if the additional youth sentence is a concurrent youth sentence imposed under paragraph 42(2)(*o*), (*q*) or (*r*), the custodial portion of the youth sentence imposed under that paragraph that extends beyond the expiry date of the custodial portion of the sentence being served before the imposition of the additional sentence, or**
   - (iii) **if the additional youth sentence is a consecutive youth sentence imposed under paragraph 42(2)(*o*), (*q*) or (*r*), the custodial portion of the additional youth sentence imposed under that paragraph.**

COMMENTARY

Legal Implications

This detailed section deals specifically with the method of calculating additional sentences imposed on a young person. There are several different scenarios as a result of the different sentencing options under section 42, as well as the concepts of consecutive and concurrent sentences.

Operational Implications

Some youths have more than one sentence imposed upon them at the same time or imposed on another youth court date. Multiple sentences under the *Young Offenders Act* were always complicated, but the introduction of community supervision following custody further complicates sentence calculation. Sentences run concurrently with each other unless the court orders the sentences to be consecutive. In order to achieve the intended result of the sentence, youth justice courts and/or Crowns need to be aware, or advised, of the expiry date of merged sentences the young person is currently serving as well as the status of the custody and community portions. If the new sentence does not expire later than any existing sentence the young person is already serving, the young person will not serve any further time in custody or in the community.

45. (1) *Supervision when additional youth sentence extends the period in custody* **— If a young person has begun to serve a portion of a youth sentence in the community subject to conditions under paragraph 42(2)(*n*) or under conditional supervision under paragraph 42(2)(*o*), (*q*) or (*r*) at the time an additional youth sentence is imposed under one of those paragraphs, and, as a result of the application of section 44, the custodial portion of the young person's youth sentence ends on a day that is later than the day on which the young person received the additional youth sentence, the serving of a portion of the youth sentence under supervision in the community subject to conditions or under conditional supervision shall become inoperative and the young person shall be committed to custody under paragraph 102(1)(*b*) or 106(*b*) until the end of the extended portion of the youth sentence to be served in custody.**

(2) *Supervision when additional youth sentence does not extend the period in custody* **— If a youth sentence has been imposed under paragraph 42(2)(*n*), (*o*), (*q*) or (*r*) on a young person who is under supervision in the community subject to conditions under paragraph 42(2)(*n*) or under conditional supervision under paragraph 42(2)(*o*), (*q*) or (*r*), and the additional youth sentence would not modify the expiry date of the youth sentence that the young person was serving at the time the additional youth sentence was imposed, the young person may be remanded to the youth custody facility that the provincial director considers appropriate. The provincial director shall review the case and, no later than forty-eight hours after the remand of the young person, shall either refer the case to the youth justice court for a review under section 103 or 109 or release the young person to continue the supervision in the community or the conditional supervision.**

(3) *Supervision when youth sentence additional to supervision* **— If a youth sentence has been imposed under paragraph 42(2)(*n*), (*o*), (*q*) or (*r*) on a young person who is under conditional supervision under paragraph**

94(19)(b) or subsection 96(5), the young person shall be remanded to the youth custody facility that the provincial director considers appropriate. The provincial director shall review the case and, no later than forty-eight hours after the remand of the young person, shall either refer the case to the youth justice court for a review under section 103 or 109 or release the young person to continue the conditional supervision.

COMMENTARY

Legal Implications

When a young person receives a custodial sentence, a portion of that sentence is served in custody, and a portion is served in the community. When additional sentences are imposed, the young person may still be in custody or may be in the community under community or conditional supervision. The new sentence may terminate the community portion of the sentence and result in the young person going back to custody, or the sentence may continue to be served in the community. The rules for making this decision are set out in this section.

Operational Implications

Calculating this new sentence is straightforward for a single sentence, but requires close adherence to calculation rules for combined and multiple sentences. Provinces and territories have worked together to develop sentence calculation rules and a sentence calculation manual to provide sentence administrators with national consistency when calculating sentences imposed under the *Youth Criminal Justice Act*.

46. *Exception when youth sentence in respect of earlier offence* **— The total of the custodial portions of a young person's youth sentences shall not exceed six years calculated from the beginning of the youth sentence that is determined in accordance with section 43 if**

- (a) **a youth sentence is imposed under paragraph 42(2)(n), (o), (q) or (r) on the young person already serving a youth sentence under one of those paragraphs; and**
- (b) **the later youth sentence imposed is in respect of an offence committed before the commencement of the earlier youth sentence.**

COMMENTARY

Legal Implications

This is one of the many technical provisions relating to the rules on sentencing and the determination of the length of the sentence. There is a limit of six years placed on the custodial portion of the sentence if the second sentence is for an offence committed before the commencement of the first sentence.

47. (1) *Committal to custody deemed continuous* — Subject to subsections (2) and (3), a young person who is sentenced under paragraph 42(2)(*n*) is deemed to be committed to continuous custody for the custodial portion of the sentence.

(2) *Intermittent custody* —If the sentence does not exceed ninety days, the youth justice court may order that the custodial portion of the sentence be served intermittently if it is consistent with the purpose and principles set out in section 38.

(3) *Availability of place of intermittent custody* — Before making an order of committal to intermittent custody, the youth justice court shall require the prosecutor to make available to the court for its consideration a report of the provincial director as to the availability of a youth custody facility in which an order of intermittent custody can be enforced and, if the report discloses that no such youth custody facility is available, the court shall not make the order.

COMMENTARY

Legal Implications

Most custodial sentences are served continuously, meaning that once the young person enters the custodial facility, the sentence begins to run and will continue to run until the young person is released from custody.

Like most rules, there is an exception. Provided the provincial director advises there is a youth custody facility available, the judge may order a sentence to be served intermittently. This means that the young person may serve the sentence a few days at a time, usually on weekends.

Operational Implications

Intermittent sentences were provided for in the *Young Offenders Act*; however, they were used infrequently, and in some jurisdictions not at all. An intermittent sentence may be used for a youth who, although he or she has been found guilty of a charge that warrants a custodial sentence, is employed, or in school during the week, and a custody sentence would interfere with his or her progress. An intermittent sentence would allow the youth to serve the custodial time on weekends. Before the youth justice court can make an order for intermittent sentence, the provincial director is required to provide the court with a report indicating that a youth custody facility is available. Intermittent sentences are disruptive to the individual as well as to the custody facility and do not allow sufficient program opportunities to address a young person's needs.

48. *Reasons for the sentence* — When a youth justice court imposes a youth sentence, it shall state its reasons for the sentence in the record of the case and shall, on request, give or cause to be given a copy of the sentence and the reasons for the sentence to

(a) the young person, the young person's counsel, a parent of the young person, the provincial director and the prosecutor; and

(b) in the case of a committal to custody under paragraph 42(2)(n), (o), (q) or (r), the review board.

COMMENTARY

Legal Implications

Judges are required to give reasons when sentencing a young person and, in a climate of full disclosure, are required to provide copies of those reasons to the young person, his or her counsel, the parent and the prosecutor. A copy should also be given to the review board in the event of a custodial sentence.

Operational Implications

The duty for a judge to give reasons for the sentence has not been changed from the *Young Offenders Act*, but the factors the judge must consider (section 39(3)) are more detailed in this legislation and must be part of the reasons for the sentence. This section acts as a check or safeguard, for the sake of the young person, to ensure that every possible option outside of the formal court system has been considered.

49. (1) *Warrant of committal* —When a young person is committed to custody, the youth justice court shall issue or cause to be issued a warrant of committal.

(2) *Custody during transfer* — A young person who is committed to custody may, in the course of being transferred from custody to the court or from the court to custody, be held under the supervision and control of a peace officer or in any place of temporary detention referred to in subsection 30(1) that the provincial director may specify.

(3) *Subsection 30(3) applies* — Subsection 30(3) (detention separate from adults) applies, with any modifications that the circumstances require, in respect of a person held in a place of temporary detention under subsection (2).

COMMENTARY

Legal Implications

This section has not been changed from the *Young Offenders Act*. It provides some of the rules for holding a young person in custody. These rules provide for a warrant of committal (a document that authorizes a custody facility to keep the young person in custody), the transport of the young person between court and the custodial facility and the transfer of the young person between facilities.

This section also gives direction for keeping a youth in a place of temporary detention.

Operational Implications

Unlike the *Young Offenders Act*, this legislation does not include definitions of open or secure custody. Instead, levels of custody are defined by the degree of restraint. This legislation does not place restrictions on where a youth may be detained, or on the level of detainment. In some jurisdictions the child welfare legislation prescribes standards for detaining a young person in an open or secure facility. The *Youth Criminal Justice Act* does maintain the important principle of keeping youths separate and apart from adults (see sections 84 and 85).

50. (1) *Application of Part XXIII of Criminal Code* — Subject to section 74 (application of *Criminal Code* to adult sentences), Part XXIII (sentencing) of the *Criminal Code* does not apply in respect of proceedings under this Act except for paragraph 718.2(*e*) (sentencing principle for aboriginal offenders), sections 722 (victim impact statements), 722.1 (copy of statement) and 722.2 (inquiry by court), subsection 730(2) (court process continues in force) and sections 748 (pardons and remissions), 748.1 (remission by the Governor in Council) and 749 (royal prerogative) of that Act, which provisions apply with any modifications that the circumstances require.

(2) *Section 787 of Criminal Code does not apply* — Section 787 (general penalty) of the *Criminal Code* does not apply in respect of proceedings under this Act.

COMMENTARY

Legal Implications

These sentencing provisions have not been changed from the *Young Offenders Act* except for the reference to adult sentences. These provisions are particular to youths and they differ from the provisions for adults. The rule is that the sentencing provisions applicable to adults do not apply. There are exceptions to this rule, and these are set out in this section. The victim impact provisions are good examples of adult sentencing provisions that are an exception to the general rule and apply only to youths.

51. (1) *Mandatory prohibition order* — Despite section 42 (youth sentences), when a young person is found guilty of an offence referred to in any of paragraphs 109(1)(*a*) to (*d*) of the *Criminal Code*, the youth justice court shall, in addition to imposing a sentence under section 42 (youth sentences), make an order prohibiting the young person from possessing any firearm, cross-bow, prohibited weapon, restricted weapon, prohibited device, ammunition, prohibited ammunition or explosive substance during

the period specified in the order as determined in accordance with subsection (2).

(2) *Duration of prohibition order* — An order made under subsection (1) begins on the day on which the order is made and ends not earlier than two years after the young person has completed the custodial portion of the sentence or, if the young person is not subject to custody, after the time the young person is found guilty of the offence.

(3) *Discretionary prohibition order* — Despite section 42 (youth sentences), where a young person is found guilty of an offence referred to in paragraph 110(1)(*a*) or (*b*) of the *Criminal Code*, the youth justice court shall, in addition to imposing a sentence under section 42 (youth sentences), consider whether it is desirable, in the interests of the safety of the young person or of any other person, to make an order prohibiting the young person from possessing any firearm, cross-bow, prohibited weapon, restricted weapon, prohibited device, ammunition, prohibited ammunition or explosive substance, or all such things, and where the court decides that it is so desirable, the court shall so order.

(4) *Duration of prohibition order* — An order made under subsection (3) against a young person begins on the day on which the order is made and ends not later than two years after the young person has completed the custodial portion of the sentence or, if the young person is not subject to custody, after the time the young person is found guilty of the offence.

(5) *Reasons for the prohibition order* — When a youth justice court makes an order under this section, it shall state its reasons for making the order in the record of the case and shall give or cause to be given a copy of the order and, on request, a transcript or copy of the reasons to the young person against whom the order was made, the counsel and a parent of the young person and the provincial director.

(6) *Reasons* — When the youth justice court does not make an order under subsection (3), or when the youth justice court does make such an order but does not prohibit the possession of everything referred to in that subsection, the youth justice court shall include in the record a statement of the youth justice court's reasons.

(7) *Application of Criminal Code* — Sections 113 to 117 (firearm prohibition orders) of the *Criminal Code* apply in respect of any order made under this section.

(8) *Report* — Before making an order referred to in section 113 (lifting firearms order) of the *Criminal Code* in respect of a young person, the youth justice court may require the provincial director to cause to be prepared, and to submit to the youth justice court, a report on the young person.

COMMENTARY

Legal Implications

This section gives the youth justice court the power to prohibit a young person from possessing a firearm, ammunition or other weapons. It is a unique sentence because the mandatory order of prohibition is for a minimum period of two years, whereas all of the other sentences in the *Youth Criminal Justice Act* are at the discretion of the youth justice court.

The prohibition order provisions in the *Criminal Code* of Canada are complex and have been developed with a primary view of protecting the public. This concern has been extended to young persons by making these provisions apply to youths. This section of the *Youth Criminal Justice Act* references sections of the *Criminal Code* that deal with prohibition orders. It is necessary to refer to the *Criminal Code* in order to understand the prohibition orders under the *Youth Criminal Justice Act*.

Operational Impacts

This section authorizes the youth justice court to order a report to be prepared before the court can make an order to lift a firearm prohibition order. This is an added responsibility for provincial directors and for those preparing the reports for the court. Guidance regarding the content of the report is found in the relevant section of the *Criminal Code*, not in this Act.

52. (1) *Review of order made under section 51* — **A youth justice court may, on application, review an order made under section 51 at any time after the end of the period set out in subsection 119(2) (period of access to records) that applies to the record of the offence that resulted in the order being made.**

(2) *Grounds* — **In conducting a review under this section, the youth justice court shall take into account**

- (*a*) **the nature and circumstances of the offence in respect of which the order was made; and**
- (*b*) **the safety of the young person and of other persons.**

(3) *Decision of review* — **When a youth justice court conducts a review under this section, it may, after giving the young person, a parent of the young person, the Attorney General and the provincial director an opportunity to be heard,**

- (*a*) **confirm the order;**
- (*b*) **revoke the order; or**
- (*c*) **vary the order as it considers appropriate in the circumstances of the case.**

(4) *New order not to be more onerous* — No variation of an order made under paragraph (3)(*c*) may be more onerous than the order being reviewed.

(5) *Application of provisions* — Subsections 59(3) to (5) apply, with any modifications that the circumstances require, in respect of a review under this section.

COMMENTARY

Legal Implications

This section provides for a review of the prohibition order made under the previous section and sets out the procedure to be followed. A youth justice court may confirm, revoke or vary the order, but the court cannot make it more onerous than the original order.

Operational Implications

Generally, applications for review are brought forward when the youth's circumstances have changed. A youth or a parent may advise the provincial director, the Crown or defence counsel to make application to the court on behalf of the young person.

53. (1) *Funding for victims* — The lieutenant governor in council of a province may order that, in respect of any fine imposed in the province under paragraph 42(2)(*d*), a percentage of the fine as fixed by the lieutenant governor in council be used to provide such assistance to victims of offences as the lieutenant governor in council may direct from time to time.

(2) *Victim fine surcharge* — If the lieutenant governor in council of a province has not made an order under subsection (1), a youth justice court that imposes a fine on a young person under paragraph 42(2)(*d*) may, in addition to any other punishment imposed on the young person, order the young person to pay a victim fine surcharge in an amount not exceeding fifteen per cent of the fine. The surcharge shall be used to provide such assistance to victims of offences as the lieutenant governor in council of the province in which the surcharge is imposed may direct from time to time.

COMMENTARY

Legal Implications

This section is new and authorizes the province to set a victim fine surcharge, or a percentage of any fine up to a maximum of 15 per cent, to be ordered by a youth justice court and used to provide assistance to victims.

Operational Implications

Victims of criminal offences should be treated with respect during the criminal process, and one way of ensuring this is to develop programs with the objective of providing assistance to victims. This is an optional program, and jurisdictions may elect not to establish a victim fine surcharge; however, this approach could provide some funding when the sentence imposed by the court is a fine. Many jurisdictions currently have victim fine surcharge programs for adult offenders.

54. (1) *Where a fine or other payment is ordered* — **The youth justice court shall, in imposing a fine under paragraph 42(2)(*d*) or in making an order under paragraph 42(2)(*e*) or (*g*), have regard to the present and future means of the young person to pay.**

(2) *Discharge of fine or surcharge* — **A young person on whom a fine is imposed under paragraph 42(2)(*d*), including any percentage of a fine imposed under subsection 53(1), or on whom a victim fine surcharge is imposed under subsection 53(2), may discharge the fine or surcharge in whole or in part by earning credits for work performed in a program established for that purpose**

- (*a*) **by the lieutenant governor in council of the province in which the fine or surcharge was imposed; or**
- (*b*) **by the lieutenant governor in council of the province in which the young person resides, if an appropriate agreement is in effect between the government of that province and the government of the province in which the fine or surcharge was imposed.**

(3) *Rates, crediting and other matters* — **A program referred to in subsection (2) shall determine the rate at which credits are earned and may provide for the manner of crediting any amounts earned against the fine or surcharge and any other matters necessary for or incidental to carrying out the program.**

(4) *Representations respecting orders under paragraphs 42(2)(e) to (h)* — **In considering whether to make an order under any of paragraphs 42(2)(*e*) to (*h*), the youth justice court may consider any representations made by the person who would be compensated or to whom restitution or payment would be made.**

(5) *Notice of orders under paragraphs 42(2)(e) to (h)* — **If the youth justice court makes an order under any of paragraphs 42(2)(*e*) to (*h*), it shall cause notice of the terms of the order to be given to the person who is to be compensated or to whom restitution or payment is to be made.**

(6) *Consent of person to be compensated* — **No order may be made under paragraph 42(2)(*h*) unless the youth justice court has secured the consent of the person to be compensated.**

(7) *Orders under paragraph 42(2)(h), (i) or (m)* — No order may be made under paragraph 42(2)(h), (i) or (m) unless the youth justice court is satisfied that

- (a) the young person against whom the order is made is a suitable candidate for such an order; and
- (b) the order does not interfere with the normal hours of work or education of the young person.

(8) *Duration of order for service* — No order may be made under paragraph 42(2)(h) or (i) to perform personal or community services unless those services can be completed in two hundred and forty hours or less and within twelve months after the date of the order.

(9) *Community service order* — No order may be made under paragraph 42(2)(i) unless

- (a) the community service to be performed is part of a program that is approved by the provincial director; or
- (b) the youth justice court is satisfied that the person or organization for whom the community service is to be performed has agreed to its performance.

(10) *Application for further time to complete youth sentence* — A youth justice court may, on application by or on behalf of the young person in respect of whom a youth sentence has been imposed under any of paragraphs 42(2)(d) to (i), allow further time for the completion of the sentence subject to any regulations made under paragraph 155(b) and to any rules made by the youth justice court under subsection 17(1).

COMMENTARY

Legal Implications

This section covers a number of specific issues related to the following sentences: fines, compensation orders, restitution, order to pay a victim, order to compensate a victim, community service and an order to attend a program. The provisions are very much the same as in the *Young Offenders Act*, with the addition of the ability for a youth to have the victim fine or surcharge discharged for work performed under a program established for that purpose.

55. (1) *Conditions that must appear in orders* — The youth justice court shall prescribe, as conditions of an order made under paragraph 42(2)(k) or (l), that the young person

- (a) keep the peace and be of good behaviour; and
- (b) appear before the youth justice court when required by the court to do so.

(2) Conditions that may appear in orders — A youth justice court may prescribe, as conditions of an order made under paragraph 42(2)(k) or (l), that a young person do one or more of the following that the youth justice court considers appropriate in the circumstances:

- (a) report to and be supervised by the provincial director or a person designated by the youth justice court;
- (b) notify the clerk of the youth justice court, the provincial director or the youth worker assigned to the case of any change of address or any change in the young person's place of employment, education or training;
- (c) remain within the territorial jurisdiction of one or more courts named in the order;
- (d) make reasonable efforts to obtain and maintain suitable employment;
- (e) attend school or any other place of learning, training or recreation that is appropriate, if the youth justice court is satisfied that a suitable program for the young person is available there;
- (f) reside with a parent, or any other adult that the youth justice court considers appropriate, who is willing to provide for the care and maintenance of the young person;
- (g) reside at a place that the provincial director may specify;
- (h) comply with any other conditions set out in the order that the youth justice court considers appropriate, including conditions for securing the young person's good conduct and for preventing the young person from repeating the offence or committing other offences; and
- (i) not own, possess or have the control of any weapon, ammunition, prohibited ammunition, prohibited device or explosive substance, except as authorized by the order.

COMMENTARY

Legal Implications

Probation orders and intensive support and supervision orders are both subject to two mandatory conditions listed in this section. Optional conditions may also appear in the probation order. These orders are the same as those listed in the *Young Offenders Act*, with an additional condition prohibiting the possession or control of weapons, ammunition or explosive substances.

Operational Implications

The conditions of a probation order serve two purposes: enforcement and rehabilitation. A probation order is the legal mandate to supervise a young person in the community as ordered by the court while at the same time serving to support more appropriate behaviour on the part of the young person and address the issues that may have led to the inappropriate behaviour in order to facilitate rehabilitation. For example, a probation order may contain a condition that names individuals a young person is not to associate with in an attempt to steer the youth away from negative peer influence.

56. (1) *Communication of order* — A youth justice court that makes an order under paragraph 42(2)(k) or (l) shall

(a) cause the order to be read by or to the young person bound by it;
(b) explain or cause to be explained to the young person the purpose and effect of the order, and confirm that the young person understands it; and
(c) cause a copy of the order to be given to the young person, and to any parent of the young person who is in attendance at the sentencing hearing.

(2) *Copy of order to parent* — A youth justice court that makes an order under paragraph 42(2)(k) or (l) may cause a copy to be given to a parent of the young person who is not in attendance at the proceedings if the parent is, in the opinion of the court, taking an active interest in the proceedings.

(3) *Endorsement of order by young person* — After the order has been read and explained under subsection (1), the young person shall endorse on the order an acknowledgement that the young person has received a copy of the order and had its purpose and effect explained.

(4) *Validity of order* — The failure of a young person to endorse the order or of a parent to receive a copy of the order does not affect the validity of the order.

(5) *Commencement of order* — An order made under paragraph 42(2)(k) or (l) comes into force

(a) on the date on which it is made; or
(b) if a young person receives a sentence that includes a period of continuous custody and supervision, at the end of the period of supervision.

(6) *Effect of order in case of custody* — If a young person is subject to a sentence that includes both a period of continuous custody and supervision and an order made under paragraph 42(2)(k) or (l), and the court orders under subsection 42(12) a delay in the start of the period of custody, the court may divide the period that the order made under paragraph 42(2)(k) or (l) is in effect, with the first portion to have effect from the date on which it is made until the start of the period of custody, and the remainder to take effect at the end of the period of supervision.

(7) *Notice to appear* — A young person may be given notice either orally or in writing to appear before the youth justice court under paragraph 55(1)(b).

(8) *Warrant in default of appearance* — **If service of a notice in writing is proved and the young person fails to attend court in accordance with the notice, a youth justice court may issue a warrant to compel the appearance of the young person.**

COMMENTARY

Legal Implications

Probation orders and intensive support and supervision orders are more detailed than most sentences; therefore, there are provisions to make sure that the young person understands the order and that the parent has an opportunity to see the order as well as the conditions in the order. Section 56(6) allows for a probation order or intensive support and supervision order to be divided into two periods. The order can commence on the day it is made prior to the start of a period of custody and resume at the end of the community portion of custody.

Operational Implications

Language has been added in this section to clarify that failure to give a parent a copy of the order does not affect the validity of the order. This was often an issue when a young person had to be returned to court for breaching a probation order. A common defence under the *Young Offenders Act* was to attack the validity of the order.

The use of probation orders is different under the *Youth Criminal Justice Act*. According to the principles of sentencing, any conditions that are incorporated into a probation order must be the least restrictive and the most likely to rehabilitate and reintegrate the young person. The primary focus of the probation is rehabilitation and reintegration, with supervision as the secondary focus. Often, there are too many conditions placed on a youth subject to probation. These sentencing principles provide closer scrutiny of the conditions added to probation orders. The sections pertaining to probation orders also apply to intensive support and supervision programs, wherever the program is available. This new sentence is considered an intensive probation order in many jurisdictions. Ideally, the youth workers, or probation officers, assigned to youths who have been given an intensive support and supervision sentence will be responsible for fewer cases in order to dedicate more time to supervising the youths and more resources to addressing the needs of these young people and increase their opportunities for rehabilitation.

57. (1) *Transfer of youth sentence* — **When a youth sentence has been imposed under any of paragraphs 42(2)(*d*) to (*i*), (*k*), (*l*) or (*s*) in respect of a young person and the young person or a parent with whom the young person resides is or becomes a resident of a territorial division outside the jurisdiction of the youth justice court that imposed the youth sentence, whether in the same or in another province, a youth justice court judge in the territorial division in which the youth sentence was imposed may, on the application of the Attorney General or on the application of the young**

person or the young person's parent, with the consent of the Attorney General, transfer to a youth justice court in another territorial division the youth sentence and any portion of the record of the case that is appropriate. All subsequent proceedings relating to the case shall then be carried out and enforced by that court.

(2) *No transfer outside province before appeal completed* — No youth sentence may be transferred from one province to another under this section until the time for an appeal against the youth sentence or the finding on which the youth sentence was based has expired or until all proceedings in respect of any such appeal have been completed.

(3) *Transfer to a province when person is adult* — When an application is made under subsection (1) to transfer the youth sentence of a young person to a province in which the young person is an adult, a youth justice court judge may, with the consent of the Attorney General, transfer the youth sentence and the record of the case to the youth justice court in the province to which the transfer is sought, and the youth justice court to which the case is transferred shall have full jurisdiction in respect of the youth sentence as if that court had imposed the youth sentence. The person shall be further dealt with in accordance with this Act.

COMMENTARY

Legal Implications

When a young person receives certain non-custodial sentences, there is provision to transfer the sentence to another jurisdiction, within or outside the province or territory. This provision recognizes the fact that young persons and families may move their place of residence. The youth justice court may grant the order to transfer the sentence to the other jurisdiction based on an application made by the young person, the Attorney General or the parents. Section 57(1) does not include provisions to transfer sentences made under section 42(2)(*c*), conditional discharge. This needs to be addressed in any future amendments.

58. (1) *Interprovincial arrangements* — When a youth sentence has been imposed under any of paragraphs 42(2)(*k*) to (*r*) in respect of a young person, the youth sentence in one province may be dealt with in any other province in accordance with any agreement that may have been made between those provinces.

(2) *Youth justice court retains jurisdiction* — Subject to subsection (3), when a youth sentence imposed in respect of a young person is dealt with under this section in a province other than that in which the youth sentence was imposed, the youth justice court of the province in which the youth sentence was imposed retains, for all purposes of this Act, exclusive jurisdiction over the young person as if the youth sentence were dealt with within that province, and any warrant or process issued in respect of the

young person may be executed or served in any place in Canada outside the province where the youth sentence was imposed as if it were executed or served in that province.

(3) *Waiver of jurisdiction* — When a youth sentence imposed in respect of a young person is dealt with under this section in a province other than the one in which the youth sentence was imposed, the youth justice court of the province in which the youth sentence was imposed may, with the consent in writing of the Attorney General of that province and the young person, waive its jurisdiction, for the purpose of any proceeding under this Act, to the youth justice court of the province in which the youth sentence is dealt with, in which case the youth justice court in the province in which the youth sentence is dealt with shall have full jurisdiction in respect of the youth sentence as if that court had imposed the youth sentence.

COMMENTARY

Legal Implications

Provinces and territories are authorized by this section to enter into agreements for the transfer of custodial and certain non-custodial sentences. This provision gives direction over the technical and important aspect of the youth justice court's authority to enforce the sentence. The original court that sentenced the young person may retain jurisdiction over the young person, or it may give that authority to the youth justice court in the new jurisdiction.

Operational Implications

When a youth relocates to another jurisdiction, it is often the best practice to apply to the court to give authority to the new jurisdiction. However, when the youth is transferred temporarily, it is best to maintain the original jurisdiction. When a youth moves to another province for a given period of time in order to attend a particular program that will assist in his or her rehabilitation, it is necessary to maintain the authority in the original jurisdiction to support the youth's reintegration. Jurisdictions have policies and procedures in place to transfer youths interprovincially and to maintain an appropriate level of supervision and service.

59. (1) *Review of youth sentences not involving custody* — When a youth justice court has imposed a youth sentence in respect of a young person, other than a youth sentence under paragraph 42(2)(*n*), (*o*), (*q*) or (*r*), the youth justice court shall, on the application of the young person, the young person's parent, the Attorney General or the provincial director, made at any time after six months after the date of the youth sentence or, with leave of a youth justice court judge, at any earlier time, review the youth sentence if the court is satisfied that there are grounds for a review under subsection (2).

(2) *Grounds for review* — A review of a youth sentence may be made under this section

  (*a*) on the ground that the circumstances that led to the youth sentence have changed materially;
  (*b*) on the ground that the young person in respect of whom the review is to be made is unable to comply with or is experiencing serious difficulty in complying with the terms of the youth sentence;
  (*c*) on the ground that the young person in respect of whom the review is to be made has contravened a condition of an order made under paragraph 42(2)(*k*) or (*l*) without reasonable excuse;
  (*d*) on the ground that the terms of the youth sentence are adversely affecting the opportunities available to the young person to obtain services, education or employment; or
  (*e*) on any other ground that the youth justice court considers appropriate.

(3) *Progress report* — The youth justice court may, before reviewing under this section a youth sentence imposed in respect of a young person, require the provincial director to cause to be prepared, and to submit to the youth justice court, a progress report on the performance of the young person since the youth sentence took effect.

(4) *Subsections 94(10) to (12) apply* — Subsections 94(10) to (12) apply, with any modifications that the circumstances require, in respect of any progress report required under subsection (3).

(5) *Subsections 94(7) and (14) to (18) apply* — Subsections 94(7) and (14) to (18) apply, with any modifications that the circumstances require, in respect of reviews made under this section and any notice required under subsection 94(14) shall also be given to the provincial director.

(6) *Compelling appearance of young person* — The youth justice court may, by summons or warrant, compel a young person in respect of whom a review is to be made under this section to appear before the youth justice court for the purposes of the review.

(7) *Decision of the youth justice court after review* — When a youth justice court reviews under this section a youth sentence imposed in respect of a young person, it may, after giving the young person, a parent of the young person, the Attorney General and the provincial director an opportunity to be heard,

  (*a*) confirm the youth sentence;
  (*b*) terminate the youth sentence and discharge the young person from any further obligation of the youth sentence; or
  (*c*) vary the youth sentence or impose any new youth sentence under section 42, other than a committal to custody, for any period of time, not exceeding the remainder of the period of the earlier youth

sentence, that the court considers appropriate in the circumstances of the case.

(8) *New youth sentence not to be more onerous* — Subject to subsection (9), when a youth sentence imposed in respect of a young person is reviewed under this section, no youth sentence imposed under subsection (7) shall, without the consent of the young person, be more onerous than the remainder of the youth sentence reviewed.

(9) *Exception* — A youth justice court may under this section extend the time within which a youth sentence imposed under paragraphs 42(2)(*d*) to (*i*) is to be complied with by a young person if the court is satisfied that the young person requires more time to comply with the youth sentence, but in no case shall the extension be for a period of time that expires more than twelve months after the date the youth sentence would otherwise have expired.

COMMENTARY

Legal Implications

Youth justice courts have the authority to review a youth sentence after the sentence has been in force, usually for a minimum of six months. This allows courts to take into consideration a number of factors listed in this section, including a material change in circumstances, the inability to comply with the conditions of the sentence, a breach of the conditions or the fact that the conditions of the sentence may be preventing the young person from obtaining services, employment or education. These provisions were also contained in the *Young Offenders Act*.

Operational Implications

Probation officers can use this section as an alternative to laying a charge for failure to comply with a community sentence under section 137. When a young person fails to comply, the probation officer should review the circumstances and the severity of the breach along with the youth's progress towards rehabilitation, and consider whether a court review to alter conditions of the order would be sufficient to hold the young person accountable.

When reviewing a sentence under this section, the youth justice court may request a progress report, which will usually be prepared by the probation officer. Progress reports identify any change in circumstances since the sentence took effect as well as the young person's progress with respect to rehabilitation and may make recommendations to the court.

60. *Provisions applicable to youth sentences on review* — **This Part and Part 5 (custody and supervision) apply with any modifications that the circumstances require to orders made in respect of reviews of youth sentences under sections 59 and 94 to 96.**

COMMENTARY

Legal Implications

This new section deals with issues of procedure for reviews of sentence. There are procedures set out in both Parts 4 and 5 of the *Youth Criminal Justice Act*, and rather than repeat all of the provisions from Part 5, this section simply incorporates them by this reference.

ADULT SENTENCE AND ELECTION

61. *Age for purpose of presumptive offences* — **The lieutenant governor in council of a province may by order fix an age greater than fourteen years but not more than sixteen years for the purpose of the application of the provisions of this Act relating to presumptive offences.**

COMMENTARY

Legal Implications

Sections 61-81, which are new, set out the rules for adult sentences for youths and replace the sections on the transfer to ordinary court (adult court) hearings and procedures in the *Young Offenders Act*.

In 1995, the *Young Offenders Act* introduced the concept of a presumption of an adult sentence for four offences: murder, attempted murder, manslaughter and aggravated sexual assault committed by young persons 16 or 17 years of age. The *Youth Criminal Justice Act* expanded this concept by adding a fifth category of offence for young persons who have a pattern of convictions for serious violent offences for which there is now a presumption of an adult sentence.

In addition, the *Youth Criminal Justice Act* sets the age for the presumption at 14 in the definition of "presumption offence", but at the same time authorizes the lieutenant governor in council of a province to elect to choose the age of 15 or 16 for this presumption.

On March 31, 2003, the Quebec Court of Appeal in *Reference re: Bill C-7 Respecting the Criminal Justice System for Young Persons*, [2003] Q.J. No. 2850 (Que. C.A.), ruled that the provisions of presumptive offences violate the principles of fundamental justice (section 7) of the *Canadian Charter of Rights and Freedoms* by placing the burden of proof on the young person who has committed the presumptive offence.

As a result amendments are being considered to the relevant sections of this Act that deal with presumptive offences.

Operational Implications

The need for a transfer hearing to determine if a young person's case should be heard in ordinary court has been eliminated, and the youth court judge has authority to order an adult sentence where applicable. The transfer hearing under the *Young Offenders Act* was always a complicated and lengthy hearing under the best of circumstances, so removing the hearing before conviction should make the process timelier. Allowing the youth court judge to order an adult sentence is a much better option than transferring a youth to an adult court. A youth court judge is more familiar with the kinds of programs and services in the community and can ensure the sentence imposed addresses the young person's needs.

Providing jurisdictions with the option of choosing the age of presumption of an adult sentence is part of the flexibility that is incorporated into many sections of this legislation. With the exception of Quebec, most jurisdictions support lowering the age of presumption to 14 years; however, there is potential for creating a nation where youths are treated differently based on location. For example, a youth could be presumed to be an adult at 14 years of age in Alberta, 15 years of age in Nova Scotia and 16 years of age in British Columbia. This could mean entirely different sentences for the same offence. However, this may become irrelevant should the federal government amend the Act to remove the presumption of an adult sentence.

62. *Imposition of adult sentence* — An adult sentence shall be imposed on a young person who is found guilty of an indictable offence for which an adult is liable to imprisonment for a term of more than two years in the following cases:

(*a*) **in the case of a presumptive offence, if the youth justice court makes an order under subsection 70(2) or paragraph 72(1)(*b*); or**

(*b*) **in any other case, if the youth justice court makes an order under subsection 64(5) or paragraph 72(1)(*b*) in relation to an offence committed after the young person attained the age of fourteen years.**

COMMENTARY

Legal Implications

This section describes when an adult sentence will be imposed upon a young person. It is a technical section that must be read together with the other sections in this Part, in particular sections 61-73, which, taken together, authorize a youth justice court to order an adult sentence.

However, the Quebec Court of Appeal in *Reference re: Bill C-7 Respecting the Criminal Justice System for Young Persons*, [2003] Q.J. No. 2850 (C.A.), has ruled that sections 62, 63, 64(1) and (5), 70, 72(1) and (2) and 73(1) violate section 7 of the *Canadian Charter of Rights and Freedoms* insofar as they place on the young person who has committed a presumptive offence the burden of proving the factors that justify imposing a youth sentence instead of an adult sentence.

In essence, the Quebec Court of Appeal has put an end to presumptive offences and the presumption of an adult sentence unless this is challenged by other jurisdictions.

63. (1) *Application by young person* — A young person who is charged with, or found guilty of, a presumptive offence may, at any time before evidence is called as to sentence or, where no evidence is called, before submissions are made as to sentence, make an application for an order that he or she is not liable to an adult sentence and that a youth sentence must be imposed.

(2) *Application unopposed* — If the Attorney General gives notice to the youth justice court that the Attorney General does not oppose the application, the youth justice court shall, without a hearing, order that the young person, if found guilty, is not liable to an adult sentence and that a youth sentence must be imposed.

COMMENTARY

Legal Implications

This section allows the young person to apply for a youth sentence for a presumptive offence, and, if the Attorney General agrees with the young person, then no hearing is necessary, and a youth sentence will apply.

This section may be subject to amendment as a result of the decision of the Quebec Court of Appeal in *Reference re: Bill C-7 Respecting the Criminal Justice System for Young Persons*, [2003] Q.J. No. 2850 (C.A.).

Operational Implications

This section, which empowers the youth justice court to impose a youth sentence, entitles a young person to apply for a youth sentence and allows the court to conduct a hearing to determine which sentence should apply.

64. (1) *Application by Attorney General* — The Attorney General may, following an application under subsection 42(9) (judicial determination of serious violent offence), if any is made, and before evidence is called as to sentence or, where no evidence is called, before submissions are made as to sentence, make an application for an order that a young person is liable to an adult sentence if the young person is or has been found guilty of an offence, other than a presumptive offence, for which an adult is liable to imprisonment for a term of more than two years, that was committed after the young person attained the age of fourteen years.

(2) *Notice of intention to seek adult sentence* — If the Attorney General intends to seek an adult sentence for an offence by making an application under subsection (1), or by establishing that the offence is a presumptive offence within the meaning of paragraph (*b*) of the definition "presumptive offence" in subsection 2(1), the Attorney General shall, before the young person enters a plea or with leave of the youth justice court before the commencement of the trial, give notice to the young person and the youth justice court of the intention to seek an adult sentence.

(3) *Included offences* — A notice of intention to seek an adult sentence given in respect of an offence is notice in respect of any included offence of which the young person is found guilty for which an adult is liable to imprisonment for a term of more than two years.

(4) *Notice to young person* — If a young person is charged with an offence, other than an offence set out in paragraph (*a*) of the definition "presumptive offence" in subsection 2(1), and the Attorney General intends to establish, after a finding of guilt, that the offence is a serious violent offence and a presumptive offence within the meaning of paragraph (*b*) of the definition "presumptive offence" in subsection 2(1) for which the young person is liable to an adult sentence, the Attorney General shall, before the young person enters a plea or, with leave of the youth justice court under subsection (2), before the commencement of the trial, give notice of that intention to the young person.

(5) *Application unopposed* — If the young person gives notice to the youth justice court that the young person does not oppose the application for an adult sentence, the youth justice court shall, without a hearing, order that if the young person is found guilty of an offence for which an adult is liable to imprisonment for a term of more than two years, an adult sentence must be imposed.

COMMENTARY

Legal Implications

The Attorney General may make an application to have a young person sentenced as an adult if the young person is found guilty of an offence, for which an adult is liable to imprisonment for a term of more than two years, committed after the young person was 14. If the Attorney General intends to ask the youth justice court for an adult sentence for a presumptive offence, an application must be made, the rules for which are set out in this section.

The Attorney General must give the young person notice that an adult sentence may be imposed. The young person has the right to oppose or not to oppose the application of the Attorney General for an adult sentence.

This section may be subject to amendment as a result of the decision of the Quebec Court of Appeal in *Reference re: Bill C-7 Respecting the Criminal Justice System for Young Persons*, [2003] Q.J. No. 2850 (C.A.).

65. *Presumption does not apply* — If the Attorney General at any stage of proceedings gives notice to the youth justice court that an adult sentence will not be sought in respect of a young person who is alleged to have committed an offence set out in paragraph (*a*) of the definition "presumptive offence" in subsection 2(1), the court shall order that the young person is not liable to an adult sentence, and the court shall order a ban on publication of information that would identify the young person as having been dealt with under this Act.

COMMENTARY

Legal Implications

In the case of an offence where it is presumed that the young person will receive an adult sentence, the Attorney General may give notice that an adult sentence will not be sought if a youth sentence would be sufficient to hold the young person accountable. The youth justice court would then order that the young person is not liable to an adult sentence and order a ban on publication of information that would identify the youth.

This section may be subject to amendment as a result of the decision of the Quebec Court of Appeal in *Reference re: Bill C-7 Respecting the Criminal Justice System for Young Persons*, [2003] Q.J. No. 2850 (C.A.).

66. *No election if youth sentence* — If the youth justice court has made an order under subsection 63(2) or section 65 before a young person is required to be put to an election under section 67, the young person shall not be put to an election unless the young person is alleged to have committed first degree murder or second degree murder within the meaning of section 231 of the *Criminal Code*.

COMMENTARY

Legal Implications

When it is clear to the youth justice court that a youth sentence will be imposed, then it is not necessary for the youth justice court to give the young person a choice as to where the trial will take place.

However, when the young person is charged with murder, the youth justice court must give him or her the choice of court, as the Charter guarantees the right to a jury trial if the possible penalty is five years or more. The youth sentence for murder is greater than five years; therefore, the young person has a Charter right to a jury trial and a choice of court.

67. (1) *Election – adult sentence* — Subject to section 66, the youth justice court shall, before a young person enters a plea, put the young person to his or her election in the words set out in subsection (2) if

- **(*a*) the young person is charged with having committed an offence set out in paragraph (*a*) of the definition "presumptive offence" in subsection 2(1);**
- **(*b*) the Attorney General has given notice under subsection 64(2) of the intention to seek an adult sentence for an offence committed after the young person has attained the age of fourteen years;**
- **(*c*) the young person is charged with having committed first or second degree murder within the meaning of section 231 of the *Criminal Code* before the young person has attained the age of fourteen years; or**

(d) the person to whom section 16 (status of accused uncertain) applies is charged with having, after attaining the age of fourteen years, committed an offence for which an adult would be entitled to an election under section 536 of the *Criminal Code*, or over which a superior court of criminal jurisdiction would have exclusive jurisdiction under section 469 of that Act.

(2) *Wording of election* — The youth justice court shall put the young person to his or her election in the following words:

> You have the option to elect to be tried by a youth justice court judge without a jury and without having had a preliminary inquiry; or you may elect to be tried by a judge without a jury; or you may elect to be tried by a court composed of a judge and jury. If you do not elect now, you are deemed to have elected to be tried by a court composed of a judge and jury. If you elect to be tried by a judge without a jury or by a court composed of a judge and jury or if you are deemed to have elected to be tried by a court composed of a judge and jury, you will have a preliminary inquiry only if you or the prosecutor requests one. How do you elect to be tried?

(3) *Election – Nunavut* — Subject to section 66, in respect of proceedings in Nunavut, the youth justice court shall, before a young person enters a plea, put the young person to his or her election in the words set out in subsection (4) if

(a) the young person is charged with having committed an offence set out in paragraph (a) of the definition "presumptive offence" in subsection 2(1);
(b) the Attorney General has given notice under subsection 64(2) of the intention to seek an adult sentence for an offence committed after the young person has attained the age of fourteen years;
(c) the young person is charged with having committed first or second degree murder within the meaning of section 231 of the *Criminal Code* before the young person has attained the age of fourteen years; or
(d) the person to whom section 16 (status of accused uncertain) applies is charged with having, after attaining the age of fourteen years, committed an offence for which an adult would be entitled to an election under section 536.1 of the *Criminal Code*.

(4) *Wording of election* — The youth justice court shall put the young person to his or her election in the following words:

> You have the option to elect to be tried by a judge of the Nunavut Court of Justice alone, acting as a youth justice court without a jury and without a preliminary inquiry; or you may elect to be tried by a judge of the Nunavut Court of Justice, acting as a youth justice court without a jury; or you may elect to be tried by a judge of the Nunavut

Court of Justice, acting as a youth justice court with a jury. If you elect to be tried by a judge without a jury or by a judge, acting as a youth justice court, with a jury or if you are deemed to have elected to be tried by a judge, acting as a youth justice court, with a jury, you will have a preliminary inquiry only if you or the prosecutor requests one. How do you elect to be tried?

(5) *Mode of trial where co-accused are young persons* — When two or more young persons who are charged with the same offence, who are jointly charged in the same information or indictment or in respect of whom the Attorney General seeks joinder of counts that are set out in separate informations or indictments are put to their election, then, unless all of them elect or re-elect or are deemed to have elected, as the case may be, the same mode of trial, the youth justice court judge

- (*a*) may decline to record any election, re-election or deemed election for trial by a youth justice court judge without a jury, a judge without a jury or, in Nunavut, a judge of the Nunavut Court Justice without a jury; and
- (*b*) if the judge declines to do so, shall hold a preliminary inquiry, if requested to do so by one of the parties, unless a preliminary inquiry has been held prior to the election, re-election or deemed election.

(6) *Attorney General may require trial by jury* — The Attorney General may, even if a young person elects under subsection (1) or (3) to be tried by a youth justice court judge without a jury or a judge without a jury, require the young person to be tried by a court composed of a judge and jury.

(7) *Preliminary inquiry* — When a young person elects to be tried by a judge without a jury, or elects or is deemed to have elected to be tried by a court composed of a judge and jury, the youth justice court referred to in subsection 13(1) shall, on the request of the young person or the prosecutor made at that time or within the period fixed by rules of court made under section 17 or 155 or, if there are no such rules, by the youth justice court judge, conduct a preliminary inquiry and if, on its conclusion, the young person is ordered to stand trial, the proceedings shall be conducted

- (*a*) before a judge without a jury or a court composed of a judge and jury, as the case may be; or
- (*b*) in Nunavut, before a judge of the Nunavut Court of Justice acting as a youth justice court, with or without a jury, as the case may be.

(7.1) *Preliminary inquiry if two or more accused* — If two or more young persons are jointly charged in an information and one or more of them make a request for a preliminary inquiry under subsection (7), a preliminary inquiry must be held with respect to all of them.

(7.2) *When no request for preliminary inquiry* — If no request for a preliminary inquiry is made under subsection (7), the youth justice court shall fix the date for the trial or the date on which the young person must appear in the trial court to have the date fixed.

(8) *Preliminary inquiry provisions of Criminal Code* — The preliminary inquiry shall be conducted in accordance with the provisions of Part XVIII (procedure on preliminary inquiry) of the *Criminal Code*, except to the extent that they are inconsistent with this Act.

(9) *Parts XIX and XX of Criminal Code* — Proceedings under this Act before a judge without a jury or a court composed of a judge and jury or, in Nunavut, a judge of the Nunavut Court of Justice acting as a youth justice court, with or without a jury, as the case may be, shall be conducted in accordance with the provisions of Parts XIX (indictable offences — trial without jury) and XX (procedure in jury trials and general provisions) of the *Criminal Code*, with any modifications that the circumstances require, except that

    (*a*) the provisions of this Act respecting the protection of privacy of young persons prevail over the provisions of the *Criminal Code*; and

    (*b*) the young person is entitled to be represented in court by counsel if the young person is removed from court in accordance with subsection 650(2) of the *Criminal Code*.

[S.C. 2002, c. 13, s. 91]

COMMENTARY

Legal Implications

This section provides specific wording that must be used by the youth justice court when requesting the young person to elect the way in which the case will proceed. The young person has three choices:

- to have a trial before a youth justice court;
- to have a trial before a judge acting as a youth justice court and to have a preliminary inquiry to see if there is enough evidence to have a trial; and
- to have a trial before a judge sitting with a jury and to have a preliminary inquiry.

All cases will be heard by youth justice courts and youth justice court judges, and they will either be so designated or deemed to be so (see section 13).

In cases where a young person chooses not to elect, the youth court will deem the youth to have elected to have a preliminary inquiry and to be tried by a court composed of a judge and jury. Section 67 also gives the Attorney General the authority to require the young person to be tried by a judge and jury even if he or she had not elected to do so.

In addition to setting out the choices for trial, this section also includes a number of technical procedural rules necessary to provide guidance for the lawyers and the judge on the following: the election, joint trials, application of the *Criminal Code* and the procedure for the preliminary inquiry. Specific reference is made to Nunavut due to the fact that it has a single-level court.

Section 67(2), (4), (5), (7.1) and (7.2) has been amended to address the issue of requesting a preliminary inquiry.

68. (1) *Proof of notice under subsection 64(4)* — **When a young person is found guilty of an offence, other than an offence set out in paragraph (*a*) of the definition "presumptive offence" in subsection 2(1), committed after he or she attained the age of fourteen years, and the Attorney General seeks to establish that the offence is a serious violent offence and a presumptive offence within the meaning of paragraph (*b*) of the definition "presumptive offence" in subsection 2(1), the Attorney General must satisfy the youth justice court that the young person, before entering a plea, was given notice under subsection 64(4) (intention to prove prior serious violent offences).**

(2) *Determination of serious violent offence* — If the youth justice court is satisfied that the young person was given notice under subsection 64(4) (intention to prove prior serious violent offences), the Attorney General may make an application in accordance with subsection 42(9) (judicial determination of serious violent offence).

(3) *Inquiry by court and proof* — If the youth justice court determines that the offence is a serious violent offence, it shall ask whether the young person admits to the previous judicial determinations of serious violent offences made at different proceedings. If the young person does not admit to any of it, the Attorney General may adduce evidence as proof of the previous judicial determinations in accordance with section 667 of the *Criminal Code*, with any modifications that the circumstances require. For the purposes of that section, a certified copy of the information or indictment endorsed in accordance with subsection 42(9) (judicial determination of serious violent offence) or a certified copy of a court decision is deemed to be a certificate.

(4) *Determination by court* — If the youth justice court, after making its inquiry under subsection (3), is satisfied that the offence is a presumptive offence within the meaning of paragraph (*b*) of the definition "presumptive offence" in subsection 2(1), the youth justice court shall endorse the information or indictment accordingly.

(5) *Determination by court* — If the youth justice court, after making its inquiry under subsection (3), is not satisfied that the offence is a presumptive offence within the meaning of paragraph (*b*) of the definition "presumptive offence" in subsection 2(1), the Attorney General may make an application under subsection 64(1) (application for adult sentence).

COMMENTARY

Legal Implications

Section 42(9) of the Act includes a reference to judicial determination of serious violent offence. If there are three findings of a serious violent offence, they can lead to a presumption of an adult sentence. This section explains the procedures for giving notice to the young person of the intention to seek a finding of serious violent offence and on proving the prior judicial determination of a serious violent offence to seek the presumption of adult sentence.

This section may be subject to amendment as a result of the decision of the Quebec Court of Appeal in *Reference re: Bill C-7 Respecting the Criminal Justice System for Young Persons*, [2003] Q.J. No. 2850 (C.A.).

Operational Implications

When a youth is found guilty of a third serious violent offence and the criteria are met, a presumption of an adult sentence arises. Once the presumption of adult sentence arises, the young person could be eligible for an intensive rehabilitation custody and supervision order that is imposed by the youth justice court, subject to the provincial director's approval of the program. This order could actually address the reasons the youth committed serious violent offences. Unfortunately, the determination of a serious violent offence is based only on serious violent convictions. As a result, charges that have been reduced through the plea bargaining process may make a young person who might otherwise benefit from this sentence ineligible.

Another example of a missed opportunity for a young person to benefit from this sentence is in *R. v. J.M.M.*, [2003] A.J. No. 1159, 2003 ABPC 169, where the Alberta Provincial Court denied a serious violent offender determination based on the fact that the offence pre-dated the coming into force of the *Youth Criminal Justice Act* and therefore fell into the definition of punishment within section 11(*i*) of the Charter.

69. (1) *Paragraph (a) "presumptive offence" – included offences* **— If a young person who is charged with an offence set out in paragraph (*a*) of the definition "presumptive offence" in subsection 2(1) is found guilty of committing an included offence for which an adult is liable to imprisonment for a term of more than two years, other than another presumptive offence set out in that paragraph,**

- (*a*) **the Attorney General may make an application under subsection 64(1) (application for adult sentence) without the necessity of giving notice under subsection 64(2), if the finding of guilt is for an offence that is not a presumptive offence; or**
- (*b*) **subsections 68(2) to (5) apply without the necessity of the Attorney General giving notice under subsection 64(2) (intention to seek adult sentence) or (4) (intention to prove prior serious violent offences), if the finding of guilt is for an offence that would be a presumptive offence within the meaning of paragraph (*b*) of the**

definition "presumptive offence" in subsection 2(1) if a judicial determination is made that the offence is a serious violent offence and on proof of previous judicial determinations of a serious violent offence.

(2) *Other serious offences – included offences* — If the Attorney General has given notice under subsection 64(2) of the intention to seek an adult sentence and the young person, after he or she has attained the age of fourteen years, is found guilty of committing an included offence for which an adult is liable to imprisonment for a term of more than two years, the Attorney General may make an application under subsection 64(1) (application for adult sentence) or seek to apply the provisions of section 68.

COMMENTARY

Legal Implications

An accused person is sometimes found guilty of an offence other than that charged by the police. Some offences are included with the offence charged. For example, assault is included in the offence of robbery because in order for a robbery to occur, there must be an assault and a theft. When the trial fails to prove in evidence a theft, but proves an assault, then the court may find the young person guilty of assault, even though the original charge was robbery.

This section sets out the rules for the operation of included offences when dealing with the possibility of adult sentences.

This section may be subject to amendment as a result of the decision of the Quebec Court of Appeal in *Reference re: Bill C-7 Respecting the Criminal Justice System for Young Persons*, [2003] Q.J. No. 2850 (C.A.).

70. (1) *Inquiry by court to young person* — The youth justice court, after hearing an application under subsection 42(9) (judicial determination of serious violent offence), if any is made, and before evidence is called or, where no evidence is called, before submissions are made as to sentence, shall inquire whether a young person wishes to make an application under subsection 63(1) (application for youth sentence) and if so, whether the Attorney General would oppose it, if

(*a*) the young person has been found guilty of a presumptive offence;
(*b*) the young person has not already made an application under subsection 63(1); and
(*c*) no order has been made under section 65 (young person not liable to adult sentence).

(2) *No application by young person* — If the young person indicates that he or she does not wish to make an application under subsection 63(1) (application for youth sentence) or fails to give an indication, the court shall order that an adult sentence be imposed.

COMMENTARY

Legal Implications

This section protects the rights of a young person when he or she is presumed to receive an adult sentence. The court must ask the young person if he or she wishes to make an application to have a youth sentence. This provision is intended to make sure that the young person is aware of his or her right to apply for a youth sentence. This section may be subject to amendment as a result of the decision of the Quebec Court of Appeal in *Reference re: Bill C-7 Respecting the Criminal Justice System for Young Persons*, [2003] Q.J. No. 2850 (C.A.).

71. Hearing – adult sentences — The youth justice court shall, at the commencement of the sentencing hearing, hold a hearing in respect of an application under subsection 63(1) (application for youth sentence) or 64(1) (application for adult sentence), unless the court has received notice that the application is not opposed. Both parties and the parents of the young person shall be given an opportunity to be heard at the hearing.

COMMENTARY

Legal Implications

The *Young Offenders Act* provided for a transfer hearing, before a finding of guilt, to determine whether a youth should be tried in adult court. The hearing provided for in this section takes place after the young person has been found guilty, and determines whether a youth or adult sentence is appropriate.

72. (1) *Test – adult sentences* — In making its decision on an application heard in accordance with section 71, the youth justice court shall consider the seriousness and circumstances of the offence, and the age, maturity, character, background and previous record of the young person and any other factors that the court considers relevant, and

- (*a*) **if it is of the opinion that a youth sentence imposed in accordance with the purpose and principles set out in subparagraph 3(1)(*b*)(ii) and section 38 would have sufficient length to hold the young person accountable for his or her offending behaviour, it shall order that the young person is not liable to an adult sentence and that a youth sentence must be imposed; and**
- (*b*) **if it is of the opinion that a youth sentence imposed in accordance with the purpose and principles set out in subparagraph 3(1)(*b*)(ii) and section 38 would not have sufficient length to hold the young person accountable for his or her offending behaviour, it shall order that an adult sentence be imposed.**

(2) *Onus* — The onus of satisfying the youth justice court as to the matters referred to in subsection (1) is with the applicant.

(3) *Pre-sentence reports* — **In making its decision, the youth justice court shall consider a pre-sentence report.**

(4) *Court to state reasons* — **When the youth justice court makes an order under this section, it shall state the reasons for its decision.**

(5) *Appeals* — **For the purposes of an appeal in accordance with section 37, an order under subsection (1) is part of the sentence.**

COMMENTARY

Legal Implications

When the youth justice court does hold a hearing to determine whether a youth or adult sentence should be imposed, the court must apply a test, that is, whether a youth sentence imposed under the principles of this Act would have sufficient length to hold the young person accountable for his or her offending behaviour. The onus is on the young person to satisfy the youth justice court that a youth sentence would be sufficient in the case of a presumptive offence, and otherwise the onus is on the Attorney General when applying for an adult sentence.

In addition to setting out the test, there are also a number of procedural rules for the operation of the hearing and a provision that makes a finding by the youth justice court part of the sentence should the young person, or the Attorney General, wish to have the decision reviewed by a higher court through an appeal.

This section may be subject to amendment as a result of the decision of the Quebec Court of Appeal in *Reference re: Bill C-7 Respecting the Criminal Justice System for Young Persons*, [2003] Q.J. No. 2850 (C.A.).

Operational Implications

This test is a significant change from that in the *Young Offenders Act,* where the transfer hearing pitted the rehabilitation of the young person against the protection of the public when in fact these concepts were not in opposition to each other.

73. (1) *Court must impose adult sentence* — **When the youth justice court makes an order under subsection 64(5) or 70(2) or paragraph 72(1)(*b*) in respect of a young person, the court shall, on a finding of guilt, impose an adult sentence on the young person.**

(2) *Court must impose youth sentence* — **When the youth justice court makes an order under subsection 63(2), section 65 or paragraph 72(1)(*a*) in respect of a young person, the court shall, on a finding of guilt, impose a youth sentence on the young person.**

COMMENTARY

Legal Implications

There are a number of provisions that lead the youth justice court to impose a youth or adult sentence. This section sets out all the provisions where a court would make an order for youth and adult sentences.

This section may be subject to amendment as a result of the decision of the Quebec Court of Appeal in *Reference re: Bill C-7 Respecting the Criminal Justice System for Young Persons*, [2003] Q.J. No. 2850 (C.A.). This decision was endorsed by the Ontario Superior Court of Justice in the case of *R. v. D.B.*, [2004] O.J. No. 3823 (C.A.).

74. (1) *Application of Parts XXIII and XXIV of Criminal Code* — Parts XXIII (sentencing) and XXIV (dangerous and long-term offenders) of the *Criminal Code* apply to a young person in respect of whom the youth justice court has ordered that an adult sentence be imposed.

(2) *Finding of guilt becomes a conviction* — A finding of guilt for an offence in respect of which an adult sentence is imposed becomes a conviction once the time allowed for the taking of an appeal has expired or, if an appeal is taken, all proceedings in respect of the appeal have been completed and the appeal court has upheld an adult sentence.

(3) *Interpretation* — This section does not affect the time of commencement of an adult sentence under subsection 719(1) of the *Criminal Code*.

COMMENTARY

Legal Implications

In general, the sentencing provisions in the *Criminal Code* do not apply to a young person, as the *Youth Criminal Justice Act* provides a complete code for sentencing youths, except where the youth justice court imposes an adult sentence for a young person. This section allows sentencing and dangerous and long-term offender provisions from the *Criminal Code* to apply to young persons when sentenced as adults.

75. (1) *Inquiry by the court to the young person* — If the youth justice court imposes a youth sentence in respect of a young person who has been found guilty of having committed a presumptive offence set out in paragraph (*a*) of the definition "presumptive offence" in subsection 2(1), or an offence under paragraph (*b*) of that definition for which the Attorney General has given notice under subsection 64(2) (intention to seek adult sentence), the court shall at the sentencing hearing inquire whether the young person or the Attorney General wishes to make an application under subsection (3) for a ban on publication.

(2) No application for a ban — **If the young person and the Attorney General both indicate that they do not wish to make an application under subsection (3), the court shall endorse the information or indictment accordingly.**

(3) *Order for a ban* — **On application of the young person or the Attorney General, a youth justice court may order a ban on publication of information that would identify the young person as having been dealt with under this Act if the court considers it appropriate in the circumstances, taking into account the importance of rehabilitating the young person and the public interest.**

(4) *Appeals* — **For the purposes of an appeal in accordance with section 37, an order under subsection (3) is part of the sentence.**

COMMENTARY

Legal Implications

This section is a significant change from that in the *Young Offenders Act*. It permits the publishing of the identity of a young person convicted of a presumptive offence: murder, attempted murder, manslaughter, aggravated sexual assault or a third serious violent offence. The young person or the Attorney General may make an application for the youth justice court to order a ban on publication. The general rule contained in the *Youth Criminal Justice Act* is that when a youth justice court imposes a sentence, the name of the young person and any information that could identify that person may not be published except as described in this section.

On March 31, 2003, the Quebec Court of Appeal in *Reference re: Bill C-7 Respecting the Criminal Justice System for Young Persons*, [2003] Q.J. No. 2850 (C.A.), addressed the question of publication and the presumption of publication for presumptive offences and found that sections 75 and 110(2)(*b*) violate the *Canadian Charter of Rights and Freedoms* insofar as they require the young person to justify maintaining the ban instead of placing the burden on the prosecutor to justify lifting the ban.

The court therefore placed the burden squarely on the Crown to rebut the general rule of no publication. One of the exceptions to that rule in the *Youth Criminal Justice Act* was in the case of a presumptive offence even though the young person received a youth sentence. The court found the reversing of the onus to require the young person to show why his or her name should not be published violated the Charter.

This section may be subject to amendment as a result of the decision in *Reference re: Bill C-7 Respecting the Criminal Justice System for Young Persons*.

Operational Implications

This section recognizes the public's concern about violent offences; therefore, when the offence is one of the most serious, the right of the young person to privacy is called into question. However, a young person should be identified only when there is a threat or risk to public safety, as notoriety would interfere with the rehabilitation of the young person.

76. (1) *Placement when subject to adult sentence* — Subject to subsections (2) and (9) and sections 79 and 80 and despite anything else in this Act or any other Act of Parliament, when a young person who is subject to an adult sentence in respect of an offence is sentenced to a term of imprisonment for the offence, the youth justice court shall order that the young person serve any portion of the imprisonment in

- **(*a*) a youth custody facility separate and apart from any adult who is detained or held in custody;**
- **(*b*) a provincial correctional facility for adults; or**
- **(*c*) if the sentence is for two years or more, a penitentiary.**

(2) *When young person subject to adult penalties* — The youth justice court that sentences a young person under subsection (1) shall, unless it is satisfied that to do so would not be in the best interests of the young person or would jeopardize the safety of others,

- **(*a*) if the young person is under the age of eighteen years at the time that he or she is sentenced, order that he or she be placed in a youth custody facility; and**
- **(*b*) if the young person is eighteen years old or older at the time that he or she is sentenced, order that he or she not be placed in a youth custody facility and order that any portion of the sentence be served in a provincial correctional facility for adults or, if the sentence is two years or more, in a penitentiary.**

(3) *Opportunity to be heard* — Before making an order under subsection (1), the youth justice court shall give the young person, a parent of the young person, the Attorney General, the provincial director and representatives of the provincial and federal correctional systems an opportunity to be heard.

(4) *Report necessary* — Before making an order under subsection (1), the youth justice court shall require that a report be prepared for the purpose of assisting the court.

(5) *Appeals* — For the purposes of an appeal in accordance with section 37, an order under subsection (1) is part of the sentence.

(6) *Review* — On application, the youth justice court shall review the placement of a young person under this section and, if satisfied that the circumstances that resulted in the initial order have changed materially,

and after having given the young person, a parent of the young person, the Attorney General, the provincial director and the representatives of the provincial and federal correctional systems an opportunity to be heard, the court may order that the young person be placed in

(*a*) a youth custody facility separate and apart from any adult who is detained or held in custody;
(*b*) a provincial correctional facility for adults; or
(*c*) if the sentence is for two years or more, a penitentiary.

(7) *Who may make application* — An application referred to in this section may be made by the young person, one of the young person's parents, the provincial director, representatives of the provincial and federal correctional systems and the Attorney General, after the time for all appeals has expired.

(8) *Notice* — When an application referred to in this section is made, the applicant shall cause a notice of the application to be given to the other persons referred to in subsection (7).

(9) *Limit – age twenty* — No young person shall remain in a youth custody facility under this section after the young person attains the age of twenty years, unless the youth justice court that makes the order under subsection (1) or reviews the placement under subsection (6) is satisfied that remaining in the youth custody facility would be in the best interests of the young person and would not jeopardize the safety of others.

COMMENTARY

Legal Implications

This new section authorizes the youth justice court to place a youth with an adult sentence in a youth facility, a provincial correctional facility (adult) or a penitentiary. Unless it is not in the best interests of the youth or it would jeopardize the safety of others, the court must place the young person in a youth facility if he or she is under the age of 18. If the youth is over the age of 18, the youth must be placed in a provincial facility.

Part of this section sets out the rules for a review of the decision to place the young person and to specify that this decision is part of the sentence for the purpose of an appeal.

There is also a provision for the general rule that a young person who is 20 years of age, or turns 20 years of age, should not remain in a youth custody facility but go to an adult facility.

Operational Implications

This provision recognizes that in most cases, the youth facility has greater capacity to provide the programs and services to match a young person's risks and needs. Therefore, the court is required to obtain prior knowledge regarding what is available in each of the systems and to include this information in a pre-sentence report.

77. (1) *Obligation to inform – parole* **— When a young person is ordered to serve a portion of a sentence in a youth custody facility under paragraph 76(1)(*a*) (placement when subject to adult sentence), the provincial director shall inform the appropriate parole board.**

(2) *Applicability of Corrections and Conditional Release Act* **— For greater certainty, Part II of the** *Corrections and Conditional Release Act* **applies, subject to section 78, with respect to a young person who is the subject of an order under subsection 76(1) (placement when subject to adult sentence).**

(3) *Appropriate parole board* **— The appropriate parole board for the purposes of this section is**

  (*a*) **if subsection 112(1) of the** *Corrections and Conditional Release Act* **would apply with respect to the young person but for the fact that the young person was ordered into a youth custody facility, the parole board mentioned in that subsection; and**
  (*b*) **in any other case, the National Parole Board.**

COMMENTARY

Legal Implications

This new section requires the provincial director to advise the appropriate parole board that the young person has received an adult sentence and has been placed in a youth custody facility.

Operational Implications

Youth custody facilities are not operated in the same way in all provinces and territories. This section is especially important in those jurisdictions where ministries that are not justice ministries, such as health and social services, have responsibility for youth custody. Although justice ministries are usually familiar with the processes of the parole board, this may not be the case with other ministries. This section ensures that the proper procedures and notifications for the release of offenders are in place and that the rights of the young person are protected. In addition, since there may be two parole boards in a province or territory — one for provincial adult facilities and one for penitentiaries — it is important that the parole board that is actually dealing with the case has all the relevant information.

78. (1) *Release entitlement* **— For greater certainty, section 6 of the** *Prisons and Reformatories Act* **applies to a young person who is ordered to serve a portion of a sentence in a youth custody facility under paragraph 76(1)(*a*) (placement when subject to adult sentence) only if section 743.1**

(rules respecting sentences of two or more years) of the *Criminal Code* would direct that the young person serve the sentence in a prison.

(2) *Release entitlement* — For greater certainty, section 127 of the *Corrections and Conditional Release Act* applies to a young person who is ordered to serve a portion of a sentence in a youth custody facility under paragraph 76(1)(*a*) (placement when subject to adult sentence) only if section 743.1 (rules respecting sentences of two or more years) of the *Criminal Code* would direct that the young person serve the sentence in a penitentiary.

COMMENTARY

Legal Implications

This section deals with the technical rules relating to the release of a young person who has had an adult sentence imposed upon him or her and has served part of the sentence in a youth custody facility. The rules for the release of a young person from custody are those that apply to adults, and for purposes of clarity, this section sets the rule for when the *Prisons and Reformatories Act* and the *Corrections and Conditional Release Act* apply.

79. *If person convicted under another Act* — If a person who is serving all or a portion of a sentence in a youth custody facility under paragraph 76(1)(*a*) (placement when subject to adult sentence) is sentenced to a term of imprisonment under an Act of Parliament other than this Act, the remainder of the portion of the sentence being served in the youth custody facility shall be served in a provincial correctional facility for adults or a penitentiary, in accordance with section 743.1 (rules respecting sentences of two or more years) of the *Criminal Code*.

COMMENTARY

Legal Implications

Some offenders commit offences as young persons, while under the age of 18, and as adults, after they have reached the age of 18. The purpose of this section is to make it clear that if a young person receives an adult sentence and is placed in a youth facility, he or she will be transferred to an adult facility to serve the rest of his or her sentence if he or she is later sentenced to imprisonment under another Act of Parliament, other than this Act, *i.e.*, the *Criminal Code*, after turning 18 years of age.

Operational Implications

This section protects the youth justice system from young people over the age of 18 who may falsely believe that they can commit further offences and remain under the protection of the youth system.

80. *If person who is serving a sentence under another Act is sentenced to an adult sentence* — If a person who has been serving a sentence of imprisonment under an Act of Parliament other than this Act is sentenced to an adult sentence of imprisonment under this Act, the sentences shall be served in a provincial correctional facility for adults or a penitentiary, in accordance with section 743.1 (rules respecting sentences of two or more years) of the *Criminal Code*.

COMMENTARY

Legal Implications

This new section is similar to the last section in that it provides for a youth who has had two sentences, one an adult sentence imposed upon him or her under the *Youth Criminal Justice Act* and the other a sentence of imprisonment under another Act of Parliament. If this occurs, the youth should serve the sentences in an adult facility. The difference in this section is that the order of the sentences is reversed. In this case, the person will have been sentenced to an adult sentence as a young person after having been sentenced to an adult sentence as an adult. Both of these sections affirm that a young person who has been sentenced to an adult facility as an adult should not be placed in a youth custody facility.

81. *Procedure for application or notice* — An application or a notice to the court under section 63, 64, 65 or 76 must be made or given orally, in the presence of the other party, or in writing with a copy served personally on the other party.

COMMENTARY

Legal Implications

This new section deals with procedures for making an application to court, or to give notice to someone who is to receive notice of a court proceeding. This should be done orally, in writing with a copy given to the other party, or in court in the presence of the other party. The reference to the other party means the other persons who have an interest in the court proceedings, and whom the justice system is required to inform about what is going to happen in court.

EFFECT OF TERMINATION OF YOUTH SENTENCE

82. (1) *Effect of absolute discharge or termination of youth sentence* — Subject to section 12 (examination as to previous convictions) of the *Canada Evidence Act*, if a young person is found guilty of an offence, and a youth justice court directs under paragraph 42(2)(*b*) that the young person be discharged absolutely, or the youth sentence, or any disposition made under the *Young Offenders Act*, chapter Y-1 of the Revised Statutes of Canada, 1985, has ceased to have effect, other than an order under section 51 (mandatory prohibition order) of this Act or section 20.1 (mandatory prohibition order) of the *Young Offenders Act*, the young person is deemed not to have been found guilty or convicted of the offence except that

(a) the young person may plead *autrefois convict* in respect of any subsequent charge relating to the offence;
(b) a youth justice court may consider the finding of guilt in considering an application under subsection 63(1) (application for youth sentence) or 64(1) (application for adult sentence);
(c) any court or justice may consider the finding of guilt in considering an application for judicial interim release or in considering what sentence to impose for any offence; and
(d) the National Parole Board or any provincial parole board may consider the finding of guilt in considering an application for conditional release or pardon.

(2) *Disqualifications removed* — For greater certainty and without restricting the generality of subsection (1), an absolute discharge under paragraph 42(2)(b) or the termination of the youth sentence or disposition in respect of an offence for which a young person is found guilty removes any disqualification in respect of the offence to which the young person is subject under any Act of Parliament by reason of a finding of guilt.

(3) *Applications for employment* — No application form for or relating to the following shall contain any question that by its terms requires the applicant to disclose that he or she has been charged with or found guilty of an offence in respect of which he or she has, under this Act or the *Young Offenders Act*, chapter Y-1 of the Revised Statutes of Canada, 1985, been discharged absolutely, or has completed the youth sentence under this Act or the disposition under the *Young Offenders Act*:

(a) employment in any department, as defined in section 2 of the *Financial Administration Act*;
(b) employment by any Crown corporation, as defined in section 83 of the *Financial Administration Act*;
(c) enrolment in the Canadian Forces; or
(d) employment on or in connection with the operation of any work, undertaking or business that is within the legislative authority of Parliament.

(4) *Finding of guilt not a previous conviction* — A finding of guilt under this Act is not a previous conviction for the purposes of any offence under any Act of Parliament for which a greater punishment is prescribed by reason of previous convictions, except for

(a) the purpose of establishing that an offence is a presumptive offence within the meaning of paragraph (b) of the definition "presumptive offence" in subsection 2(1); or
(b) the purpose of determining the adult sentence to be imposed.

COMMENTARY

Legal Implications

This section, which describes the effect of a sentence ending, is, for most purposes, a statutory pardon. While it is necessary for an adult to make an application for a pardon, for young persons, it is automatic. Once a sentence has ended, the general rule is that the young person is deemed not to have been found guilty or convicted of the offence.

This section may be subject to amendment as a result of the decision of the Quebec Court of Appeal in *Reference re: Bill C-7 Respecting the Criminal Justice System for Young Persons*, [2003] Q.J. No. 2850 (C.A.).

Operational Implications

Restrictions are placed on the various departments and branches of the Government of Canada, forbidding the questioning of a young person about his or her previous criminal offences, including when he or she seeks employment or enrolls in the Canadian Forces.

The purpose of the section is to ensure that once a young person has served his or her sentence, he or she does not continue to be prejudiced by his or her previous actions and is given a chance to get on with rebuilding his or her life.

PART 5 CUSTODY AND SUPERVISION

INTRODUCTION

Custody and supervision was not part of the *Young Offenders Act*; therefore, this section, dealing with the rules for young persons who receive sentences involving custody, including a specific set of principles to be used, is new. The rehabilitation and reintegration of youths from custody to the community is the focus of this new section.

This is a particularly important part of the Act, as a period of community supervision following custody is a new concept for the youth justice system. There is no longer a designation of "open" and "secure" custody, as was the case in the *Young Offenders Act*. Instead there is a requirement for two levels of custody distinguished by the degree of restraint on the young person. The term "temporary release" from the *Young Offenders Act* is replaced with a "reintegration leave", and the leave has been extended from 15 to 30 days and can be renewed.

The Act places additional responsibilities on provincial directors and sets out specific conditions that are to be placed on youths while serving the community portion of the custody sentence.

83. (1) *Purpose* **— The purpose of the youth custody and supervision system is to contribute to the protection of society by**

(a) carrying out sentences imposed by courts through the safe, fair and humane custody and supervision of young persons; and
(b) assisting young persons to be rehabilitated and reintegrated into the community as law-abiding citizens, by providing effective programs to young persons in custody and while under supervision in the community.

(2) *Principles to be used* — In addition to the principles set out in section 3, the following principles are to be used in achieving that purpose:

(a) that the least restrictive measures consistent with the protection of the public, of personnel working with young persons and of young persons be used;
(b) that young persons sentenced to custody retain the rights of other young persons, except the rights that are necessarily removed or restricted as a consequence of a sentence under this Act or another Act of Parliament;
(c) that the youth custody and supervision system facilitate the involvement of the families of young persons and members of the public;
(d) that custody and supervision decisions be made in a forthright, fair and timely manner, and that young persons have access to an effective review procedure; and
(e) that placements of young persons where they are treated as adults not disadvantage them with respect to their eligibility for and conditions of release.

COMMENTARY

Legal Implications

This section is the first in Part 5, and sets out the purpose and principles specifically directed to young persons and the corrections system.

The purpose of the custody and supervision system is to contribute to the protection of society through safe, fair and humane measures while at the same time assisting the young person to become rehabilitated and reintegrated into society.

The principles set out in this section form part of the principles throughout the Act and supplement the general principles in section 3 of this Act.

When sentencing, in order to benefit both society, in terms of protection, and the young person, in terms of rehabilitation, the courts are obligated to address the question as to what would be the least restrictive sentence to protect society. While in custody, a youth retains the rights of other young persons except those that are necessarily removed or restricted as a consequence of the sentence. This section recognizes the importance of families and encourages their involvement.

The last principle is directed to those youths who receive an adult sentence and are placed in a youth facility. Young persons are not to be disadvantaged by their treatment as adults, but are eligible for release at a time and on conditions similar to adults.

Operational Implications

Research and common sense have shown that a young person who is released from custody without any support will likely be back in custody in a very short time. This legislation seeks to provide that support through court order. This mandatory community supervision following custody is very similar to the aftercare that was attached to probation orders under the *Juvenile Delinquents Act*, which assisted many young people with successful reintegration.

The community supervision portion of a custody sentence looks slightly different in each jurisdiction and possibly each community. For some orders, jurisdictions may interpret this supervision to be an intensive supervision and support program delivered by probation officers with a lower number of cases. Other types of supervision programs may be delivered by community agencies or contract workers based on the individual needs of the youth. Or, the community supervision program may be provided as an aftercare program by staff from a custody facility. Regardless of how the program is delivered, a plan for the youth's reintegration must be developed early on in the custody portion of the sentence. The youth worker assigned by the provincial director to the young person is legislated in section 90(1) to ensure this happens. The reintegration plan addresses issues such as where and with whom the youth will live, plans for education or employment, leisure activities, participation in any community programs to support the youth, and the nature of the supervision for the community portion of the sentence. This reintegration plan is a new requirement and is critical to the young person's rehabilitation and successful return to the community.

84. ***Young person to be held apart from adults*** **— Subject to subsection 30(3) (pre-trial detention), paragraphs 76(1)(*b*) and (*c*) (placement in adult facilities with adult sentence) and sections 89 to 93 (placement in adult facilities with youth sentence), a young person who is committed to custody shall be held separate and apart from any adult who is detained or held in custody.**

COMMENTARY

Legal Implications

As the *Young Offenders Act* did, the *Youth Criminal Justice Act* has legislated that youths, with a few exceptions, cannot be held with adults. Youths are to be held separate and apart from adults when committed to custody.

Operational Implications

When the *Young Offenders Act* was introduced, jurisdictions had to ensure that youths were held separate and apart from adults. The *Youth Criminal Justice Act* has not changed that.

85. (1) *Levels of custody* — In the youth custody and supervision system in each province there must be at least two levels of custody for young persons distinguished by the degree of restraint of the young persons in them.

(2) *Designation of youth custody facilities* — Every youth custody facility in a province that contains one or more levels of custody shall be designated by

- (*a*) in the case of a youth custody facility with only one level of custody, being the level of custody with the least degree of restraint of the young persons in it, the lieutenant governor in council or his or her delegate; and
- (*b*) in any other case, the lieutenant governor in council.

(3) *Provincial director to specify custody level – committal to custody* — The provincial director shall, when a young person is committed to custody under paragraph 42(2)(*n*), (*o*), (*q*) or (*r*) or an order is made under subsection 98(3), paragraph 103(2)(*b*), subsection 104(1) or paragraph 109(2)(*b*), determine the level of custody appropriate for the young person, after having taken into account the factors set out in subsection (5).

(4) *Provincial director to specify custody level – transfer* — The provincial director may determine a different level of custody for the young person when the provincial director is satisfied that the needs of the young person and the interests of society would be better served by doing so, after having taken into account the factors set out in subsection (5).

(5) *Factors* — The factors referred to in subsections (3) and (4) are

- (*a*) that the appropriate level of custody for the young person is the one that is the least restrictive to the young person, having regard to
    - (i) the seriousness of the offence in respect of which the young person was committed to custody and the circumstances in which that offence was committed,
    - (ii) the needs and circumstances of the young person, including proximity to family, school, employment and support services,
    - (iii) the safety of other young persons in custody, and
    - (iv) the interests of society;
- (*b*) that the level of custody should allow for the best possible match of programs to the young person's needs and behaviour, having regard to the findings of any assessment in respect of the young person; and
- (*c*) the likelihood of escape.

(6) *Placement and transfer at appropriate level* — After the provincial director has determined the appropriate level of custody for the young person under subsection (3) or (4), the young person shall be placed in the youth custody facility that contains that level of custody specified by the provincial director.

(7) *Notice* — The provincial director shall cause a notice in writing of a determination under subsection (3) or (4) to be given to the young person and a parent of the young person and set out in that notice the reasons for it.

COMMENTARY

Legal Implications

The Act requires more than one level of custody into which a young person could be placed. The *Young Offenders Act* legislated two levels of custody designated as open and secure custody. The *Youth Criminal Justice Act* provides the rules for designating the two levels of custody based on the degree of restraint, but does not name levels of custody.

This section of the Act also provides for the provincial director to determine the level of custody when the youth justice court imposes a custody order. The general rule under this Act is for the provincial director to determine the level of custody, but the lieutenant governor in council, by way of an Order in Council, under section 88, may choose to have those decisions made by the youth justice court. Conversely, under the *Young Offenders Act*, the decision was made by the youth court unless the provincial director was designated to make the determination. Under the *Youth Criminal Justice Act*, the provincial director is to give notice to the young person, and his or her parents, of the decision on the appropriate level of custody.

Operational Implications

Eliminating the designation of open and secure custody gives provinces and territories a great deal of flexibility in designating custody facilities. For example, one facility could provide two levels of custody. The physical design of many custody facilities will accommodate two levels of restraint in the same building, and the levels of restraint can also be distinguished by the programming and/or staffing provided for each level.

The authority for the provincial director to determine the level of custody is optional, as it was in the *Young Offenders Act*. Neither provinces nor territories exercised this authority under the *Young Offenders Act*, and none have opted to have the provincial director determine the level of custody under the *Youth Criminal Justice Act*. The sections that provide procedural safeguards for a young person with respect to due process rights and appeals are extremely labour-intensive for a jurisdiction to put in place and a provincial director to make decisions. There is also a concern regarding the liability for provincial directors making this kind of decision. However, if the legislation is not read carefully, the assumption would be that the provincial director is deciding the level of custody the young person receives. Courts need to be made aware of the option the province or territory elected. At the time of implementation of the *Youth Criminal Justice Act*, all provinces and territories opted to have the youth justice court determine the level of custody until further review.

86. (1) *Procedural safeguards* **— The lieutenant governor in council of a province shall ensure that procedures are in place to ensure that the due process rights of the young person are protected with respect to a determination made under subsection 85(3) or (4), including that the young person be**

- (*a*) **provided with any relevant information to which the provincial director has access in making the determination, subject to subsection (2);**
- (*b*) **given the opportunity to be heard; and**
- (*c*) **informed of any right to a review under section 87.**

(2) *Withholding of information* **— Where the provincial director has reasonable grounds to believe that providing the information referred to in paragraph (1)(*a*) would jeopardize the safety of any person or the security of a facility, he or she may authorize the withholding from the young person of as much information as is strictly necessary in order to protect such safety or security.**

COMMENTARY

Legal Implications

In order to make sure that there is due process for the determination of the level of custody and that the rights of young persons are protected, this new section sets out a number of procedures that must be followed if the provincial director determines the level of custody. These procedures include giving the young person access to information used for the decision, giving the young person the opportunity to be heard and advising the young person of the right to ask for a review of the decision if he or she does not agree with the result.

Operational Implications

This section puts a great deal of onus on the provincial director. Provinces and territories need good policy and procedures to be developed if they elect to have the provincial director determine the level of custody. Also a validated risk/need assessment instrument will be critical in assisting a provincial director in determining the level of custody that will meet a young person's needs and will not jeopardize public safety.

87. (1) *Review* **— A young person may apply for a review under this section of a determination**

(a) under subsection 85(3) that would place the young person in a facility at a level of custody that has more than a minimal degree of restraint; or
(b) under subsection 85(4) that would transfer a young person to a facility at a level of custody with a higher degree of restraint or increase the degree of restraint of the young person in the facility.

(2) *Procedural safeguards* — The lieutenant governor in council of a province shall ensure that procedures are in place for the review under subsection (1), including that

(a) the review board that conducts the review be independent;
(b) the young person be provided with any relevant information to which the review board has access, subject to subsection (3); and
(c) the young person be given the opportunity to be heard.

(3) *Withholding of information* — Where the review board has reasonable grounds to believe that providing the information referred to in paragraph (2)(b) would jeopardize the safety of any person or the security of a facility, it may authorize the withholding from the young person of as much information as is strictly necessary in order to protect such safety or security.

(4) *Factors* — The review board shall take into account the factors referred to in subsection 85(5) in reviewing a determination.

(5) *Decision is final* — A decision of the review board under this section in respect of a particular determination is final.

COMMENTARY

Legal Implications

A young person may apply to have a review of the level of custody decision made by the provincial director. The review by an independent review board is to ensure that the young person has appropriate procedural safeguards. These safeguards would include the right to access information and the right to be heard. The review board, however, may withhold information from the young person if there are safety or security issues. The decision of the review board is final and cannot be appealed further.

Operational Implications

Independent boards were established under the *Young Offenders Act* to review custody placements when required. This role could be expanded, or a review board could be established to specifically review the provincial director's decision. When a province or territory elects to have the youth justice court determine the level of custody, this section is not applicable.

88. *Functions to be exercised by youth justice court* — The lieutenant governor in council of a province may order that the power to make determinations of the level of custody for young persons and to review those determinations be exercised in accordance with the *Young Offenders Act*, chapter Y-1 of the Revised Statutes of Canada, 1985. The following provisions of that Act apply, with any modifications that the circumstances require, to the exercise of those powers:

(*a*) the definitions "review board" and "progress report" in subsection 2(1);
(*b*) section 11;
(*c*) sections 24.1 to 24.3; and
(*d*) sections 28 to 31.

COMMENTARY

Legal Implications

The lieutenant governor in council of a province may make an order to have the youth justice court judge determine the level of custody, as was the case in all jurisdictions under the *Young Offenders Act*. This section of the *Youth Criminal Justice Act* authorizes the lieutenant governor in council to make this order and to have the relevant sections of the *Young Offenders Act* apply.

Operational Implications

To date, all jurisdictions have elected to maintain judicial determination of the level of custody, as this option does not require a jurisdiction to develop additional appeal procedures. When this section is invoked by an Order in Council in a province or territory, the sections of the *Young Offenders Act* that deal with the youth court reviewing the level of custody and the provincial director being able to temporarily move a youth from open to secure custody apply as outlined in this section.

89. (1) *Exception if young person is twenty years old or older* — When a young person is twenty years old or older at the time the youth sentence is imposed on him or her under paragraph 42(2)(*n*), (*o*), (*q*) or (*r*), the young person shall, despite section 85, be committed to a provincial correctional facility for adults to serve the youth sentence.

(2) *If serving youth sentence in a provincial correctional facility* — If a young person is serving a youth sentence in a provincial correctional facility for adults pursuant to subsection (1), the youth justice court may, on application of the provincial director at any time after the young person begins to serve a portion of the youth sentence in a provincial correctional facility for adults, after giving the young person, the provincial director and representatives of the provincial and federal correctional systems an opportunity to be heard, authorize the provincial director to direct that the young person serve the remainder of the youth sentence in a penitentiary if the court considers it to be in the best interests of the young person or in the public interest and if, at the time of the application, that remainder is two years or more.

(3) *Provisions to apply* — If a young person is serving a youth sentence in a provincial correctional facility for adults or a penitentiary under subsection (1) or (2), the *Prisons and Reformatories Act* and the *Corrections and Conditional Release Act*, and any other statute, regulation or rule applicable in respect of prisoners or offenders within the meaning of those Acts, statutes, regulations and rules, apply in respect of the young person except to the extent that they conflict with Part 6 (publication, records and information) of this Act, which Part continues to apply to the young person.

COMMENTARY

Legal Implications

This new provision deals with a young person who at the time of sentence is 20 years of age or older. If the person is 20 years old at the time of sentence, he or she must serve the youth sentence in a provincial facility for adults. In addition, there is a new provision for a young person sentenced being transferred from a provincial facility for adults to a penitentiary if there are more than two years remaining on the youth sentence.

When either of these situations occurs, the rules for release applicable to the relevant adult facility apply except to the extent that they conflict with Part 6 (Publication, Records and Information) of this Act.

Operational Implications

Experience under the *Young Offenders Act* has shown that a number of young people do not get charged for offences that they committed as young persons until they are adults. This is particularly true for sexual offences, as they can be discovered years after they occur. This section gives direction for where an adult serving a youth sentence can be detained. Under the *Young Offenders Act*, defence counsel would argue that adults serving youth sentences should be detained in youth facilities. This section of the *Youth Criminal Justice Act* clarifies that issue.

90. (1) *Youth worker* — When a youth sentence is imposed committing a young person to custody, the provincial director of the province in which the young person received the youth sentence and was placed in custody shall, without delay, designate a youth worker to work with the young person to plan for his or her reintegration into the community, including the preparation and implementation of a reintegration plan that sets out the most effective programs for the young person in order to maximize his or her chances for reintegration into the community.

(2) *Role of youth worker when young person in the community* — When a portion of a young person's youth sentence is served in the community in accordance with section 97 or 105, the youth worker shall supervise the young person, continue to provide support to the young person and assist the young person to respect the conditions to which he or she is subject, and help the young person in the implementation of the reintegration plan.

COMMENTARY

Legal Implications

In order to support the young person, the Act provides for the provincial director to designate a youth worker/probation officer to begin the plan of reintegrating the young person into the community. The youth worker has the responsibility of developing a plan for the young person that will provide the best chance for his or her successful reintegration and, thus, help avoid his or her return to custody. When the young person is released into the community, the youth worker will continue to work with, and support, the young person to help make the reintegration plan successful.

Operational Implications

Reintegrating a young person into the community following a period of custody is one of the key concepts of the *Youth Criminal Justice Act*. The Act recognizes that support for the young person is required to enable a smooth transition from custody to life in the community. This section legislates good case management based on current best practices. Once the young person has been committed to custody the plan should be developed as soon as possible and reviewed regularly. It is important that the plan ensures the young person has continuity in programs, services and people to support his or her community portion of custody. The youth worker/probation officer ensures that the plan is developed with input from all of the significant people in the young person's life and ensures the plan is carried out.

91. (1) *Reintegration leave* — **The provincial director of a province may, subject to any terms or conditions that he or she considers desirable, authorize, for a young person committed to a youth custody facility in the province further to an order under paragraph 76(1)(*a*) (placement when subject to adult sentence) or a youth sentence imposed under paragraph 42(2)(*n*), (*o*), (*q*) or (*r*),**

> (*a*) a reintegration leave from the youth custody facility for a period not exceeding thirty days if, in the opinion of the provincial director, it is necessary or desirable that the young person be absent, with or without escort, for medical, compassionate or humanitarian reasons or for the purpose of rehabilitating the young person or reintegrating the young person into the community; or

(b) that the young person be released from the youth custody facility on the days and during the hours that the provincial director specifies in order that the young person may
  (i) attend school or any other educational or training institution,
  (ii) obtain or continue employment or perform domestic or other duties required by the young person's family,
  (iii) participate in a program specified by the provincial director that, in the provincial director's opinion, will enable the young person to better carry out employment or improve his or her education or training, or
  (iv) attend an out-patient treatment program or other program that provides services that are suitable to addressing the young person's needs.

(2) *Renewal of reintegration leave* — A reintegration leave authorized under paragraph (1)(a) may be renewed by the provincial director for one or more thirty-day periods on reassessment of the case.

(3) *Revocation of authorization* — The provincial director of a province may, at any time, revoke an authorization made under subsection (1).

(4) *Arrest and return to custody* — If the provincial director revokes an authorization under subsection (3) or if a young person fails to comply with any term or condition of a reintegration leave or a release from custody under this section, the young person may be arrested without warrant and returned to custody.

COMMENTARY

Legal Implications

This new section replaces and expands on the temporary release section of the *Young Offenders Act*. The maximum number of days a leave can be granted has increased from 15 days under the *Young Offenders Act* to a maximum of 30 days in this new legislation. Another significant change is the ability for the provincial director to renew the reintegration leave for one or more periods of up to 30 days. This was not an option in the *Young Offenders Act*.

The rules for reintegration leave include the purpose, time limits, revocation and arrest if necessary in the case of a breach of the conditions of the release. There is now a statutory focus on helping the young person return to the community to better his or her chances of getting on with his or her life without turning to criminal behaviour. The enforcement provisions are necessary in the case of a breach, but the focus is on the positive impact of a young person building relationships outside the custodial facility.

Operational Implications

The reintegration plan should also address the frequency, duration and schedule of the reintegration leaves. Generally, the leaves should be more frequent and of longer duration as the youth gets closer to the release date. The provision allowing reintegration leaves to be extended for one or more 30-day periods will allow greater flexibility for the youth to participate in community-based programs that will foster reintegration. The reference in this section to 30 days was not intended to be a minimum and fixed period. Reintegration leaves are also utilized to assist young persons in accessing community programs or bridging from custody to a community program. These leaves can be with or without an escort.

92. (1) *Transfer to adult facility* — **When a young person is committed to custody under paragraph 42(2)(n), (o), (q) or (r), the youth justice court may, on application of the provincial director made at any time after the young person attains the age of eighteen years, after giving the young person, the provincial director and representatives of the provincial correctional system an opportunity to be heard, authorize the provincial director to direct that the young person, subject to subsection (3), serve the remainder of the youth sentence in a provincial correctional facility for adults, if the court considers it to be in the best interests of the young person or in the public interest.**

(2) *If serving youth sentence in a provincial correctional facility* — **The youth justice court may authorize the provincial director to direct that a young person, subject to subsection (3), serve the remainder of a youth sentence in a penitentiary**

  (*a*) **if the youth justice court considers it to be in the best interests of the young person or in the public interest;**
  (*b*) **if the provincial director applies for the authorization at any time after the young person begins to serve a portion of a youth sentence in a provincial correctional facility for adults further to a direction made under subsection (1);**
  (*c*) **if, at the time of the application, that remainder is two years or more; and**
  (*d*) **so long as the youth justice court gives the young person, the provincial director and representatives of the provincial and federal correctional systems an opportunity to be heard.**

(3) *Provisions to apply* — **If the provincial director makes a direction under subsection (1) or (2), the** *Prisons and Reformatories Act* **and the** *Corrections and Conditional Release Act***, and any other statute, regulation or rule applicable in respect of prisoners and offenders within the meaning of those Acts, statutes, regulations and rules, apply in respect of the young person except to the extent that they conflict with Part 6 (publication, records and information) of this Act, which Part continues to apply to the young person.**

(4) *Placement when adult and youth sentences* — If a person is subject to more than one sentence, at least one of which is a youth sentence imposed under paragraph 42(2)(*n*), (*o*), (*q*) or (*r*) and at least one of which is a sentence referred to in either paragraph (*b*) or (*c*), he or she shall serve, in a provincial correctional facility for adults or a penitentiary in accordance with section 743.1 (rules respecting sentences of two or more years) of the *Criminal Code*, the following:

(*a*) the remainder of any youth sentence imposed under paragraph 42(2)(*n*), (*o*), (*q*) or (*r*);
(*b*) an adult sentence to which an order under paragraph 76(1)(*b*) or (*c*) (placement in adult facility) applies; and
(*c*) any sentence of imprisonment imposed otherwise than under this Act.

(5) *Youth sentence and adult sentence* — If a young person is committed to custody under a youth sentence under paragraph 42(2)(*n*), (*o*), (*q*) or (*r*) and is also already subject to an adult sentence to which an order under paragraph 76(1)(*a*) (placement when subject to adult sentence) applies, the young person may, in the discretion of the provincial director, serve the sentences, or any portion of the sentences, in a youth custody facility, in a provincial correctional facility for adults or, if the unexpired portion of the sentence is two years or more, in a penitentiary.

COMMENTARY

Legal Implications

The general rule is that young persons are to serve their sentences in a youth facility; however, upon reaching the age of 18, the provincial director may apply for a transfer to an adult facility.

The place where young persons serve their sentences requires detailed rules to provide for the numerous possibilities due to age, seriousness of offence and length of the sentence.

When a young person turns 18 and is transferred to an adult facility after an application by the provincial director, it will be to a correctional facility operated by the province or territory. Once transferred to the provincial facility, it is then possible for a further transfer to a federal adult facility (a penitentiary). There are certain conditions that need to be met before a young person can be placed in a penitentiary, including the requirement that there be at least two years left in the sentence.

This section also makes it clear that the rules for release are governed by the facility in which the young person is placed. There is even provision for the situation where a young person is subject to both youth and adult sentences.

S. 93

Operational Implications

This section gives authority for transferring a youth based on age while at the same time taking into account the best interests of the young person and public safety. Program and individual needs should also be considered when deciding to transfer a youth. It is important that young persons be held with other youths as long as possible where appropriate. Provincial directors will also consider a young person's level of physical and emotional maturity and may exercise the option of having the youth remain in the youth facility.

93. (1) *When young person reaches twenty years of age* — **When a young person who is committed to custody under paragraph 42(2)(*n*), (*o*), (*q*) or (*r*) is in a youth custody facility when the young person attains the age of twenty years, the young person shall be transferred to a provincial correctional facility for adults to serve the remainder of the youth sentence, unless the provincial director orders that the young person continue to serve the youth sentence in a youth custody facility.**

(2) *If serving youth sentence in a provincial correctional facility* — **If a young person is serving a portion of a youth sentence in a provincial correctional facility for adults pursuant to a transfer under subsection (1), the youth justice court may, on application of the provincial director after the transfer, after giving the young person, the provincial director and representatives of the provincial and federal correctional systems an opportunity to be heard, authorize the provincial director to direct that the young person serve the remainder of the youth sentence in a penitentiary if the court considers it to be in the best interests of the young person or in the public interest and if, at the time of the application, that remainder is two years or more.**

(3) *Provisions to apply* — **If the provincial director makes the direction, the** *Prisons and Reformatories Act* **and the** *Corrections and Conditional Release Act,* **and any other statute, regulation or rule applicable in respect of prisoners and offenders within the meaning of those Acts, statutes, regulations and rules, apply in respect of the young person except to the extent that they conflict with Part 6 (publication, records and information) of this Act, which Part continues to apply to the young person.**

COMMENTARY

Legal Implications

The previous section dealt with young persons who are 18, and this new section deals with young persons who have reached the age of 20. When a young person reaches the age of 20, the provincial director shall transfer the person to an adult correctional facility, unless the provincial director makes an order that the young person will continue to serve the sentence in the youth facility. Again, there is provision for transferring the young person to a provincial and federal facility as well as rules setting out the applicable circumstances. In addition, there is a provision to state the rules for release.

This section tries to strike a balance between protecting young persons from adults and disallowing youths who turn 18, 19, 20 or older to be in a youth facility because of the possibility of their negatively influencing other youths.

Operational Implications

A provincial director is more likely to transfer a youth who is 20 years of age than a youth who is 18. Provincial directors will need to consider the youth's program needs and level of maturity.

94. (1) *Annual review* — **When a young person is committed to custody pursuant to a youth sentence under paragraph 42(2)(*n*), (*o*), (*q*) or (*r*) for a period exceeding one year, the provincial director of the province in which the young person is held in custody shall cause the young person to be brought before the youth justice court without delay at the end of one year from the date of the most recent youth sentence imposed in respect of the offence — and at the end of every subsequent year from that date — and the youth justice court shall review the youth sentence.**

(2) *Annual review* — **When a young person is committed to custody pursuant to youth sentences imposed under paragraph 42(2)(*n*), (*o*), (*q*) or (*r*) in respect of more than one offence for a total period exceeding one year, the provincial director of the province in which the young person is held in custody shall cause the young person to be brought before the youth justice court without delay at the end of one year from the date of the earliest youth sentence imposed — and at the end of every subsequent year from that date — and the youth justice court shall review the youth sentences.**

(3) *Optional review* — **When a young person is committed to custody pursuant to a youth sentence imposed under paragraph 42(2)(*n*), (*o*), (*q*) or (*r*) in respect of an offence, the provincial director may, on the provincial director's own initiative, and shall, on the request of the young person, the young person's parent or the Attorney General, on any of the grounds set out in subsection (6), cause the young person to be brought before a youth justice court to review the youth sentence,**

  (*a*) **when the youth sentence is for a period not exceeding one year, once at any time after the expiry of the greater of**
   (i) **thirty days after the date of the youth sentence imposed under subsection 42(2) in respect of the offence, and**
   (ii) **one third of the period of the youth sentence imposed under subsection 42(2) in respect of the offence; and**
  (*b*) **when the youth sentence is for a period exceeding one year, at any time after six months after the date of the most recent youth sentence imposed in respect of the offence.**

(4) *Time for optional review* — The young person may be brought before the youth justice court at any other time, with leave of the youth justice court judge.

(5) *Review* — If a youth justice court is satisfied that there are grounds for review under subsection (6), the court shall review the youth sentence.

(6) *Grounds for review* — A youth sentence imposed in respect of a young person may be reviewed under subsection (5)

    (*a*) on the ground that the young person has made sufficient progress to justify a change in the youth sentence;
    (*b*) on the ground that the circumstances that led to the youth sentence have changed materially;
    (*c*) on the ground that new services or programs are available that were not available at the time of the youth sentence;
    (*d*) on the ground that the opportunities for rehabilitation are now greater in the community; or
    (*e*) on any other ground that the youth justice court considers appropriate.

(7) *No review if appeal pending* — Despite any other provision of this section, no review of a youth sentence in respect of which an appeal has been taken shall be made under this section until all proceedings in respect of any such appeal have been completed.

(8) *Youth justice court may order appearance of young person for review* — When a provincial director is required under subsections (1) to (3) to cause a young person to be brought before the youth justice court and fails to do so, the youth justice court may, on application made by the young person, his or her parent or the Attorney General, or on its own motion, order the provincial director to cause the young person to be brought before the youth justice court.

(9) *Progress report* — The youth justice court shall, before reviewing under this section a youth sentence imposed in respect of a young person, require the provincial director to cause to be prepared, and to submit to the youth justice court, a progress report on the performance of the young person since the youth sentence took effect.

(10) *Additional information in progress report* — A person preparing a progress report in respect of a young person may include in the report any information relating to the personal and family history and present environment of the young person that he or she considers advisable.

(11) *Written or oral report* — A progress report shall be in writing unless it cannot reasonably be committed to writing, in which case it may, with leave of the youth justice court, be submitted orally in court.

(12) *Subsections 40(4) to (10) to apply* — Subsections 40(4) to (10) (procedures respecting pre-sentence reports) apply, with any modifications that the circumstances require, in respect of progress reports.

(13) *Notice of review from provincial director* — When a youth sentence imposed in respect of a young person is to be reviewed under subsection (1) or (2), the provincial director shall cause any notice that may be directed by rules of court applicable to the youth justice court or, in the absence of such a direction, at least five clear days notice of the review to be given in writing to the young person, a parent of the young person and the Attorney General.

(14) *Notice of review from person requesting it* — When a review of a youth sentence imposed in respect of a young person is requested under subsection (3), the person requesting the review shall cause any notice that may be directed by rules of court applicable to the youth justice court or, in the absence of such a direction, at least five clear days notice of the review to be given in writing to the young person, a parent of the young person and the Attorney General.

(15) *Statement of right to counsel* — A notice given to a parent under subsection (13) or (14) shall include a statement that the young person whose youth sentence is to be reviewed has the right to be represented by counsel.

(16) *Service of notice* — A notice under subsection (13) or (14) may be served personally or may be sent by confirmed delivery service.

(17) *Notice may be waived* — Any of the persons entitled to notice under subsection (13) or (14) may waive the right to that notice.

(18) *If notice not given* — If notice under subsection (13) or (14) is not given in accordance with this section, the youth justice court may

(a) adjourn the proceedings and order that the notice be given in the manner and to the persons that it directs; or
(b) dispense with the notice if, in the opinion of the court, having regard to the circumstances, notice may be dispensed with.

(19) *Decision of the youth justice court after review* — When a youth justice court reviews under this section a youth sentence imposed in respect of a young person, it may, after giving the young person, a parent of the young person, the Attorney General and the provincial director an opportunity to be heard, having regard to the needs of the young person and the interests of society,

(a) confirm the youth sentence;
(b) release the young person from custody and place the young person under conditional supervision in accordance with the procedure set out in section 105, with any modifications that the circumstances

require, for a period not exceeding the remainder of the youth sentence that the young person is then serving; or
(c) if the provincial director so recommends, convert a youth sentence under paragraph 42(2)(r) to a youth sentence under paragraph 42(2)(q) if the offence was murder or to a youth sentence under paragraph 42(2)(n) or (o), as the case may be, if the offence was an offence other than murder.

COMMENTARY

Legal Implications

This section maintains the mandatory and optional reviews from the *Young Offenders Act*.

The new custody and supervision order should reduce the need for reviews due to the automatic period of community supervision. The time periods and rules for conducting and preparing for a review are set out in this section in some detail to ensure consistency and protection of the rights of the young person. There is particular attention given to the procedure for giving notice of the hearing and to the exchange of information to be used in the hearing. The court can dismiss an application for review as it did in *R. v. R.B.*, [2003] O.J. No. 1856 (C.J.), when Justice Weinper ruled that the young person had not made sufficient progress to justify a change in sentence and that there were greater opportunities for rehabilitation in custody than in the community.

95. *Orders are youth sentences* **— Orders under subsections 97(2) (conditions) and 98(3) (continuation of custody), paragraph 103(2)(b) (continuation of custody), subsections 104(1) (continuation of custody) and 105(1) (conditional supervision) and paragraph 109(2)(b) (continuation of suspension of conditional supervision) are deemed to be youth sentences for the purposes of section 94 (reviews).**

COMMENTARY

Legal Implications

This section clarifies that for the purpose of a review under section 94, a number of orders (set out in the section) made under the *Youth Criminal Justice Act* are youth sentences for the purpose of the review provision. This is to ensure that these orders, which affect the sentence of a young person, will be subject to review.

96. (1) *Recommendation of provincial director for conditional supervision of young person* **— When a young person is held in custody pursuant to a youth sentence under paragraph 42(2)(n), (o), (q) or (r), the provincial director may, if satisfied that the needs of the young person and the interests of society would be better served by doing so, make a recommendation to the youth**

justice court that the young person be released from custody and placed under conditional supervision.

(2) *Notice* — If the provincial director makes a recommendation, the provincial director shall cause a notice to be given in writing that includes the reasons for the recommendation and the conditions that the provincial director would recommend be set under section 105 to the young person, a parent of the young person and the Attorney General and give a copy of the notice to the youth justice court.

(3) *Application to court for review of recommendation* — If notice of a recommendation is made under subsection (2) with respect to a youth sentence imposed on a young person, the youth justice court shall, if an application for review is made by the young person, the young person's parent or the Attorney General within ten days after service of the notice, review the youth sentence without delay.

(4) *Subsections 94(7), (9) to (12) and (14) to (19) apply* — Subject to subsection (5), subsections 94(7) (no review of appeal pending), (9) to (12) (progress reports) and (14) to (19) (provisions respecting notice and decision of the youth justice court) apply, with any modifications that the circumstances require, in respect of reviews made under this section and any notice required under subsection 94(14) shall also be given to the provincial director.

(5) *If no application for review made under subsection (3)* — A youth justice court that receives a notice under subsection (2) shall, if no application for a review is made under subsection (3),

    (*a*) order the release of the young person and place the young person under conditional supervision in accordance with section 105, having regard to the recommendations of the provincial director; or

    (*b*) if the court considers it advisable, order that the young person not be released.

For greater certainty, an order under this subsection may be made without a hearing.

(6) *Notice when no release ordered* — When a youth justice court orders that the young person not be released under paragraph (5)(*b*), it shall cause a notice of its order to be given to the provincial director without delay.

(7) *Provincial director may request review* — When the provincial director is given a notice under subsection (6), he or she may request a review under this section.

(8) *When provincial director requests a review* — When the provincial director requests a review under subsection (7),

(a) the provincial director shall cause any notice that may be directed by rules of court applicable to the youth justice court or, in the absence of such a direction, at least five clear days notice of the review to be given in writing to the young person, a parent of the young person and the Attorney General; and
(b) the youth justice court shall review the youth sentence without delay after the notice required under paragraph (a) is given.

COMMENTARY

Legal Implications

The provincial director may make a recommendation under this section that a young person serving the custody portion of a sentence be released on conditional supervision. The notice is given to the youth justice court. Upon this recommendation, a notice must be given to the interested parties, who may then make an application for the review of the sentence. If no application for review is made, then the youth justice court shall make an order to release, or not release, the young person. This order may be made without a hearing. When the order is made not to release the young person, the provincial director may give notice and request a review of the sentence.

Operational Implications

This section adds increased responsibility to the role of the provincial director. The provincial director may recommend the release of a youth from custody before the community supervision is scheduled to begin. The legislation recognizes that those working with the young person are best able to advise or inform the court when the young person has made sufficient progress to be released from custody.

97. (1) *Conditions to be included in custody and supervision order* — **Every youth sentence imposed under paragraph 42(2)(n) shall contain the following conditions, namely, that the young person, while serving the portion of the youth sentence under supervision in the community,**

(a) keep the peace and be of good behaviour;
(b) report to the provincial director and then be under the supervision of the provincial director;
(c) inform the provincial director immediately on being arrested or questioned by the police;
(d) report to the police, or any named individual, as instructed by the provincial director;
(e) advise the provincial director of the young person's address of residence and report immediately to the provincial director any change
   (i) in that address,

(ii) in the young person's normal occupation, including employment, vocational or educational training and volunteer work,
(iii) in the young person's family or financial situation, and
(iv) that may reasonably be expected to affect the young person's ability to comply with the conditions of the sentence; and

(f) not own, possess or have the control of any weapon, ammunition, prohibited ammunition, prohibited device or explosive substance, except as authorized in writing by the provincial director for the purposes of the young person participating in a program specified in the authorization.

(2) *Other conditions* — The provincial director may set additional conditions that support and address the needs of the young person, promote the reintegration of the young person into the community and offer adequate protection to the public from the risk that the young person might otherwise present. The provincial director shall, in setting the conditions, take into account the needs of the young person, the most effective programs for the young person in order to maximize his or her chances for reintegration into the community, the nature of the offence and the ability of the young person to comply with the conditions.

(3) *Communication of conditions* — The provincial director shall

(a) cause the conditions to be read by or to the young person bound by them;
(b) explain or cause to be explained to the young person the purpose and effect of the conditions, and confirm that the young person understands them; and
(c) cause a copy of the conditions to be given to the young person, and to a parent of the young person.

(4) *Provisions to apply* — Subsections 56(3) (endorsement of order by young person) and (4) (validity of order) apply, with any modifications that the circumstances require, in respect of conditions under this section.

COMMENTARY

Legal Implications

This new section sets out the list of mandatory supervision conditions that are imposed as part of the community supervision portion of every custody and supervision order. Additional community supervision conditions may be set at the discretion of the provincial director. The section also sets out the procedure for communicating these conditions to the young person. In addition, there is provision for the young person signing the document setting out the conditions, and provision for the validity of this portion of the sentence.

Operational Implications

The role of the provincial director is significantly expanded in this legislation to include a number of increased responsibilities. While the court sets mandatory conditions for community supervision, the provincial director may set additional conditions related to the needs of the young person, such as those that require the young person to participate in a community program or restrict a youth from communicating with another individual, in order to facilitate reintegration and ensure that the public is adequately protected. These conditions for supervision are treated very much like a probation order, with the provincial director ensuring that the order be communicated and signed by the young person. The legislation makes no provisions for any variations or amendments of the conditions that are set by the provincial director; therefore, if a young person is doing well and the provincial director feels the conditions should be varied, the young person must make application under section 94 for an optional review.

98. (1) *Application for continuation of custody* — **Within a reasonable time before the expiry of the custodial portion of a young person's youth sentence, the Attorney General or the provincial director may apply to the youth justice court for an order that the young person remain in custody for a period not exceeding the remainder of the youth sentence.**

(2) *Continuation of custody* — **If the hearing for an application under subsection (1) cannot be completed before the expiry of the custodial portion of the youth sentence, the court may order that the young person remain in custody pending the determination of the application if the court is satisfied that the application was made in a reasonable time, having regard to all the circumstances, and that there are compelling reasons for keeping the young person in custody.**

(3) *Decision* — **The youth justice court may, after giving both parties and a parent of the young person an opportunity to be heard, order that a young person remain in custody for a period not exceeding the remainder of the youth sentence, if it is satisfied that there are reasonable grounds to believe that**

> (*a*) **the young person is likely to commit a serious violent offence before the expiry of the youth sentence he or she is then serving; and**
>
> (*b*) **the conditions that would be imposed on the young person if he or she were to serve a portion of the youth sentence in the community would not be adequate to prevent the commission of the offence.**

(4) *Factors* — **For the purpose of determining an application under subsection (1), the youth justice court shall take into consideration any factor that is relevant to the case of the young person, including**

> (*a*) **evidence of a pattern of persistent violent behaviour and, in particular,**

(i) the number of offences committed by the young person that caused physical or psychological harm to any other person,
(ii) the young person's difficulties in controlling violent impulses to the point of endangering the safety of any other person,
(iii) the use of weapons in the commission of any offence,
(iv) explicit threats of violence,
(v) behaviour of a brutal nature associated with the commission of any offence, and
(vi) a substantial degree of indifference on the part of the young person as to the reasonably foreseeable consequences, to other persons, of the young person's behaviour;
(b) psychiatric or psychological evidence that a physical or mental illness or disorder of the young person is of such a nature that the young person is likely to commit, before the expiry of the youth sentence the young person is then serving, a serious violent offence;
(c) reliable information that satisfies the youth justice court that the young person is planning to commit, before the expiry of the youth sentence the young person is then serving, a serious violent offence;
(d) the availability of supervision programs in the community that would offer adequate protection to the public from the risk that the young person might otherwise present until the expiry of the youth sentence the young person is then serving;
(e) whether the young person is more likely to reoffend if he or she serves his or her youth sentence entirely in custody without the benefits of serving a portion of the youth sentence in the community under supervision; and
(f) evidence of a pattern of committing violent offences while he or she was serving a portion of a youth sentence in the community under supervision.

COMMENTARY

Legal Implications

This section allows for the community portion of the custody and community supervision sentence to be served in custody, under certain circumstances, on application by the provincial director or the Attorney General for a continuation of custody. This section provides for notice to the parties and the parents of the young person as well as a list of the factors to be considered by the youth justice court when making the decision to continue custody.

Operational Implications

The list of factors the court must take into consideration when granting a continuation of custody focuses on a young person's repeated violent behaviour and risk to reoffend. One of the factors is psychiatric or psychological evidence that the young person has a physical or mental disorder, yet there is no requirement that a section 34 assessment be ordered. Technically, provincial directors could make a case for the continuation of custody for any young person, provided community supervision programs are not available to provide the public with adequate protection. The practice of applying for continuation of custody is new in this Act and needs to continue to be monitored carefully to ensure that custody is not routinely continued, particularly if custody is being used in the absence of community programs or services.

An application for the continuation of custody under this section was denied by the Saskatchewan Provincial Youth Court in *R. v. S.T.T.* (2003), 239 Sask. R. 71, [2003] S.J. No. 636 (Prov. Ct.), as the youth court judge noted that an application for the continuation of custody must not be used to revisit the wisdom of the original sentence, or to influence co-operation in the rehabilitation and reintegration plan.

99. (1) *Report* **— For the purpose of determining an application under section 98 (application for continuation of custody), the youth justice court shall require the provincial director to cause to be prepared, and to submit to the youth justice court, a report setting out any information of which the provincial director is aware with respect to the factors set out in subsection 98(4) that may be of assistance to the court.**

(2) *Written or oral report* **— A report referred to in subsection (1) shall be in writing unless it cannot reasonably be committed to writing, in which case it may, with leave of the youth justice court, be submitted orally in court.**

(3) *Provisions apply* **— Subsections 40(4) to (10) (procedures respecting pre-sentence reports) apply, with any modifications that the circumstances require, in respect of a report referred to in subsection (1).**

(4) *Notice of hearing* **— When an application is made under section 98 (application for continuation of custody) in respect of a young person, the provincial director shall cause to be given, to the young person and to a parent of the young person, at least five clear days notice of the hearing in writing.**

(5) *Statement of right to counsel* **— Any notice given to a parent under subsection (4) shall include a statement that the young person has the right to be represented by counsel.**

(6) *Service of notice* **— A notice under subsection (4) may be served personally or may be sent by confirmed delivery service.**

(7) *When notice not given* **— When notice under subsection (4) is not given in accordance with this section, the youth justice court may**

    (*a*) adjourn the hearing and order that the notice be given in any manner and to any person that it directs; or

(*b*) **dispense with the giving of the notice if, in the opinion of the youth justice court, having regard to the circumstances, the giving of the notice may be dispensed with.**

COMMENTARY

Legal Implications

The provincial director is required to cause to be prepared a report for the youth justice court to consider when making a decision on whether to continue the custody portion of the youth sentence. The rules set for the preparation of pre-sentence reports (section 40(4)-(10)) apply to the preparation of this report. There is also provision for giving five days' notice of the hearing and a notice of the right for the young person to be represented at the hearing by counsel.

Operational Implications

This is another area in which the provincial director and correctional staff have increased responsibility. The provincial director must provide the court with a report to advise the court of the factors listed in section 98(4) that apply to the young person. It is also the provincial director's responsibility, not the responsibility of the court, to notify the young person and parent of the hearing in writing. Under the *Young Offenders Act*, many of the court administrative functions that were legislated functions of the court, such as the distribution of pre-disposition reports or probation orders, fell to the provincial director just to ensure they were done. The *Youth Criminal Justice Act* assigns many administrative functions, like this notice and communication of conditions of community supervision, to the provincial director, rather than to the court.

100. *Reasons* — **When a youth justice court makes an order under subsection 98(3) (decision for continued custody), it shall state its reasons for the order in the record of the case and shall provide, or cause to be provided, to the young person in respect of whom the order was made, the counsel and a parent of the young person, the Attorney General and the provincial director**

  (*a*) **a copy of the order; and**
  (*b*) **on request, a transcript or copy of the reasons for the order.**

COMMENTARY

Legal Implications

This section requires the youth justice court to provide a copy of the decision for continued custody and, if requested, a copy of the reasons to the young person, counsel for the young person, the parent, the Attorney General and the provincial director.

101. (1) *Review of youth justice court decision* — An order made under subsection 98(3) (decision for continued custody) in respect of a young person, or the refusal to make such an order, shall, on application of the young person, the young person's counsel, the Attorney General or the provincial director made within thirty days after the decision of the youth justice court, be reviewed by the court of appeal, and that court may, in its discretion, confirm or reverse the decision of the youth justice court.

(2) *Extension of time to make application* — The court of appeal may, at any time, extend the time within which an application under subsection (1) may be made.

(3) *Notice of application* — A person who proposes to apply for a review under subsection (1) shall give notice of the application in the manner and within the period of time that may be directed by rules of court.

COMMENTARY

Legal Implications

The court of appeal may review the decision of the youth justice court to continue or refuse to continue the custody of the young person on application within 30 days of the decision. Proper notices must be given to the interested parties. If necessary, the court of appeal may extend the time for the giving of the notices.

Operational Implications

The introduction of custody and community supervision in this legislation is unfamiliar to courts and provincial directors. There was some very limited previous experience in the application for continuance of custody under the *Young Offenders Act* in supervision of a conditional supervision disposition.

102. (1) *Breach of conditions* — If the provincial director has reasonable grounds to believe that a young person has breached or is about to breach a condition to which he or she is subject under section 97 (conditions to be included in custody and supervision orders), the provincial director may, in writing,

(*a*) permit the young person to continue to serve a portion of his or her youth sentence in the community, on the same or different conditions; or

(*b*) if satisfied that the breach is a serious one that increases the risk to public safety, order that the young person be remanded to any youth custody facility that the provincial director considers appropriate until a review is conducted.

(2) *Provisions apply* — Sections 107 (apprehension) and 108 (review by provincial director) apply, with any modifications that the circumstances require, to an order under paragraph (1)(*b*).

COMMENTARY

Legal Implications

This section authorizes the provincial director, if there are reasonable grounds to believe there has been a breach of a community supervision condition, to take action to deal with the breach. The provincial director can either do nothing, set different conditions or, if the breach is a serious one that increases the risk to public safety, order the young person to be remanded into custody in a youth custody facility in order for a review to take place.

Operational Implications

This section provides another area of increased responsibility for the provincial director and, subsequently, the youth worker. Once the provincial director is satisfied that a breach of the community supervision conditions has occurred, the provincial director begins the process. This section relies on section 107 to apprehend the young person if the breach is serious and increases the risk to public safety, and on section 108 to review the breach. This section empowers the provincial director as the decision maker. When a young person does not comply with a condition of community supervision, it is not an offence as is the case when a young person fails to comply with a condition of a probation order. Failure to comply with a condition of community supervision requires the provincial director to review and make certain decisions. Police officers are having some difficulty with the fact that they are not in a position of authority when a young person breaches a condition of community supervision. Unlike a breach of a probation condition, a police officer who believes a young person has breached a condition of community supervision cannot detain or charge the young person. The police officer only has the authority to advise the provincial director of what was believed to be a breach and it is the provincial director's decision to act upon it.

103. (1) *Review by youth justice court* — **When the case of a young person is referred to the youth justice court under section 108 (review by provincial director), the provincial director shall, without delay, cause the young person to be brought before the youth justice court, and the youth justice court shall, after giving the young person an opportunity to be heard,**

  (*a*) **if the court is not satisfied on reasonable grounds that the young person has breached or was about to breach one of the conditions under which he or she was being supervised in the community, order that the young person continue to serve a portion of his or** her youth sentence in the community, on the same or different conditions; or

(b) if the court is satisfied on reasonable grounds that the young person has breached or was about to breach one of the conditions under which he or she was being supervised in the community, make an order under subsection (2).

(2) *Order* — On completion of a review under subsection (1), the youth justice court

(a) shall order that the young person continue to serve the remainder of the youth sentence the young person is then serving in the community, and when the court does so, the court may vary the existing conditions or impose new conditions; or

(b) shall, despite paragraph 42(2)(n) (custody and supervision order), order that the young person remain in custody for a period that does not exceed the remainder of the youth sentence the young person is then serving, if the youth justice court is satisfied that the breach of the conditions was serious.

(3) *Provisions apply* — Subsections 109(4) to (8) apply, with any modifications that the circumstances require, in respect of a review under this section.

COMMENTARY

Legal Implications

The provincial director may refer a young person to the youth justice court for a review under section 108 to determine whether the young person should be released or detained in custody as the result of a breach of a condition (section 102) under which the young person was being supervised in the community.

This section sets out the rules and procedures for the court to follow in a case where the provincial director has referred the case to the court. At the end of the review, the court will order the young person to continue to serve the remainder of the sentence in the community, or order the young person to remain in custody for a period not to exceed the remainder of the sentence, if the breach of the conditions was serious.

In *R. v. K.P.A.* (2004), 243 Sask. R. 180, [2004] S.J. No. 47 (Prov. Ct.), the Saskatchewan Youth Justice Court questioned the obligation of the provincial director to inform the young person of his right to counsel under section 25(1) at any stage of the proceedings, including the point where the provincial director reviews the breach of conditions under sections 102 and 108 of the Act. The youth justice court also noted that the timeliness of the youth justice court review is paramount, as the intent of the legislation is for the sentence to continue to run pending a review.

104. (1) *Continuation of custody* — When a young person on whom a youth sentence under paragraph 42(2)(*o*), (*q*) or (*r*) has been imposed is held in custody and an application is made to the youth justice court by the Attorney General, within a reasonable time before the expiry of the custodial portion of the youth sentence, the provincial director of the province in which the young person is held in custody shall cause the young person to be brought before the youth justice court and the youth justice court may, after giving both parties and a parent of the young person an opportunity to be heard and if it is satisfied that there are reasonable grounds to believe that the young person is likely to commit an offence causing the death of or serious harm to another person before the expiry of the youth sentence the young person is then serving, order that the young person remain in custody for a period not exceeding the remainder of the youth sentence.

(2) *Continuation of custody* — If the hearing of an application under subsection (1) cannot be completed before the expiry of the custodial portion of the youth sentence, the court may order that the young person remain in custody until the determination of the application if the court is satisfied that the application was made in a reasonable time, having regard to all the circumstances, and that there are compelling reasons for keeping the young person in custody.

(3) *Factors* — For the purpose of determining an application under subsection (1), the youth justice court shall take into consideration any factor that is relevant to the case of the young person, including

- (*a*) evidence of a pattern of persistent violent behaviour and, in particular,
    - (i) the number of offences committed by the young person that caused physical or psychological harm to any other person,
    - (ii) the young person's difficulties in controlling violent impulses to the point of endangering the safety of any other person,
    - (iii) the use of weapons in the commission of any offence,
    - (iv) explicit threats of violence,
    - (v) behaviour of a brutal nature associated with the commission of any offence, and
    - (vi) a substantial degree of indifference on the part of the young person as to the reasonably foreseeable consequences, to other persons, of the young person's behaviour;
- (*b*) psychiatric or psychological evidence that a physical or mental illness or disorder of the young person is of such a nature that the young person is likely to commit, before the expiry of the youth sentence the young person is then serving, an offence causing the death of or serious harm to another person;
- (*c*) reliable information that satisfies the youth justice court that the young person is planning to commit, before the expiry of the youth sentence the young person is then serving, an offence causing the death of or serious harm to another person; and

(*d*) the availability of supervision programs in the community that would offer adequate protection to the public from the risk that the young person might otherwise present until the expiry of the youth sentence the young person is then serving.

(4) *Youth justice court to order appearance of young person* — If a provincial director fails to cause a young person to be brought before the youth justice court under subsection (1), the youth justice court shall order the provincial director to cause the young person to be brought before the youth justice court without delay.

(5) *Provisions to apply* — Sections 99 to 101 apply, with any modifications that the circumstances require, in respect of an order made, or the refusal to make an order, under this section.

(6) *If application denied* — If an application under this section is denied, the court may, with the consent of the young person, the Attorney General and the provincial director, proceed as though the young person had been brought before the court as required under subsection 105(1).

COMMENTARY

Legal Implications

This section incorporates section 26.1 of the *Young Offenders Act* and applies it to youths who are subject to conditional supervision on the community portion of their sentence for presumptive offences, first and second degree murder sentences and intensive rehabilitation custody and supervision orders. It authorizes the Attorney General to apply to continue the custodial portion of the sentence.

If the youth justice court is satisfied that there are reasonable grounds to believe that the young person is likely to commit an offence causing the death of, or serious harm to, another person before the expiry of the sentence, the court may order the young person to remain in custody for a period not to exceed the remainder of the sentence.

This section sets out the factors to be considered by the court in considering the application of the Attorney General and the general procedures to be followed.

Operational Implications

The list of factors the court must take into consideration when considering a continuation of custody for these sentences is similar to those set out in section 98(4) and focuses on a young person's repeated violent behaviour and risk to reoffend. In these cases, it is not the provincial director who applies for continuation of custody, but the Attorney General, obviously on the advice of the provincial director. The young persons in this category are even more vulnerable, and meet many of the factors for continuance of custody, especially those persons with an intensive rehabilitation custody and supervision order where the criteria to be eligible for the order in many ways mirror the factors needed to continue custody. These young persons pose the greatest risk to public safety and, therefore, present a challenge to authorities to adequately support them in the community (conditional) supervision portion of the sentence and not to force them to continue the custody portion of the sentence. The practice of applying for continuation of custody is new in this Act and needs to be monitored carefully, as it has the potential to reduce the impact of the use of community supervision for successful reintegration of a young person into the community.

105. (1) *Conditional supervision* — The provincial director of the province in which a young person on whom a youth sentence under paragraph 42(2)(*o*), (*q*) or (*r*) has been imposed is held in custody or, if applicable, with respect to whom an order has been made under subsection 104(1) (continuation of custody), shall cause the young person to be brought before the youth justice court at least one month before the expiry of the custodial portion of the youth sentence. The court shall, after giving the young person an opportunity to be heard, by order, set the conditions of the young person's conditional supervision.

(2) *Conditions to be included in order* — The youth justice court shall include in the order under subsection (1) the following conditions, namely, that the young person

- (*a*) keep the peace and be of good behaviour;
- (*b*) appear before the youth justice court when required by the court to do so;
- (*c*) report to the provincial director immediately on release, and then be under the supervision of the provincial director or a person designated by the youth justice court;
- (*d*) inform the provincial director immediately on being arrested or questioned by the police;
- (*e*) report to the police, or any named individual, as instructed by the provincial director;
- (*f*) advise the provincial director of the young person's address of residence on release and after release report immediately to the clerk of the youth justice court or the provincial director any change
  - (i) in that address,
  - (ii) in the young person's normal occupation, including employment, vocational or educational training and volunteer work,
  - (iii) in the young person's family or financial situation, and
  - (iv) that may reasonably be expected to affect the young person's ability to comply with the conditions of the order;
- (*g*) not own, possess or have the control of any weapon, ammunition, prohibited ammunition, prohibited device or explosive substance, except as authorized by the order; and

(*h*) comply with any reasonable instructions that the provincial director considers necessary in respect of any condition of the conditional supervision in order to prevent a breach of that condition or to protect society.

(3) *Other conditions* — In setting conditions for the purposes of subsection (1), the youth justice court may include in the order the following conditions, namely, that the young person

(*a*) on release, travel directly to the young person's place of residence, or to any other place that is noted in the order;
(*b*) make reasonable efforts to obtain and maintain suitable employment;
(*c*) attend school or any other place of learning, training or recreation that is appropriate, if the court is satisfied that a suitable program is available for the young person at such a place;
(*d*) reside with a parent, or any other adult that the court considers appropriate, who is willing to provide for the care and maintenance of the young person;
(*e*) reside in any place that the provincial director may specify;
(*f*) remain within the territorial jurisdiction of one or more courts named in the order;
(*g*) comply with conditions set out in the order that support and address the needs of the young person and promote the reintegration of the young person into the community; and
(*h*) comply with any other conditions set out in the order that the court considers appropriate, including conditions for securing the young person's good conduct and for preventing the young person from repeating the offence or committing other offences.

(4) *Temporary conditions* — When a provincial director is required under subsection (1) to cause a young person to be brought before the youth justice court but cannot do so for reasons beyond the young person's control, the provincial director shall so advise the youth justice court and the court shall, by order, set any temporary conditions for the young person's conditional supervision that are appropriate in the circumstances.

(5) *Conditions to be set at first opportunity* — When an order is made under subsection (4), the provincial director shall bring the young person before the youth justice court as soon after the order is made as the circumstances permit and the court shall then set the conditions of the young person's conditional supervision.

(6) *Report* — For the purpose of setting conditions under this section, the youth justice court shall require the provincial director to cause to be prepared, and to submit to the youth justice court, a report setting out any information that may be of assistance to the court.

(7) *Provisions apply* — Subsections 99(2) to (7) (provisions respecting reports and notice) and 104(4) (ordering appearance of young person) apply, with any modifications that the circumstances require, in respect of any proceedings held under subsection (1).

(8) *Provisions apply* — Subsections 56(1) to (4) (provisions respecting probation orders), (7) (notice to appear) and (8) (warrant in default) and section 101 (review of youth justice court decision) apply, with any modifications that the circumstances require, in respect of an order made under subsection (1).

COMMENTARY

Legal Implications

This section requires that all youths subject to conditional supervision for the community portion of their sentence be brought before the youth justice court at least one month before the expiry of the custodial portion of their sentence. Section 26.2 of the *Young Offenders Act* is the basis for this section and deals only with youths who are subject to conditional supervision on the community portion of their sentence for presumptive offences, first and second degree murder sentences and intensive rehabilitation custody and supervision orders or through an annual review under section 94.

The youth court sets the mandatory and optional conditions that young persons are to follow while serving the community portion of their sentence. This section also sets out the procedures for the hearing and for the provincial director's preparation of a report.

Operational Implications

Although the sections dealing with conditional supervision were originally contained in the *Young Offenders Act*, there were very few cases of conditional supervision under that Act; therefore, most jurisdictions are not as familiar with this part of the legislation. Nevertheless, the role for conditional supervision has been expanded under the *Youth Criminal Justice Act*.

Should a police officer have a reasonable belief that a young person has breached or is about to breach a condition of conditional supervision, the police officer only has the authority to advise the provincial director of what was believed to be a breach and it is the provincial director's decision to act upon it.

106. *Suspension of conditional supervision* — If the provincial director has reasonable grounds to believe that a young person has breached or is about to breach a condition of an order made under subsection 105(1), the provincial director may, in writing,

    (*a*) suspend the conditional supervision; and
    (*b*) order that the young person be remanded to any youth custody facility that the provincial director considers appropriate until a

review is conducted under section 108 and, if applicable, section 109.

COMMENTARY

Legal Implications

The provincial director is authorized by this section to suspend the conditional supervision portion of the young person's sentence, as was the case in section 26.3 of the *Young Offenders Act*, and to have the youth remanded to a youth custody facility until a review is conducted.

The provincial director must have reasonable grounds to believe that the young person has breached, or is about to breach, one of the conditions set by the court under section 105(2).

Operational Implications

Should a police officer have a reasonable belief that a young person has breached, or is about to breach, a condition of conditional supervision, the police officer only has the authority to advise the provincial director of what was believed to be a breach and it is the provincial director's decision to act upon it.

107. (1) *Apprehension* — **If the conditional supervision of a young person is suspended under section 106, the provincial director may issue a warrant in writing, authorizing the apprehension of the young person and, until the young person is apprehended, the young person is deemed not to be continuing to serve the youth sentence the young person is then serving.**

(2) *Warrants* — **A warrant issued under subsection (1) shall be executed by any peace officer to whom it is given at any place in Canada and has the same force and effect in all parts of Canada as if it had been originally issued or subsequently endorsed by a provincial court judge or other lawful authority having jurisdiction in the place where it is executed.**

(3) *Peace officer may arrest* — **If a peace officer believes on reasonable grounds that a warrant issued under subsection (1) is in force in respect of a young person, the peace officer may arrest the young person without the warrant at any place in Canada.**

(4) *Requirement to bring before provincial director* — **If a young person is arrested under subsection (3) and detained, the peace officer making the arrest shall cause the young person to be brought before the provincial director or a person designated by the provincial director**

  (*a*) if the provincial director or the designated person is available within a period of twenty-four hours after the young person is arrested, without unreasonable delay and in any event within that period; and

(b) if the provincial director or the designated person is not available within that period, as soon as possible.

(5) *Release or remand in custody* — If a young person is brought before the provincial director or a person designated by the provincial director under subsection (4), the provincial director or the designated person

- (a) if not satisfied that there are reasonable grounds to believe that the young person is the young person in respect of whom the warrant referred to in subsection (1) was issued, shall release the young person; or
- (b) if satisfied that there are reasonable grounds to believe that the young person is the young person in respect of whom the warrant referred to in subsection (1) was issued, may remand the young person in custody to await execution of the warrant, but if no warrant for the young person's arrest is executed within a period of forty-eight hours after the time the young person is remanded in custody, the person in whose custody the young person then is shall release the young person.

COMMENTARY

Legal Implications

This section sets out the rules for the apprehension of a young person whom the provincial director has ordered to be remanded. The provincial director may issue a warrant for the arrest of the young person, and a peace officer may execute this warrant anywhere in Canada, as was the case in section 26.4 of the *Young Offenders Act*.

Upon arrest, the young person should be brought before the provincial director within 24 hours, or as soon as possible, and the provincial director should be satisfied that it is the young person for whom the warrant was issued, or release the young person.

Operational Implications

This section of the *Youth Criminal Justice Act* authorizes police to apprehend a young person who is believed to have failed to comply with community/conditional supervision conditions only if the provincial director has issued a warrant. If there is no warrant issued, the police cannot detain the youth. There is no requirement for a provincial director to be available to the police on a 24-hour basis. The young person is to be brought before the provincial director within 24 hours, *or as soon as possible*. Once the warrant is issued, the sentence stops until the young person is apprehended.

108. *Review by provincial director* — **Without delay after the remand to custody of a young person whose conditional supervision has been suspended under section 106, or without delay after being informed of the**

arrest of such a young person, the provincial director shall review the case and, within forty-eight hours, cancel the suspension of the conditional supervision or refer the case to the youth justice court for a review under section 109.

COMMENTARY

Legal Implications

Once the young person has been arrested or remanded, the provincial director should review the case within 48 hours of being informed of the arrest. The provincial director may then cancel the suspension of the conditional supervision and release the young person, or refer the case to a youth justice court for a review of the decision, as was done in section 26.5 of the *Young Offenders Act*.

Operational Implications

This section of the *Youth Criminal Justice Act* reinforces the concept of timeliness but also provides some flexibility. The provincial director is to review the conditional supervision of a young person within 48 hours of the young person's remand to custody, or within 48 hours of the provincial director being notified. The interpretation of this section is very important. The provincial director responsible for reviewing a young person's conditional supervision should be a community-based provincial director who is familiar with the young person and the circumstances of the breach. The provincial director who issued the warrant should review the young person's remand. Ideally the provincial director would review the young person's circumstances with the probation officer who is the case manager and who developed the reintegration plan. The provision in this section to begin the clock after the provincial director has *been informed*, not at the time the young person was apprehended, is critical to good case management and decision making. It ensures that the right people are considering the correct information when deciding a young person's future status in the community.

109. (1) *Review by youth justice court* — **If the case of a young person is referred to the youth justice court under section 108, the provincial director shall, without delay, cause the young person to be brought before the youth justice court, and the youth justice court shall, after giving the young person an opportunity to be heard,**

   (*a*) **if the court is not satisfied on reasonable grounds that the young person has breached or was about to breach a condition of the conditional supervision, cancel the suspension of the conditional supervision; or**
   (*b*) **if the court is satisfied on reasonable grounds that the young person has breached or was about to breach a condition of the conditional supervision, review the decision of the provincial**

director to suspend the conditional supervision and make an order under subsection (2).

(2) *Order* — On completion of a review under subsection (1), the youth justice court shall order

  (*a*) the cancellation of the suspension of the conditional supervision, and when the court does so, the court may vary the conditions of the conditional supervision or impose new conditions;
  (*b*) in a case other than a deferred custody and supervision order made under paragraph 42(2)(*p*), the continuation of the suspension of the conditional supervision for any period of time, not to exceed the remainder of the youth sentence the young person is then serving, that the court considers appropriate, and when the court does so, the court shall order that the young person remain in custody; or
  (*c*) in the case of a deferred custody and supervision order made under paragraph 42(2)(*p*), that the young person serve the remainder of the order as if it were a custody and supervision order under paragraph 42(2)(*n*).

(3) *Custody and supervision order* — After a court has made a direction under paragraph (2)(*c*), the provisions of this Act applicable to orders under paragraph 42(2)(*n*) apply in respect of the deferred custody and supervision order.

(4) *Factors to be considered* — In making its decision under subsection (2), the court shall consider the length of time the young person has been subject to the order, whether the young person has previously contravened it, and the nature of the contravention, if any.

(5) *Reasons* — When a youth justice court makes an order under subsection (2), it shall state its reasons for the order in the record of the case and shall give, or cause to be given, to the young person in respect of whom the order was made, the counsel and a parent of the young person, the Attorney General and the provincial director,

  (*a*) a copy of the order; and
  (*b*) on request, a transcript or copy of the reasons for the order.

(6) *Report* — For the purposes of a review under subsection (1), the youth justice court shall require the provincial director to cause to be prepared, and to submit to the youth justice court, a report setting out any information of which the provincial director is aware that may be of assistance to the court.

(7) *Provisions apply* — Subsections 99(2) to (7) (provisions respecting reports and notice) and 105(6) (report for the purpose of setting conditions) apply, with any modifications that the circumstances require, in respect of a review under this section.

(8) *Provisions apply* — Section 101 (review of youth justice court decision) applies, with any modifications that the circumstances require, in respect of an order made under subsection (2).

COMMENTARY

Legal Implications

When the provincial director refers a case to the youth justice court for review, the court should first determine if there has been a breach of the conditions of the conditional supervision order. If the court is not satisfied that there has been a breach of the conditions, then the suspension of the conditional supervision should be conceded, and the young person should be released from custody. If the court is satisfied, on reasonable grounds, that there has been a breach, then the youth justice court should order the cancellation of the suspension, including a variation of the conditions if appropriate, or continue the cancellation of the conditional supervision.

If the youth justice court continues the cancellation in cases other than a deferred custody and supervision order, it may continue the suspension for any period of time that does not exceed the term of the original order, and the young person will remain in custody for the period of the suspension.

If the youth justice court continues the cancellation in the case of a deferred custody and supervision order, the young person will serve the remainder of the sentence as if that remainder was a custody and supervision order, with a period of custody and community supervision.

Operational Implications

Although these procedures were in place in section 26.6 of the *Young Offenders Act*, the review of conditional supervision under this new legislation is used far more regularly, as it applies to a greater number of sentences than it did under the *Young Offenders Act*. It is difficult enough for cases to proceed through youth justice court in a timely, expedient manner. This process requires more court time and could result in each young person returning to court several times.

PART 6 PUBLICATION, RECORDS AND INFORMATION

INTRODUCTION

The next 20 sections set out the rules for the keeping and use of young persons' records. Care has been taken to limit the use of records that identify youths as having been involved in the criminal justice system. It is recognized that the rehabilitation of young persons may be adversely affected by the publication of their names and information that would lead to their identification.

There is a general prohibition on the publication of names and identifying information. At the same time, the system should be able to access information that gives a true profile of young persons involved in the system. There are rules that set out the limitations on the release and sharing of information, including references to the persons to whom records may be shared, and the purposes for which records may be released, as well as the time period in which records remain active.

These provisions, which strike a balance between the need for information and the need for privacy, provide the best opportunity for rehabilitation of the young person. It is particularly important for persons who keep records to be familiar with these rules. So far, these sections have proven to be confusing and unclear and should be reviewed in future amendments

PROTECTION OF PRIVACY OF YOUNG PERSONS

110. (1) *Identity of offender not to be published* — Subject to this section, no person shall publish the name of a young person, or any other information related to a young person, if it would identify the young person as a young person dealt with under this Act.

(2) *Limitation* — Subsection (1) does not apply

(*a*) in a case where the information relates to a young person who has received an adult sentence;

(*b*) subject to sections 65 (young person not liable to adult sentence) and 75 (youth sentence imposed despite presumptive offence), in a case where the information relates to a young person who has received a youth sentence for an offence set out in paragraph (*a*) of the definition "presumptive offence" in subsection 2(1), or an offence set out in paragraph (*b*) of that definition for which the Attorney General has given notice under subsection 64(2) (intention to seek adult sentence); and

(*c*) in a case where the publication of information is made in the course of the administration of justice, if it is not the purpose of the publication to make the information known in the community.

(3) *Exception* — A young person referred to in subsection (1) may, after he or she attains the age of eighteen years, publish or cause to be published information that would identify him or her as having been dealt with under this Act or the *Young Offenders Act*, chapter Y-1 of the Revised Statutes of Canada, 1985, provided that he or she is not in custody pursuant to either Act at the time of the publication.

(4) *Ex parte application for leave to publish* — A youth justice court judge shall, on the *ex parte* application of a peace officer, make an order permitting any person to publish information that identifies a young person as having committed or allegedly committed an indictable offence, if the judge is satisfied that

(*a*) there is reason to believe that the young person is a danger to others; and

(b) publication of the information is necessary to assist in apprehending the young person.

(5) *Order ceases to have effect* — An order made under subsection (4) ceases to have effect five days after it is made.

(6) *Application for leave to publish* — The youth justice court may, on the application of a young person referred to in subsection (1), make an order permitting the young person to publish information that would identify him or her as having been dealt with under this Act or the *Young Offenders Act*, chapter Y-1 of the Revised Statutes of Canada, 1985, if the court is satisfied that the publication would not be contrary to the young person's best interests or the public interest.

COMMENTARY

Legal Implications

The general rule of non-publication of names or information that would identify a young person as having been dealt with under this Act, as well as the limitations, has been adopted from section 38 of the *Young Offenders Act*, with some exceptions. There is a presumption of publication if a young person receives a youth sentence for the offences of murder, attempted murder, manslaughter, aggravated assault or three serious violent offences. A young person 18 years of age may publish information that would identify him or her provided he or she is not in custody at the time of the publication. There is also a special rule which allows a young person to make an application to a youth justice court to permit publication of his or her name if it would not be contrary to his or her best interests or those of the public.

On March 31, 2003, the Quebec Court of Appeal in *Reference re: Bill C-7 Respecting the Criminal Justice System for Young Persons*, [2003] Q.J. No. 2850 (C.A.), addressed the question of publication and the presumption of publication for presumptive offences and found that sections 75 and 110(2)(*b*) violate the *Canadian Charter of Rights and Freedoms* insofar as they require the young person to justify maintaining the ban instead of placing the burden on the prosecutor to justify lifting the ban.

The court, therefore, placed the burden squarely on the Crown to rebut the general rule of no publication. The general rule is no publication, and one of the exceptions to that rule in the *Youth Criminal Justice Act* was in the case of a presumptive offence even though the young person received a youth sentence. The court found the reversing of the onus to require the young person to show why his or her name should not be published violated the Charter.

Operational Implications

The onus to convince the court to impose a publication ban for a young person who receives a youth sentence for the offences of murder, attempted murder, manslaughter, aggravated assault or three serious violent offences will be on the applicant (subject to any future amendments based on the Quebec Court of

Appeal decision in *Reference re: Bill C-7 Respecting the Criminal Justice System for Young Persons*, [2003] Q.J. No. 2850), be it the young person and counsel, or the Attorney General (see section 75).

Allowing a young person to publish information about his or her criminal behaviour strays far from the confidentiality of the *Young Offenders Act*, so it is difficult to know if this will open a Pandora's box. It may shed some much-needed light on the "good news" stories of young persons in the youth justice system. The *Young Offenders Act* was not clear about whether a young person, upon becoming an adult, could release information that would identify him or her as a young offender, or if there was still a prohibition against the disclosure, release and publication of this information. The *Youth Criminal Justice Act* makes this clear.

111. (1) *Identity of victim or witness not to be published* — **Subject to this section, no person shall publish the name of a child or young person, or any other information related to a child or a young person, if it would identify the child or young person as having been a victim of, or as having appeared as a witness in connection with, an offence committed or alleged to have been committed by a young person.**

(2) *Exception* — **Information that would serve to identify a child or young person referred to in subsection (1) as having been a victim or a witness may be published, or caused to be published, by**

- **(a) that child or young person after he or she attains the age of eighteen years or before that age with the consent of his or her parents; or**
- **(b) the parents of that child or young person if he or she is deceased.**

(3) *Application for leave to publish* — **The youth justice court may, on the application of a child or a young person referred to in subsection (1), make an order permitting the child or young person to publish information that would identify him or her as having been a victim or a witness if the court is satisfied that the publication would not be contrary to his or her best interests or the public interest.**

COMMENTARY

Legal Implications

This legislation also protects the identity of children under the age of 12, and young persons who are victims or witnesses of an offence committed by a young person. The rule is that there shall be no publication of information that would identify a child or young person who is a victim of a young person's offence.

There is, of course, an exception to this rule of non-publication, for example, when the child or young person has reached the age of 18 and wants to publish his or her name, or in a situation where the parents of a deceased child or young person wishes to publish the name.

The child or young person may seek an order from the youth justice court to publish the name if it would not be contrary to the interests of the child, the young person or the public.

Operational Implications

Pre-sentence reports, which contain victim information, are distributed to the young person and his or her parent(s), usually without instructions regarding the distribution or destruction of the report. Often, these reports can be found on the bench in the lobby of the courtroom. Since victim information needs to be protected, it may not be a necessary component in reports that are distributed outside the youth justice system.

112. ***Non-application*** **— Once information is published under subsection 110(3) or (6) or 111(2) or (3), subsection 110(1) (identity of offender not to be published) or 111(1) (identity of victim or witness not to be published), as the case may be, no longer applies in respect of the information.**

COMMENTARY

Legal Implications

This new section clarifies that once the name of a young person, a child or a young person who is a victim or witness is published under this Act, the general prohibition against publication no longer applies.

FINGERPRINTS AND PHOTOGRAPHS

113. (1) ***Identification of Criminals Act applies*** **— The** ***Identification of Criminals Act*** **applies in respect of young persons.**

(2) ***Limitation*** **— No fingerprint, palmprint or photograph or other measurement, process or operation referred to in the** ***Identification of Criminals Act*** **shall be taken of, or applied in respect of, a young person who is charged with having committed an offence except in the circumstances in which an adult may, under that Act, be subjected to the measurements, processes and operations.**

COMMENTARY

Legal Implications

The *Identification of Criminals Act* applies to young persons, as it did under the *Young Offenders Act*. This allows the police to photograph, fingerprint, palmprint and use other means of measuring identification as set out in that Act. However, these methods of measuring identification are limited to circumstances where they could be used for adults.

RECORDS THAT MAY BE KEPT

114. *Youth justice court, review board and other courts* — A youth justice court, review board or any court dealing with matters arising out of proceedings under this Act may keep a record of any case that comes before it arising under this Act.

COMMENTARY

Legal Implications

This section is the same as in the *Young Offenders Act* in that it authorizes the keeping of records for proceedings that arise under the *Youth Criminal Justice Act*. There are limitations on the keeping and use of records dealing with young persons, but this provision ensures that a record of proceedings may be kept.

115. (1) *Police records* — A record relating to any offence alleged to have been committed by a young person, including the original or a copy of any fingerprints or photographs of the young person, may be kept by any police force responsible for or participating in the investigation of the offence.

(2) *Police records* — When a young person is charged with having committed an offence in respect of which an adult may be subjected to any measurement, process or operation referred to in the *Identification of Criminals Act*, the police force responsible for the investigation of the offence may provide a record relating to the offence to the Royal Canadian Mounted Police. If the young person is found guilty of the offence, the police force shall provide the record.

(3) *Records held by R.C.M.P.* — The Royal Canadian Mounted Police shall keep the records provided under subsection (2) in the central repository that the Commissioner of the Royal Canadian Mounted Police may, from time to time, designate for the purpose of keeping criminal history files or records of offenders or keeping records for the identification of offenders.

COMMENTARY

Legal Implications

This section combines sections 41 and 42 of the *Young Offenders Act*. Police records are essential in order to keep track of previous criminal behaviour committed by young persons. This section authorizes the police to keep records of alleged offences and offences charged, as well as records which arise out of the *Identification of Criminal Records Act*. The RCMP are also authorized to keep records of police forces across Canada in a central repository for the use of all police. The central repository enables police across the country to access important information about young persons who are engaged in criminal behaviour anywhere in the country. This information is essential for police to make good policing decisions about release after arrest and to make decisions about extrajudicial measures.

Operational Implications

Police records are essential in order to understand the trends and patterns of youth crime, particularly in this legislation. The *Youth Criminal Justice Act* authorizes a number of offences to be dealt with outside the formal justice system. Following tradition, justice statistics are gathered in the formal system once a conviction has been registered. This section of the legislation allows the police to keep formal records and authorizes the RCMP to keep records in a central repository. It also authorizes the police to keep records of any offence alleged to have been committed. However, the reality is that there are a wide variety of data collection systems being used by police across the country and within a province, so the ability to track young persons and identify patterns and trends is very limited. The Canada-wide system, the Canadian Police Information Centre (CPIC), remains the only national offender database, and CPIC cannot record data outside the formal justice system as it is not part of a young person's record and therefore should not be available on a national database.

116. (1) *Government records* **— A department or an agency of any government in Canada may keep records containing information obtained by the department or agency**

- **(*a*) for the purposes of an investigation of an offence alleged to have been committed by a young person;**
- **(*b*) for use in proceedings against a young person under this Act;**
- **(*c*) for the purpose of administering a youth sentence or an order of the youth justice court;**
- **(*d*) for the purpose of considering whether to use extrajudicial measures to deal with a young person; or**
- **(*e*) as a result of the use of extrajudicial measures to deal with a young person.**

(2) *Other records* **— A person or organization may keep records containing information obtained by the person or organization**

- **(*a*) as a result of the use of extrajudicial measures to deal with a young person; or**
- **(*b*) for the purpose of administering or participating in the administration of a youth sentence.**

COMMENTARY

Legal Implications

The *Youth Criminal Justice Act* has strict control over the keeping and use of information pertaining to a young person and has set strict rules to ensure that the privacy of young persons is protected while at the same time balancing the need for access to information to ensure an effective and efficient youth justice system.

This section authorizes departments and agencies of government, as well as persons and organizations, to keep records for various purposes. A person or organization is limited to the purposes of the use of extrajudicial measures and for the purpose of the administration of a youth sentence.

ACCESS TO RECORDS

117. *Exception – adult sentence* **— Sections 118 to 129 do not apply to records kept in respect of an offence for which an adult sentence has been imposed once the time allowed for the taking of an appeal has expired or, if an appeal is taken, all proceedings in respect of the appeal have been completed and the appeal court has upheld an adult sentence. The record shall be dealt with as a record of an adult and, for the purposes of the** *Criminal Records Act***, the finding of guilt in respect of the offence for which the record is kept is deemed to be a conviction.**

COMMENTARY

Legal Implications

Generally, access to records that show that a young person has been dealt with under this Act is prohibited. This section, however, removes that general prohibition in the case where a young person has received an adult sentence. The decision of the youth justice court to impose an adult sentence must be final, with all appeals being exhausted, before the information can be treated as an adult record.

118. (1) *No access unless authorized* **— Except as authorized or required by this Act, no person shall be given access to a record kept under sections 114 to 116, and no information contained in it may be given to any person, where to do so would identify the young person to whom it relates as a young person dealt with under this Act.**

(2) *Exception for employees* **— No person who is employed in keeping or maintaining records referred to in subsection (1) is restricted from doing anything prohibited under subsection (1) with respect to any other person so employed.**

COMMENTARY

Legal Implications

This section, which incorporates part of section 46 of the *Young Offenders Act*, contains a general prohibition for anyone to access records kept by the youth justice court, or any other court, review board, police or government, that would identify a young person as having been dealt with under this Act. This prohibition does not apply to persons who are specifically authorized or required by this Act to have access to the records. This exception is necessary in order for the authorized information to be kept available for access when it is needed for the purposes permitted by the Act.

119. (1) *Persons having access to records* — Subject to subsections (4) to (6), from the date that a record is created until the end of the applicable period set out in subsection (2), the following persons, on request, shall be given access to a record kept under section 114, and may be given access to a record kept under sections 115 and 116:

- (*a*) the young person to whom the record relates;
- (*b*) the young person's counsel, or any representative of that counsel;
- (*c*) the Attorney General;
- (*d*) the victim of the offence or alleged offence to which the record relates;
- (*e*) the parents of the young person, during the course of any proceedings relating to the offence or alleged offence to which the record relates or during the term of any youth sentence made in respect of the offence;
- (*f*) any adult assisting the young person under subsection 25(7), during the course of any proceedings relating to the offence or alleged offence to which the record relates or during the term of any youth sentence made in respect of the offence;
- (*g*) any peace officer for
  - (i) law enforcement purposes, or
  - (ii) any purpose related to the administration of the case to which the record relates, during the course of proceedings against the young person or the term of the youth sentence;
- (*h*) a judge, court or review board, for any purpose relating to proceedings against the young person, or proceedings against the person after he or she becomes an adult, in respect of offences committed or alleged to have been committed by that person;
- (*i*) the provincial director, or the director of the provincial correctional facility for adults or the penitentiary at which the young person is serving a sentence;
- (*j*) a person participating in a conference or in the administration of extrajudicial measures, if required for the administration of the case to which the record relates;

(k) a person acting as ombudsman, privacy commissioner or information commissioner, whatever his or her official designation might be, who in the course of his or her duties under an Act of Parliament or the legislature of a province is investigating a complaint to which the record relates;
(l) a coroner or a person acting as a child advocate, whatever his or her official designation might be, who is acting in the course of his or her duties under an Act of Parliament or the legislature of a province;
(m) a person acting under the *Firearms Act*;
(n) a member of a department or agency of a government in Canada, or of an organization that is an agent of, or under contract with, the department or agency, who is
  (i) acting in the exercise of his or her duties under this Act,
  (ii) engaged in the supervision or care of the young person, whether as a young person or an adult, or in an investigation related to the young person under an Act of the legislature of a province respecting child welfare,
  (iii) considering an application for conditional release or pardon made by the young person, whether as a young person or an adult,
  (iv) administering a prohibition order made under an Act of Parliament or the legislature of a province, or
  (v) administering a youth sentence, if the young person has been committed to custody and is serving the custody in a provincial correctional facility for adults or a penitentiary;
(o) a person, for the purpose of carrying out a criminal record check required by the Government of Canada or the government of a province or a municipality for purposes of employment or the performance of services, with or without remuneration;
(p) an employee or agent of the Government of Canada, for statistical purposes under the *Statistics Act*;
(q) an accused or his or her counsel who swears an affidavit to the effect that access to the record is necessary to make a full answer and defence;
(r) a person or a member of a class of persons designated by order of the Governor in Council, or the lieutenant governor in council of the appropriate province, for a purpose and to the extent specified in the order; and
(s) any person or member of a class of persons that a youth justice court judge considers has a valid interest in the record, to the extent directed by the judge, if the judge is satisfied that access to the record is
  (i) desirable in the public interest for research or statistical purposes, or
  (ii) desirable in the interest of the proper administration of justice.

(2) *Period of access* — The period of access referred to in subsection (1) is

(a) if an extrajudicial sanction is used to deal with the young person, the period ending two years after the young person consents to be subject to the sanction in accordance with paragraph 10(2)(c);
(b) if the young person is acquitted of the offence otherwise than by reason of a verdict of not criminally responsible on account of mental disorder, the period ending two months after the expiry of the time allowed for the taking of an appeal or, if an appeal is taken, the period ending three months after all proceedings in respect of the appeal have been completed;
(c) if the charge against the young person is dismissed for any reason other than acquittal, the charge is withdrawn, or the young person is found guilty of the offence and a reprimand is given, the period ending two months after the dismissal, withdrawal, or finding of guilt;
(d) if the charge against the young person is stayed, with no proceedings being taken against the young person for a period of one year, at the end of that period;
(e) if the young person is found guilty of the offence and the youth sentence is an absolute discharge, the period ending one year after the young person is found guilty;
(f) if the young person is found guilty of the offence and the youth sentence is a conditional discharge, the period ending three years after the young person is found guilty;
(g) subject to paragraphs (i) and (j) and subsection (9), if the young person is found guilty of the offence and it is a summary conviction offence, the period ending three years after the youth sentence imposed in respect of the offence has been completed;
(h) subject to paragraphs (i) and (j) and subsection (9), if the young person is found guilty of the offence and it is an indictable offence, the period ending five years after the youth sentence imposed in respect of the offence has been completed;
(i) subject to subsection (9), if, during the period calculated in accordance with paragraph (g) or (h), the young person is found guilty of an offence punishable on summary conviction committed when he or she was a young person, the latest of
  (i) the period calculated in accordance with paragraph (g) or (h), as the case may be, and
  (ii) the period ending three years after the youth sentence imposed for that offence has been completed; and
(j) subject to subsection (9), if, during the period calculated in accordance with paragraph (g) or (h), the young person is found guilty of an indictable offence committed when he or she was a young person, the period ending five years after the sentence imposed for that indictable offence has been completed.

Part 6 Publication, Records and Information   S. 119

(3) *Prohibition orders not included* — Prohibition orders made under an Act of Parliament or the legislature of a province, including any order made under section 51, shall not be taken into account in determining any period referred to in subsection (2).

(4) *Extrajudicial measures* — Access to a record kept under section 115 or 116 in respect of extrajudicial measures, other than extrajudicial sanctions, used in respect of a young person shall be given only to the following persons for the following purposes:

   (a) a peace officer or the Attorney General, in order to make a decision whether to again use extrajudicial measures in respect of the young person;
   (b) a person participating in a conference, in order to decide on the appropriate extrajudicial measure;
   (c) a peace officer, the Attorney General or a person participating in a conference, if access is required for the administration of the case to which the record relates; and
   (d) a peace officer for the purpose of investigating an offence.

(5) *Exception* — When a youth justice court has withheld all or part of a report from any person under subsection 34(9) or (10) (nondisclosure of medical or psychological report) or 40(7) (nondisclosure of pre-sentence report), that person shall not be given access under subsection (1) to that report or part.

(6) *Records of assessments or forensic DNA analysis* — Access to a report made under section 34 (medical and psychological reports) or a record of the results of forensic DNA analysis of a bodily substance taken from a young person in execution of a warrant issued under section 487.05 of the *Criminal Code* may be given only under paragraphs (1)(a) to (c), (e) to (h) and (q) and subparagraph (1)(s)(ii).

(7) *Introduction into evidence* — Nothing in paragraph (1)(h) or (q) authorizes the introduction into evidence of any part of a record that would not otherwise be admissible in evidence.

(8) *Disclosures for research or statistical purposes* — When access to a record is given to a person under paragraph (1)(p) or subparagraph (1)(s)(i), the person may subsequently disclose information contained in the record, but shall not disclose the information in any form that would reasonably be expected to identify the young person to whom it relates.

(9) *Application of usual rules* — If, during the period of access to a record under any of paragraphs (2)(g) to (j), the young person is convicted of an offence committed when he or she is an adult,

(a) section 82 (effect of absolute discharge or termination of youth sentence) does not apply to the young person in respect of the offence for which the record is kept under sections 114 to 116;
(b) this Part no longer applies to the record and the record shall be dealt with as a record of an adult; and
(c) for the purposes of the *Criminal Records Act*, the finding of guilt in respect of the offence for which the record is kept is deemed to be a conviction.

(10) *Records of offences that result in a prohibition order* — Despite anything in this Act, when a young person is found guilty of an offence that results in a prohibition order being made, and the order is still in force at the end of the applicable period for which access to a record kept in respect of the order may be given under subsection (2),

(a) the record kept by the Royal Canadian Mounted Police pursuant to subsection 115(3) may be disclosed only to establish the existence of the order for purposes of law enforcement; and
(b) the record referred to in section 114 that is kept by the youth justice court may be disclosed only to establish the existence of the order in any offence involving a breach of the order.

COMMENTARY

Legal Implications

This section expands section 44.1 of the *Young Offenders Act* and sets out the general rules for the people who have access to youth records, the purposes for which they have access and the length of time that access is permitted. These general rules are detailed and are the essence of the balance struck between the privacy of a young person and the need to access information.

The persons who are authorized to have access to youth records will be given access to records of the court and review board (kept under section 114), and *may* be given access to police and government records (kept under sections 115 and 116). It is important to make this distinction because access to records of the courts and review board is mandatory, while access to police and government records is permissive.

This section includes a number of subsections that address specific issues regarding records, such as time periods, use of extrajudicial measures records, use of assessment reports and DNA analysis, disclosures for research purposes and permission to disclose a record while a prohibition order is in force in order to show the existence of the prohibition order. Prohibition orders are specifically excluded from the time periods set out in section 119(2).

In the Ontario Court of Justice decision *R. v. Keith*, [2003] O.J. No. 2256 (C.J.), Justice Wright ruled that disclosure under section 119 is mandatory with respect to records kept pursuant to section 114, and discretionary with respect to records kept under sections 115 and 116.

A key provision of this section (section 119(9)) explains what happens when an offence is committed as an adult while a youth record is still active. This part of the Act, which limits access to youth records, will no longer apply to a youth record. This means that a record, which falls within the time periods for access, will be kept active and treated as an adult record.

Operational Implications

The youth criminal justice system would not be able to function without access to any of the information about young persons. It is, therefore, necessary to allow access to records of young persons, but it is also necessary to control access to those records. It is important to restrict access to only those pieces of information that are necessary for the individual to perform his or her particular function. The Act is silent on where in the youth justice system access to records is obtained. The British Columbia Provincial Court in *R. v. D.B.M.*, [2003] B.C.J. No. 2646, 2003 BCPC 394, acknowledged that section 114 authorizes the court to maintain records but section 119(1)(*q*) is unclear as it does not specify who may provide access to those records.

120. (1) *Access to R.C.M.P. records* **— The following persons may, during the period set out in subsection (3), be given access to a record kept under subsection 115(3) in respect of an offence set out in the schedule:**

(*a*) the young person to whom the record relates;
(*b*) the young person's counsel, or any representative of that counsel;
(*c*) an employee or agent of the Government of Canada, for statistical purposes under the *Statistics Act*;
(*d*) any person or member of a class of persons that a youth justice court judge considers has a valid interest in the record, to the extent directed by the judge, if the judge is satisfied that access is desirable in the public interest for research or statistical purposes;
(*e*) the Attorney General or a peace officer, when the young person is or has been charged with another offence set out in the schedule or the same offence more than once, for the purpose of investigating any offence that the young person is suspected of having committed, or in respect of which the young person has been arrested or charged, whether as a young person or as an adult;
(*f*) the Attorney General or a peace officer to establish the existence of an order in any offence involving a breach of the order; and
(*g*) any person for the purposes of the *Firearms Act*.

(2) *Access for identification purposes* **— During the period set out in subsection (3), access to the portion of a record kept under subsection 115(3) that contains the name, date of birth and last known address of the young person to whom the fingerprints belong, may be given to a person for identification purposes if a fingerprint identified as that of the young person is found during the investigation of an offence or during an attempt to identify a deceased person or a person suffering from amnesia.**

(3) *Period of access* — For the purposes of subsections (1) and (2), the period of access to a record kept under subsection 115(3) in respect of an offence is the following:

- (*a*) if the offence is an indictable offence, other than a presumptive offence, the period starting at the end of the applicable period set out in paragraphs 119(2)(*h*) to (*j*) and ending five years later; and
- (*b*) if the offence is an offence set out in paragraph (*a*) of the definition "presumptive offence" in subsection 2(1) or an offence set out in paragraph (*b*) of that definition for which the Attorney General has given notice under subsection 64(2) (intention to seek adult sentence), the period starting at the end of the applicable period set out in paragraphs 119(2)(*h*) to (*j*) and continuing indefinitely.

(4) *Subsequent offences as young person* — If a young person was found guilty of an offence set out in the schedule is, during the period of access to a record under subsection (3), found guilty of an additional offence set out in the schedule, committed when he or she was a young person, access to the record may be given to the following additional persons:

- (*a*) a parent of the young person or any adult assisting the young person under subsection 25(7);
- (*b*) a judge, court or review board, for a purpose relating to proceedings against the young person under this Act or any other Act of Parliament in respect of offences committed or alleged to have been committed by the young person, whether as a young person or as an adult; or
- (*c*) a member of a department or agency of a government in Canada, or of an organization that is an agent of, or is under contract with, the department or agency, who is
  - (i) preparing a report in respect of the young person under this Act or for the purpose of assisting a court in sentencing the young person after the young person becomes an adult,
  - (ii) engaged in the supervision or care of the young person, whether as a young person or as an adult, or in the administration of a sentence in respect of the young person, whether as a young person or as an adult, or
  - (iii) considering an application for conditional release or pardon made by the young person after the young person becomes an adult.

(5) *Disclosure for research or statistical purposes* — A person who is given access to a record under paragraph (1)(*c*) or (*d*) may subsequently disclose information contained in the record, but shall not disclose the information in any form that would reasonably be expected to identify the young person to whom it relates.

(6) *Subsequent offences as adult* — **If, during the period of access to a record under subsection (3), the young person is convicted of an additional offence set out in the schedule, committed when he or she was an adult,**

- (*a*) **this Part no longer applies to the record and the record shall be dealt with as a record of an adult and may be included on the automated criminal conviction records retrieval system maintained by the Royal Canadian Mounted Police; and**
- (*b*) **for the purposes of the *Criminal Records Act*, the finding of guilt in respect of the offence for which the record is kept is deemed to be a conviction.**

COMMENTARY

Legal Implications

This section is specifically directed to accessing records of offences listed in the Schedule to this Act for a longer period of time than the general rule permits. It was decided that these offences require access for a greater period of time. The RCMP, authorized under section 115(3), keeps these records, for all offences for which there have been identification measurements taken, in a central repository. The period of access is at least five years longer than the time periods set out in section 119, and, in the case of adult sentence procedures, the period is indefinite.

A list of individuals authorized to have access, and a description of the limited purposes for which they have access to the information, is contained in the Act. The RCMP may release information to the persons set out and for the purposes described in the section, but they are not required to do so.

Operational Implications

This section is a response to serious crime and to the demand for access to identifying information for longer periods of time for the serious crimes specifically listed. Access is granted by the RCMP.

121. *Deemed election* — **For the purposes of sections 119 and 120, if no election is made in respect of an offence that may be prosecuted by indictment or proceeded with by way of summary conviction, the Attorney General is deemed to have elected to proceed with the offence as an offence punishable on summary conviction.**

COMMENTARY

Legal Implications

The two previous sections, which define when a record may be accessed, distinguish between indictable and summary conviction offences. Indictable offences may be accessed for a longer period of time; therefore, it is necessary to clearly distinguish between the two types of offences. This has not been changed from section 45(5) of the *Young Offenders Act*.

Operational Implications

Without a presumption, there could be a problem making the distinction between indictable and summary conviction offences, as many offences are hybrid, and the Crown Attorney has a choice to proceed in court by indictment, or by summary conviction. This section makes it clear that when the Crown does not elect, the proceedings are deemed to be by summary conviction, which is the less serious of the two procedures.

122. *Disclosure of information and copies of record* **— A person who is required or authorized to be given access to a record under section 119, 120, 123 or 124 may be given any information contained in the record and may be given a copy of any part of the record.**

COMMENTARY

Legal Implications

Records are generally not made available for inspection. The previous sections give certain people access to records for specific purposes and for specific periods of time. This section makes it clear that those who will be responsible for allowing access to the records are authorized to give the information in the record and may give a copy of any part of the record.

Operational Implications

The *Young Offenders Act* never made it clear that a copy of a record could be given to those who were authorized under the legislation. This new section removes any confusion about actually giving out a copy of any part of the record. It will end countless debates on the legality of copying a record but does not solve the issue of who — what department — actually gives a copy of a record. A young person's record may contain court documents, custody documents, reintegration plans generated by probation, community sentence reports, school or medical information and many other related documents. Policies and procedures need to be in place to identify who in the justice system should be given a copy of a record and what part of the record they are authorized to copy.

123. (1) *Where records may be made available* **— A youth justice court judge may, on application by a person after the end of the applicable period set out in subsection 119(2), order that the person be given access to all or part of a record kept under sections 114 to 116 or that a copy of the record or part be given to that person,**

(*a*) if the youth justice court judge is satisfied that
  (i) the person has a valid and substantial interest in the record or part,
  (ii) it is necessary for access to be given to the record or part in the interest of the proper administration of justice, and
  (iii) disclosure of the record or part or the information in it is not prohibited under any other Act of Parliament or the legislature of a province; or
(*b*) if the youth court judge is satisfied that access to the record or part is desirable in the public interest for research or statistical purposes.

(2) *Restriction for paragraph (1)(a)* — Paragraph (1)(*a*) applies in respect of a record relating to a particular young person or to a record relating to a class of young persons only if the identity of young persons in the class at the time of the making of the application referred to in that paragraph cannot reasonably be ascertained and the disclosure of the record is necessary for the purpose of investigating any offence that a person is suspected on reasonable grounds of having committed against a young person while the young person is, or was, serving a sentence.

(3) *Notice* — Subject to subsection (4), an application for an order under paragraph (1)(*a*) in respect of a record shall not be heard unless the person who makes the application has given the young person to whom the record relates and the person or body that has possession of the record at least five days notice in writing of the application, and the young person and the person or body that has possession have had a reasonable opportunity to be heard.

(4) *Where notice not required* — A youth justice court judge may waive the requirement in subsection (3) to give notice to a young person when the judge is of the opinion that

(*a*) to insist on the giving of the notice would frustrate the application; or
(*b*) reasonable efforts have not been successful in finding the young person.

(5) *Use of record* — In any order under subsection (1), the youth justice court judge shall set out the purposes for which the record may be used.

(6) *Disclosure for research or statistical purposes* — When access to a record is given to any person under paragraph (1)(*b*), that person may subsequently disclose information contained in the record, but shall not disclose the information in any form that would reasonably be expected to identify the young person to whom it relates.

COMMENTARY

Legal Implications

This section incorporates and adds to section 45.1 of the *Young Offenders Act*. The general rules that set out the time periods for gaining access to various youth records are set out in section 119(2) of this legislation; however, this section permits an application to be made to a youth court judge to make an order that would permit access to youth records after the time periods in section 119(2) have expired.

When the judge makes an order permitting access, the purpose for which the record may be used is limited. One of the permitted categories for the release of a record under this section is for research and statistical purposes. Another permitted purpose is the investigation of offences against a young person while he or she is, or was, serving a sentence.

Notice of an application to gain access to a record under this section requires five days' notice to the young person and to the person or body holding the record unless the youth court judge orders otherwise.

124. *Access to record by young person* — **A young person to whom a record relates and his or her counsel may have access to the record at any time.**

COMMENTARY

Legal Implications

This new section makes it clear that a young person and his or her counsel may have access to his or her record at any time.

DISCLOSURE OF INFORMATION IN A RECORD

125. (1) *Disclosure by peace officer during investigation* — **A peace officer may disclose to any person any information in a record kept under section 114 (court records) or 115 (police records) that it is necessary to disclose in the conduct of the investigation of an offence.**

(2) *Disclosure by Attorney General* — **The Attorney General may, in the course of a proceeding under this Act or any other Act of Parliament, disclose the following information in a record kept under section 114 (court reports) or 115 (police records):**

- **(a) to a person who is a co-accused with the young person in respect of the offence for which the record is kept, any information contained in the record; and**
- **(b) to an accused in a proceeding, if the record is in respect of a witness in the proceeding, information that identifies the witness as a young person who has been dealt with under this Act.**

(3) *Information that may be disclosed to a foreign state* — The Attorney General or a peace officer may disclose to the Minister of Justice of Canada information in a record that is kept under section 114 (court records) or 115 (police records) to the extent that it is necessary to deal with a request to or by a foreign state under the *Mutual Legal Assistance in Criminal Matters Act*, or for the purposes of any extradition matter under the *Extradition Act*. The Minister of Justice of Canada may disclose the information to the foreign state in respect of which the request was made, or to which the extradition matter relates, as the case may be.

(4) *Disclosure to insurance company* — A peace officer may disclose to an insurance company information in a record that is kept under section 114 (court records) or 115 (police records) for the purpose of investigating a claim arising out of an offence committed or alleged to have been committed by the young person to whom the record relates.

(5) *Preparation of reports* — The provincial director or a youth worker may disclose information contained in a record if the disclosure is necessary for procuring information that relates to the preparation of a report required by this Act.

(6) *Schools and others* — The provincial director, a youth worker, the Attorney General, a peace officer or any other person engaged in the provision of services to young persons may disclose to any professional or other person engaged in the supervision or care of a young person — including a representative of any school board or school or any other educational or training institution — any information contained in a record kept under sections 114 to 116 if the disclosure is necessary

   (*a*) to ensure compliance by the young person with an authorization under section 91 or an order of the youth justice court;
   (*b*) to ensure the safety of staff, students or other persons; or
   (*c*) to facilitate the rehabilitation of the young person.

(7) *Information to be kept separate* — A person to whom information is disclosed under subsection (6) shall

   (*a*) keep the information separate from any other record of the young person to whom the information relates;
   (*b*) ensure that no other person has access to the information except if authorized under this Act, or if necessary for the purposes of subsection (6); and
   (*c*) destroy their copy of the record when the information is no longer required for the purpose for which it was disclosed.

(8) *Time limit* — No information may be disclosed under this section after the end of the applicable period set out in subsection 119(2) (period of access to records).

S. 126 A Guide to the Youth Criminal Justice Act

COMMENTARY

Legal Implications

A list of specific purposes for which records may be released is set out in this section to assist in administering justice in the most general sense. The purposes are as follows:

- the peace officer may disclose information in the conduct of an investigation of an offence, or to an insurance company investigating a claim;
- the Attorney General may disclose information to a co-accused and also to an accused if the youth record is in respect of a witness;
- the Minister of Justice may release information to a foreign state in order to deal with a request under the *Mutual Legal Assistance in Criminal Matters Act*, or for the purposes of any extradition under provisions of the *Extradition Act*;
- the provincial director may disclose information as necessary in order to prepare a report required by this Act;
- the information may be released to schools and school boards in order to ensure compliance with an order, to ensure the safety of students and staff and to facilitate the rehabilitation of the young person.

Any information that is released under this section must be kept separate from other records, have limited access and be destroyed when no longer required for the purpose it was disclosed. The time periods set out in section 119(2) set the ceiling for the retention of records disclosed under this section, and no disclosure may take place after those time periods have passed except as otherwise permitted by this Act.

Operational Implications

The disclosure of information on a young person may be verbal or in writing. Individuals authorized to receive information are subject to the confidentiality provisions of the legislation. Verbal information should not be disclosed in a public place or where individuals not entitled to the information could overhear. Many probation offices have developed protocols to deal with disclosures to schools and to other agencies assisting in the administration of a sentence, and this ensures that disclosure rules are followed.

126. *Records in the custody, etc., of archivists* — **When records originally kept under sections 114 to 116 are under the custody or control of the Librarian and Archivist of Canada or the archivist for any province, that person may disclose any information contained in the records to any other person if**

> **(a) a youth justice court judge is satisfied that the disclosure is desirable in the public interest for research or statistical purposes; and**

(*b*) the person to whom the information is disclosed undertakes not to disclose the information in any form that could reasonably be expected to identify the young person to whom it relates.

[S.C. 2004, c. 11, s. 48]

COMMENTARY

Legal Implications

This section replicates section 45.2 of the *Young Offenders Act*, giving the youth justice court, rather than the Attorney General, or agent, as was the case under the *Young Offenders Act*, authority to order access to records kept by the Librarian and Archivist of Canada, and by the provincial archivist, for research and statistical purposes, provided it is in the public interest. The person to whom this information is disclosed must give an undertaking not to disclose any information that could reasonably be expected to identify the young person. This section recognizes the importance of maintaining archival records and, at the same time, balancing the privacy of the young person with public interest.

127. (1) *Disclosure with court order* — **The youth justice court may, on the application of the provincial director, the Attorney General or a peace officer, make an order permitting the applicant to disclose to the person or persons specified by the court any information about a young person that is specified, if the court is satisfied that the disclosure is necessary, having regard to the following circumstances:**

(*a*) **the young person has been found guilty of an offence involving serious personal injury;**
(*b*) **the young person poses a risk of serious harm to persons; and**
(*c*) **the disclosure of the information is relevant to the avoidance of that risk.**

(2) *Opportunity to be heard* — **Subject to subsection (3), before making an order under subsection (1), the youth justice court shall give the young person, a parent of the young person and the Attorney General an opportunity to be heard.**

(3) *Ex parte application* — **An application under subsection (1) may be made *ex parte* by the Attorney General where the youth justice court is satisfied that reasonable efforts have been made to locate the young person and that those efforts have not been successful.**

(4) *Time limit* — **No information may be disclosed under subsection (1) after the end of the applicable period set out in subsection 119(2) (period of access to records).**

COMMENTARY

Legal Implications

This section was originally contained in section 38(1.5)-(1.8) of the *Young Offenders Act*, and it permits disclosure of information to persons specified by the court when the young person has been convicted of a serious personal injury offence, and there is a risk of harm to someone. The release of the information should be for the purpose of reducing the risk of harm.

The Attorney General, the parent(s) of the young person, and the young person himself or herself, if the young person can be located, must be given the chance to be heard on the application, which should be made within the time limits set out in section 119(2), in order to release this information.

DISPOSITION OR DESTRUCTION OF RECORDS AND PROHIBITION ON USE AND DISCLOSURE

128. (1) *Effect of end of access periods* — **Subject to sections 123, 124 and 126, after the end of the applicable period set out in section 119 or 120 no record kept under sections 114 to 116 may be used for any purpose that would identify the young person to whom the record relates as a young person dealt with under this Act or the *Young Offenders Act*, chapter Y-1 of the Revised Statutes of Canada, 1985.**

(2) *Disposal of records* — **Subject to paragraph 125(7)(c), any record kept under sections 114 to 116, other than a record kept under subsection 115(3), may, in the discretion of the person or body keeping the record, be destroyed or transmitted to the Librarian and Archivist of Canada or the archivist for any province, at any time before or after the end of the applicable period set out in section 119.**

(3) *Disposal of R.C.M.P. records* — **All records kept under subsection 115(3) shall be destroyed or, if the Librarian and Archivist of Canada requires it, transmitted to the Librarian and Archivist, at the end of the applicable period set out in section 119 or 120.**

(4) *Purging CPIC* — **The Commissioner of the Royal Canadian Mounted Police shall remove a record from the automated criminal conviction records retrieval system maintained by the Royal Canadian Mounted Police at the end of the applicable period referred to in section 119; however, information relating to a prohibition order made under an Act of Parliament or the legislature of a province shall be removed only at the end of the period for which the order is in force.**

(5) *Exception* — **Despite subsections (1), (2) and (4), an entry that is contained in a system maintained by the Royal Canadian Mounted Police to match crime scene information and that relates to an offence committed or alleged to have been committed by a young person shall be dealt with in the same manner as information that relates to an offence committed by an**

adult for which a pardon granted under the *Criminal Records Act* is in effect.

(6) *Authority to inspect* — The Librarian and Archivist of Canada may, at any time, inspect records kept under sections 114 to 116 that are under the control of a government institution as defined in section 2 of the *Library and Archives of Canada Act*, and the archivist for a province may at any time inspect any records kept under those sections that the archivist is authorized to inspect under any Act of the legislature of the province.

(7) *Definition of "destroy"* — For the purposes of subsections (2) and (3), "destroy", in respect of a record, means

- (*a*) to shred, burn or otherwise physically destroy the record, in the case of a record other than a record in electronic form; and
- (*b*) to delete, write over or otherwise render the record inaccessible, in the case of a record in electronic form.

[S.C. 2004, c. 11, s. 49]

COMMENTARY

Legal Implications

This part of the Act sets out rules for the keeping and sharing of records, including time periods for giving access to these records, and clarifies the definition of "destroy". After the time periods for sharing and giving access have expired, records may be destroyed. In the case of the records kept by the RCMP in the central repository, authorized by section 115(3), they will be destroyed or transferred to the Librarian and Archivist of Canada.

This section makes a number of references to the Librarian and Archivist of Canada and to the archivist for a province. In addition to this Act, there is federal and provincial legislation that applies to the handling of records. One specific provision permits the use of records that are kept by the RCMP to match crime scene information to be used after the time periods for access have passed. When a young person is alleged to have committed an offence, access to the information held by the RCMP for the purpose of matching a crime scene will be the same as for adults who have been granted a pardon.

129. *No subsequent disclosure* — No person who is given access to a record or to whom information is disclosed under this Act shall disclose that information to any other person unless the disclosure is authorized under this Act.

COMMENTARY

Legal Implications

When someone has been given access to a youth record under the provisions of this Act, there is to be no further disclosure of the information received unless this Act specifically authorizes the disclosure. This makes it clear that the rules limiting access to information still apply to records that have been released under the Act.

PART 7   GENERAL PROVISIONS

INTRODUCTION

This part of the *Youth Criminal Justice Act* contains the necessary provisions for the day-to-day administration of justice. Most of these provisions were in the *Young Offenders Act* and have been clarified or expanded in this legislation. One significant change is in the provision for admissibility of statements where a young person can waive his or her right to consult by audiotape, as well as by the previous methods of videotape, or in writing, as was the case in the *Young Offenders Act*.

DISQUALIFICATION OF JUDGE

130. (1) *Disqualification of judge* — **Subject to subsection (2), a youth justice court judge who, prior to an adjudication in respect of a young person charged with an offence, examines a pre-sentence report made in respect of the young person in connection with that offence or has, after a guilty plea or a finding of guilt, heard submissions as to sentence and then there has been a change of plea, shall not in any capacity conduct or continue the trial of the young person for the offence and shall transfer the case to another judge to be dealt with according to law.**

(2) *Exception* — **A youth justice court judge may, in the circumstances referred to in subsection (1), with the consent of the young person and the prosecutor, conduct or continue the trial of the young person if the judge is satisfied that he or she has not been predisposed by a guilty plea or finding of guilt, or by information contained in the pre-sentence report or submissions as to sentence.**

COMMENTARY

Legal Implications

The principle that justice should not only be done but appear to be done is reflected in this section, which describes when a judge should disqualify himself or herself and transfer the case to another judge. This principle was contained in section 15 of the *Young Offenders Act* and is expanded upon in this section. When a judge has heard information relating to a sentence and to a young person's confirmation of guilt, and then the young person changes his or her plea, it may be perceived that the judge could be predisposed to a finding of guilt if a trial takes place. In a case where this information has been received, the judge may continue to hear the case if the parties consent, and if the judge is satisfied that they are not predisposed to finding the young person guilty.

SUBSTITUTION OF JUDGE

131. (1) *Powers of substitute youth justice court judge* — **A youth justice court judge who acts in the place of another youth justice court judge under subsection 669.2(1) (continuation of proceedings) of the** *Criminal Code* **shall**

- (*a*) **if an adjudication has been made, proceed to sentence the young person or make the order that, in the circumstances, is authorized by law; or**
- (*b*) **if no adjudication has been made, recommence the trial as if no evidence had been taken.**

(2) *Transcript of evidence already given* — **A youth justice court judge who recommences a trial under paragraph (1)(*b*) may, if the parties consent, admit into evidence a transcript of any evidence already given in the case.**

COMMENTARY

Legal Implications

This section, which is reproduced from section 64 of the *Young Offenders Act*, describes how a judge is to proceed when he or she has replaced another judge. It is permissible for a judge, with the consent of the parties, to use a transcript from any of the proceedings that may have already taken place before the other judge. These provisions are intended to prevent a repeat of what has already taken place.

EXCLUSION FROM HEARING

132. (1) *Exclusion from hearing* — **Subject to subsection (2), a court or justice before whom proceedings are carried out under this Act may exclude any person from all or part of the proceedings if the court or justice considers that the person's presence is unnecessary to the conduct of the proceedings and the court or justice is of the opinion that**

- (*a*) **any evidence or information presented to the court or justice would be seriously injurious or seriously prejudicial to**
  - (i) **the young person who is being dealt with in the proceedings,**
  - (ii) **a child or young person who is a witness in the proceedings, or**

(iii) a child or young person who is aggrieved by or the victim of the offence charged in the proceedings; or
(b) it would be in the interest of public morals, the maintenance of order or the proper administration of justice to exclude any or all members of the public from the court room.

(2) *Exception* — Subject to section 650 (accused to be present) of the *Criminal Code* and except if it is necessary for the purposes of subsection 34(9) (nondisclosure of medical or psychological report) of this Act, a court or justice may not, under subsection (1), exclude from proceedings under this Act

(a) the prosecutor;
(b) the young person who is being dealt with in the proceedings, the counsel or a parent of the young person or any adult assisting the young person under subsection 25(7);
(c) the provincial director or his or her agent; or
(d) the youth worker to whom the young person's case has been assigned.

(3) *Exclusion after adjudication or during review* — A youth justice court, after it has found a young person guilty of an offence, or a youth justice court or a review board, during a review, may, in its discretion, exclude from the court or from a hearing of the review board any person other than the following, when it is being presented with information the knowledge of which might, in its opinion, be seriously injurious or seriously prejudicial to the young person:

(a) the young person or his or her counsel;
(b) the provincial director or his or her agent;
(c) the youth worker to whom the young person's case has been assigned; and
(d) the Attorney General.

(4) *Exception* — The exception set out in paragraph (3)(a) is subject to subsection 34(9) (nondisclosure of medical or psychological report) of this Act and section 650 (accused to be present) of the *Criminal Code*.

COMMENTARY

Legal Implications

Judges are given the power to control the proceedings in order to ensure that justice is done. For example, judges have the power to exclude any person from the court for all or part of the proceedings. The guidelines set out in this section are the same as those that were in section 39 of the *Young Offenders Act*.

The general rule is that an accused has the right to be present for his or her trial and all proceedings related to the trial. Section 650 of the *Criminal Code*, which deals specifically with the accused being present for his or her trial and being excluded in certain limited circumstances, has been incorporated into this section of the *Youth Criminal Justice Act*.

It is also possible, where the court orders, for an accused to appear in court by way of closed circuit television or any other means that would permit simultaneous visual and oral communication. There are also rules relating to the exclusion of documents or reports that may be sensitive and may not be in the interest of the administration of justice.

Operational Implications

This section is carried over from the *Young Offenders Act* and, together with section 142(3) of the *Youth Criminal Justice Act*, compels the court to order the adherence to section 650 of the *Criminal Code* and the possible simultaneous use of visual and oral communication. Video remands already occur in some local regions. This section gives the authority to continue the use of video remands for young persons.

TRANSFER OF CHARGES

133. *Transfer of charges* — **Despite subsections 478(1) and (3) of the *Criminal Code*, a young person charged with an offence that is alleged to have been committed in one province may, if the Attorney General of the province consents, appear before a youth justice court of any other province and**

- **(*a*) if the young person pleads guilty to that offence and the youth justice court is satisfied that the facts support the charge, the court shall find the young person guilty of the offence alleged in the information or indictment; and**
- **(*b*) if the young person pleads not guilty to that offence, or pleads guilty but the court is not satisfied that the facts support the charge, the young person shall, if he or she was detained in custody prior to the appearance, be returned to custody and dealt with according to law.**

COMMENTARY

Legal Implications

Trials and criminal proceedings usually take place in the area where the offence occurred. According to the Act, and as was the case under section 18 of the *Young Offenders Act*, it is possible for a young person to ask the court in a province or territory to hear a case that arose from an alleged offence in another province or territory. The usual practice for the young person is to advise the Attorney General in the province where he or she would like the case to proceed, and that he or she is prepared to plead guilty to an offence, or offences, that took place in another province. The charge may then be transferred with the consent of the Attorney General, a guilty plea entered and sentence imposed.

Operational Implications

This provision lends some convenience to the parties, and avoids the necessity of an accused having multiple trials in more than one province. For example, a young person may live in Ontario and have charges in Ontario while at the same time have charges in Quebec. When this is the case, it is possible for all the charges to be dealt with in the province where the young person lives, and thus avoid the inconvenience and expense of two separate trials in two different provinces.

FORFEITURE OF RECOGNIZANCES

134. *Applications for forfeiture of recognizances* — **Applications for the forfeiture of recognizances of young persons shall be made to the youth justice court.**

COMMENTARY

Legal Implications

This section is the same as section 48 of the *Young Offenders Act* and clarifies that an application for the forfeiture of a recognizance is made to the youth justice court.

135. (1) *Proceedings in case of default* — **When a recognizance binding a young person has been endorsed with a certificate under subsection 770(1) of the *Criminal Code*, a youth justice court judge shall**

- (*a*) **on the request of the Attorney General, fix a time and place for the hearing of an application for the forfeiture of the recognizance; and**
- (*b*) **after fixing a time and place for the hearing, cause to be sent by confirmed delivery service, not less than ten days before the time so fixed, to each principal and surety named in the recognizance, directed to his or her latest known address, a notice requiring him or her to appear at the time and place fixed by the judge to show cause why the recognizance should not be forfeited.**

(2) *Order for forfeiture of recognizance* — **When subsection (1) is complied with, the youth justice court judge may, after giving the parties an opportunity to be heard, in his or her discretion grant or refuse the application and make any order with respect to the forfeiture of the recognizance that he or she considers proper.**

(3) *Judgment debtors of the Crown* — If, under subsection (2), a youth justice court judge orders forfeiture of a recognizance, the principal and his or her sureties become judgment debtors of the Crown, each in the amount that the judge orders him or her to pay.

(4) *Order may be filed* — An order made under subsection (2) may be filed with the clerk of the superior court or, in the province of Quebec, the prothonotary and, if an order is filed, the clerk or the prothonotary shall issue a writ of *fieri facias* in Form 34 set out in the *Criminal Code* and deliver it to the sheriff of each of the territorial divisions in which any of the principal and his or her sureties resides, carries on business or has property.

(5) *If a deposit has been made* — If a deposit has been made by a person against whom an order for forfeiture of a recognizance has been made, no writ of *fieri facias* shall issue, but the amount of the deposit shall be transferred by the person who has custody of it to the person who is entitled by law to receive it.

(6) *Subsections 770(2) and (4) of Criminal Code do not apply* — Subsections 770(2) (transmission of recognizance) and (4) (transmission of deposit) of the *Criminal Code* do not apply in respect of proceedings under this Act.

(7) *Sections 772 and 773 of Criminal Code apply* — Sections 772 (levy under writ) and 773 (committal when writ not satisfied) of the *Criminal Code* apply in respect of writs of *fieri facias* issued under this section as if they were issued under section 771 (proceedings in case of default) of that Act.

COMMENTARY

Legal Implications

This section, like section 49 of the *Young Offenders Act*, sets out the details for an application for a forfeiture of a recognizance, the provisions of the *Criminal Code* that do, and do not, apply and the mechanism for collecting the funds. This provision is not likely to be used against a young person, but it is necessary for rare cases.

OFFENCES AND PUNISHMENT

COMMENTARY

Legal Implications

These sections (sections 136-139) deal with offences that were scattered throughout sections 50, 26, 38(2), 38(3), 46(4), 7.2 and 36(4) of the *Young Offenders Act* and have been brought together in the *Youth Criminal Justice Act*.

These sections have a transitional aspect that provides for offences that were committed after this Act came into force and the *Young Offenders Act* was repealed. This transitional aspect covers events that have arisen out of a disposition imposed, records created, proceedings taken or other obligations created under the *Young Offenders Act*. There is also a new offence of failing or refusing to pay a victim fine surcharge if one is ordered.

136. (1) *Inducing a young person, etc.* — **Every person who**

(a) **induces or assists a young person to leave unlawfully a place of custody or other place in which the young person has been placed in accordance with a youth sentence or a disposition imposed under the** *Young Offenders Act***, chapter Y-1 of the Revised Statutes of Canada, 1985,**

(b) **unlawfully removes a young person from a place referred to in paragraph (a),**

(c) **knowingly harbours or conceals a young person who has unlawfully left a place referred to in paragraph (a),**

(d) **wilfully induces or assists a young person to breach or disobey a term or condition of a youth sentence or other order of the youth justice court, or a term or condition of a disposition or other order under the** *Young Offenders Act***, chapter Y-1 of the Revised Statutes of Canada, 1985, or**

(e) **wilfully prevents or interferes with the performance by a young person of a term or condition of a youth sentence or other order of the youth justice court, or a term or condition of a disposition or other order under the** *Young Offenders Act***, chapter Y-1 of the Revised Statutes of Canada, 1985,**

is guilty of an indictable offence and liable to imprisonment for a term not exceeding two years or is guilty of an offence punishable on summary conviction.

(2) *Absolute jurisdiction of provincial court judge* — **The jurisdiction of a provincial court judge to try an adult charged with an indictable offence under this section is absolute and does not depend on the consent of the accused.**

COMMENTARY

Legal Implications

This section expands section 50 of the *Young Offenders Act* and classifies a number of offences, all of which relate to people interfering with the justice system. This interference involves encouraging a young person to leave a place ordered by the court, removing the young person from that place, hiding a young person the police are looking for or encouraging or preventing non-compliance with a court order. There is also a provision to clarify that when an adult is charged with an offence under this Act, the provincial court judge has absolute jurisdiction.

137. *Failure to comply with sentence or disposition* — **Every person who is subject to a youth sentence imposed under any of paragraphs 42(2)(*c*) to (*m*) or (*s*) of this Act, to a victim fine surcharge ordered under subsection 53(2) of this Act or to a disposition made under any of paragraphs 20(1)(*a*.1) to (*g*), (*j*) or (*l*) of the** *Young Offenders Act***, chapter Y-1 of the Revised Statutes of Canada, 1985, and who wilfully fails or refuses to comply with that sentence, surcharge or disposition is guilty of an offence punishable on summary conviction.**

COMMENTARY

Legal Implications

This section, which has classified an offence for a person who fails or refuses to comply with a sentence imposed under this Act, expands on section 26, willful failure to comply, of the *Young Offenders Act* to add a transitional provision to cover dispositions imposed under the *Young Offenders Act*. This provision is necessary because the *Youth Criminal Justice Act* repealed the *Young Offenders Act* on April 1, 2003, and many dispositions were not completed. Added to this section is the offence of failing to pay a victim fine surcharge.

It is important to note that this section is applicable only to community-based sentences. A young person cannot be charged for failing to comply with a condition of the community portion of a custody sentence, including a deferred custody and supervision order.

138. (1) *Offences* — **Every person who contravenes subsection 110(1) (identity of offender not to be published), 111(1) (identity of victim or witness not to be published), 118(1) (no access to records unless authorized) or 128(3) (disposal of R.C.M.P. records) or section 129 (no subsequent disclosure) of this Act, or subsection 38(1) (identity not to be published), (1.12) (no subsequent disclosure), (1.14) (no subsequent disclosure by school) or (1.15) (information to be kept separate), 45(2) (destruction of records) or 46(1) (prohibition against disclosure) of the** *Young Offenders Act***, chapter Y-1 of the Revised Statutes of Canada, 1985,**

    (*a*) **is guilty of an indictable offence and liable to imprisonment for a term not exceeding two years; or**

    (*b*) **is guilty of an offence punishable on summary conviction.**

(2) *Provincial court judge has absolute jurisdiction on indictment* — **The jurisdiction of a provincial court judge to try an adult charged with an offence under paragraph (1)(*a*) is absolute and does not depend on the consent of the accused.**

COMMENTARY

Legal Implications

This section incorporates sections 38(2), 45(2) and 46(4) from the *Young Offenders Act* and includes offences for breaches of certain provisions that deal with records: sharing of records, keeping of records, subsequent disclosures of information received and publication. This section expands on and clarifies offences relating to records. The intent of these provisions is to balance the rehabilitation of the young person with the right of the public to have access to information that identifies the young person as having been dealt with under the *Youth Criminal Justice Act*. In addition, adults may be prosecuted in adult provincial court for an offence under this section.

139. (1) *Offence and punishment* — Every person who wilfully fails to comply with section 30 (designated place of temporary detention), or with an undertaking entered into under subsection 31(3) (condition of placement),

  (a) is guilty of an indictable offence and liable to imprisonment for a term not exceeding two years; or
  (b) is guilty of an offence punishable on summary conviction.

(2) *Offence and punishment* — Every person who wilfully fails to comply with section 7 (designated place of temporary detention) of the *Young Offenders Act*, chapter Y-1 of the Revised Statutes of Canada, 1985, or with an undertaking entered into under subsection 7.1(2) (condition of placement) of that Act is guilty of an offence punishable on summary conviction.

(3) *Punishment* — Any person who uses or authorizes the use of an application form in contravention of subsection 82(3) (application for employment) is guilty of an offence punishable on summary conviction.

COMMENTARY

Legal Implications

This section deals with three offences that appeared in the *Young Offenders Act* in sections 7.2 and 36(4). These sections have been brought together to make the enforcement aspect of the *Youth Criminal Justice Act* easier to follow.

An important change from the *Young Offenders Act* is the increase in the penalty for a violation of the undertaking given to the court by a person who has agreed to be responsible for a young person released from detention to his or her care. Under the *Young Offenders Act*, the offence could be prosecuted by summary conviction only, whereas the *Youth Criminal Justice Act* makes it possible for the prosecution to proceed by indictment, which could lead to a penalty of up to two years, which is far more onerous than the previous six months' maximum summary conviction. This same change in penalty also applies to any violation of the temporary placement provisions.

Operational Implications

There were very few charges brought before the court under sections 7.2 and 36(4) of the *Young Offenders Act* and likely will be very few under this legislation. The interesting part of this section is the possibility of charges that may arise out of an application for employment with specified employers that ask a young person to disclose a youth record.

APPLICATION OF CRIMINAL CODE

140. *Application of Criminal Code* — **Except to the extent that it is inconsistent with or excluded by this Act, the provisions of the *Criminal Code* apply, with any modifications that the circumstances require, in respect of offences alleged to have been committed by young persons.**

COMMENTARY

Legal Implications

This section, taken from section 51 of the *Young Offenders Act*, states that the general rule is that the *Criminal Code* applies to proceedings against young persons unless there is an inconsistency with the *Youth Criminal Justice Act*.

141. (1) *Sections of Criminal Code applicable* — **Except to the extent that they are inconsistent with or excluded by this Act, section 16 (defence of mental disorder) and Part XX.1 (mental disorder) of the *Criminal Code*, except sections 672.65 (capping of offences) and 672.66 (hearing application procedures), apply, with any modifications that the circumstances require, in respect of proceedings under this Act in relation to offences alleged to have been committed by young persons.**

(2) *Notice and copies to counsel and parents* — **For the purposes of subsection (1),**

- (*a*) wherever in Part XX.1 (mental disorder) of the *Criminal Code* a reference is made to a copy to be sent or otherwise given to an accused or a party to the proceedings, the reference shall be read as including a reference to a copy to be sent or otherwise given to
  - (i) any counsel representing the young person,
  - (ii) a parent of the young person who is in attendance at the proceedings against the young person, and
  - (iii) a parent of the young person not in attendance at the proceedings who is, in the opinion of the youth justice court or Review Board, taking an active interest in the proceedings; and

(b) wherever in Part XX.1 (mental disorder) of the *Criminal Code* a reference is made to notice to be given to an accused or a party to proceedings, the reference shall be read as including a reference to notice to be given to a parent of the young person and any counsel representing the young person.

(3) *Proceedings not invalid* — Subject to subsection (4), failure to give a notice referred to in paragraph (2)(b) to a parent of a young person does not affect the validity of proceedings under this Act.

(4) *Exception* — Failure to give a notice referred to in paragraph (2)(b) to a parent of a young person in any case renders invalid any subsequent proceedings under this Act relating to the case unless

    (a) a parent of the young person attends at the court or Review Board with the young person; or
    (b) a youth justice court judge or Review Board before whom proceedings are held against the young person
        (i) adjourns the proceedings and orders that the notice be given in the manner and to the persons that the judge or Review Board directs, or
        (ii) dispenses with the notice if the youth justice court or Review Board is of the opinion that, having regard to the circumstances, the notice may be dispensed with.

(5) *No hospital order assessments* — A youth justice court may not make an order under section 672.11 (assessment order) of the *Criminal Code* in respect of a young person for the purpose of assisting in the determination of a matter mentioned in paragraph (e) of that section.

(6) *Considerations of court or Review Board making a disposition* — Before making or reviewing a disposition in respect of a young person under Part XX.1 (mental disorder) of the *Criminal Code*, a youth justice court or Review Board shall consider the age and special needs of the young person and any representations or submissions made by a parent of the young person.

(7) *Cap applicable to young persons* — Subject to subsection (9), for the purpose of applying subsection 672.64(3) (cap for various offences) of the *Criminal Code* to proceedings under this Act in relation to an offence alleged to have been committed by a young person, the applicable cap shall be the maximum period during which the young person would be subject to a youth sentence by the youth justice court if found guilty of the offence.

(8) *Application to increase cap of unfit young person subject to adult sentence* — If a young person is charged with a presumptive offence or notice has been given under subsection 64(2) (intention to seek adult sentence), and the young person is found unfit to stand trial, the Attorney

General may apply to the court to increase the cap that will apply to the young person.

(9) *Consideration of youth justice court for increase in cap* — The youth justice court, after giving the Attorney General and the counsel and a parent of the young person in respect of whom subsection (8) applies an opportunity to be heard, shall take into consideration

- (*a*) the seriousness and circumstances of the alleged offence,
- (*b*) the age, maturity, character and background of the young person and any previous criminal record,
- (*c*) the likelihood that the young person will cause significant harm to any person if released on expiry of the cap that applies to the young person under subsection (7), and
- (*d*) the respective caps that would apply to the young person under this Act and under the *Criminal Code*.

If the court is satisfied that it would make an order under subsection 64(5) (application for adult sentence unopposed) or 70(2) (no application by young person to avoid adult sentence) or paragraph 72(1)(*b*) (imposition of adult sentence) if the young person were fit to stand trial, it shall apply to the young person the cap that would apply to an adult for the same offence.

(10) *Prima facie case to be made every year* — For the purpose of applying subsection 672.33(1) (fitness to stand trial) of the *Criminal Code* to proceedings under this Act in relation to an offence alleged to have been committed by a young person, wherever in that subsection a reference is made to two years, there shall be substituted a reference to one year.

(11) *Designation of hospitals for young persons* — A reference in Part XX.1 (mental disorder) of the *Criminal Code* to a hospital in a province shall be construed as a reference to a hospital designated by the Minister of Health for the province for the custody, treatment or assessment of young persons.

(12) *Definition of "Review Board"* — In this section, "Review Board" has the meaning assigned by section 672.1 of the *Criminal Code*.

COMMENTARY

Legal Implications

This section deals with the special procedures that apply in the case of a young person who suffers from a mental disorder. It expands on section 13.2 of the *Young Offenders Act* with an adjustment for the new adult sentencing procedure and a clarification that the reference to a review board is the review board under the *Criminal Code*.

142. (1) *Part XXVII and summary conviction trial provisions of Criminal Code to apply* — Subject to this section and except to the extent that they are inconsistent with this Act, the provisions of Part XXVII (summary conviction offences) of the *Criminal Code*, and any other provisions of that Act that apply in respect of summary conviction offences and relate to trial proceedings, apply to proceedings under this Act

    (*a*) in respect of an order under section 810 (recognizance — fear of injury or damage), 810.01 (recognizance — fear of criminal organization offence) or 810.2 (recognizance — fear of serious personal injury offence) of that Act or an offence under section 811 (breach of recognizance) of that Act;

    (*b*) in respect of a summary conviction offence; and

    (*c*) in respect of an indictable offence as if it were defined in the enactment creating it as a summary conviction offence.

(2) *Indictable offences* — For greater certainty and despite subsection (1) or any other provision of this Act, an indictable offence committed by a young person is, for the purposes of this Act or any other Act of Parliament, an indictable offence.

(3) *Attendance of young person* — Section 650 of the *Criminal Code* applies in respect of proceedings under this Act, whether the proceedings relate to an indictable offence or an offence punishable on summary conviction.

(4) *Limitation period* — In proceedings under this Act, subsection 786(2) of the *Criminal Code* does not apply in respect of an indictable offence.

(5) *Costs* — Section 809 of the *Criminal Code* does not apply in respect of proceedings under this Act.

COMMENTARY

Legal Implications

This section adopts the provisions of Part XXVII and other provisions set out in the *Criminal Code* that apply to summary conviction proceedings. These provisions apply in the youth justice court not only to summary conviction offences but also to indictable offences as well as certain peace bond applications, the reference to which has been added to the *Youth Criminal Justice Act*. The section also clarifies that certain sections of the *Criminal Code* apply or are excluded from application.

Procedure

143. *Counts charged in information* — Indictable offences and offences punishable on summary conviction may under this Act be charged in the same information or indictment and tried jointly.

COMMENTARY

Legal Implications

This is a simple and important section that was contained in section 53 of the *Young Offenders Act* and confirms that summary convictions and indictable offences may be charged together in the same information (the document that initiates criminal proceedings) and may be dealt with at the same trial.

144. (1) *Issue of subpoena* — If a person is required to attend to give evidence before a youth justice court, the subpoena directed to that person may be issued by a youth justice court judge, whether or not the person whose attendance is required is within the same province as the youth justice court.

(2) *Service of subpoena* — A subpoena issued by a youth justice court and directed to a person who is not within the same province as the youth justice court shall be served personally on the person to whom it is directed.

COMMENTARY

Legal Implications

This procedural section, formerly section 54 of the *Young Offenders Act*, gives the youth justice court the authority to issue subpoenas to require a person to appear before the court. The subpoena may be issued for someone within or outside the province.

145. *Warrant* — A warrant issued by a youth justice court may be executed anywhere in Canada.

COMMENTARY

Legal Implications

This section authorizes warrants to be issued by the youth justice court for execution anywhere in Canada, as was the case in section 55 of the *Young Offenders Act*. Like the previous few sections, this gives the youth justice court the power to control the proceedings.

EVIDENCE

146. (1) *General law on admissibility of statements to apply* — Subject to this section, the law relating to the admissibility of statements made by persons accused of committing offences applies in respect of young persons.

(2) *When statements are admissible* — No oral or written statement made by a young person who is less than eighteen years old, to a peace officer or to any other person who is, in law, a person in authority, on the arrest or detention of the young person or in circumstances where the peace officer or other person has reasonable grounds for believing that the young person has committed an offence is admissible against the young person unless

- (a) the statement was voluntary;
- (b) the person to whom the statement was made has, before the statement was made, clearly explained to the young person, in language appropriate to his or her age and understanding, that
  - (i) the young person is under no obligation to make a statement,
  - (ii) any statement made by the young person may be used as evidence in proceedings against him or her,
  - (iii) the young person has the right to consult counsel and a parent or other person in accordance with paragraph (c), and
  - (iv) any statement made by the young person is required to be made in the presence of counsel and any other person consulted in accordance with paragraph (c), if any, unless the young person desires otherwise;
- (c) the young person has, before the statement was made, been given a reasonable opportunity to consult
  - (i) with counsel, and
  - (ii) with a parent or, in the absence of a parent, an adult relative or, in the absence of a parent and an adult relative, any other appropriate adult chosen by the young person, as long as that person is not a co-accused, or under investigation, in respect of the same offence; and
- (d) if the young person consults a person in accordance with paragraph (c), the young person has been given a reasonable opportunity to make the statement in the presence of that person.

(3) *Exception in certain cases for oral statements* — The requirements set out in paragraphs (2)(b) to (d) do not apply in respect of oral statements if they are made spontaneously by the young person to a peace officer or other person in authority before that person has had a reasonable opportunity to comply with those requirements.

(4) *Waiver of right to consult* — A young person may waive the rights under paragraph (2)(c) or (d) but any such waiver

(a) must be recorded on video tape or audio tape; or
(b) must be in writing and contain a statement signed by the young person that he or she has been informed of the right being waived.

(5) *Waiver of right to consult* — When a waiver of rights under paragraph (2)(c) or (d) is not made in accordance with subsection (4) owing to a technical irregularity, the youth justice court may determine that the waiver is valid if it is satisfied that the young person was informed of his or her rights, and voluntarily waived them.

(6) *Admissibility of statements* — When there has been a technical irregularity in complying with paragraphs (2)(b) to (d), the youth justice court may admit into evidence a statement referred to in subsection (2), if satisfied that the admission of the statement would not bring into disrepute the principle that young persons are entitled to enhanced procedural protection to ensure that they are treated fairly and their rights are protected.

(7) *Statements made under duress are inadmissible* — A youth justice court judge may rule inadmissible in any proceedings under this Act a statement made by the young person in respect of whom the proceedings are taken if the young person satisfies the judge that the statement was made under duress imposed by any person who is not, in law, a person in authority.

(8) *Misrepresentation of age* — A youth justice court judge may in any proceedings under this Act rule admissible any statement or waiver by a young person if, at the time of the making of the statement or waiver,

(a) the young person held himself or herself to be eighteen years old or older;
(b) the person to whom the statement or waiver was made conducted reasonable inquiries as to the age of the young person and had reasonable grounds for believing that the young person was eighteen years old or older; and
(c) in all other circumstances the statement or waiver would otherwise be admissible.

(9) *Parent, etc., not a person in authority* — For the purpose of this section, a person consulted under paragraph (2)(c) is, in the absence of evidence to the contrary, deemed not to be a person in authority.

COMMENTARY

Legal Implications

This is one of the more important procedural changes in this legislation. This section builds on section 56 of the *Young Offenders Act* to deal with young persons giving statements and with the rules that guide that process.

The legislation recognizes that young persons are not adults; therefore, additional protections such as the right to consult a parent or other appropriate adult, and the right to have him or her present during police questioning, are given to young persons when the police take a statement from a young person (see Appendices, Form 9.1). The most significant changes from the *Young Offenders Act* expand the manner in which a young person can waive his or her rights and provide for the admission of a statement when there has been a breach of the rights of a young person.

The young person may now waive his or her rights by audiotape, as well as videotape, or in writing, as was the case in the *Young Offenders Act*. A new provision allows a youth justice court to admit a statement if these methods of waiver have not been used because of a technical irregularity and if the court is satisfied that the young person actually waived his or her rights. The most significant change is the possibility of a statement being admitted if there has been a technical irregularity.

Operational Implications

Taking a young person's statement under the *Young Offenders Act* was always viewed as a complicated process from a police perspective. The new technical provisions in the *Youth Criminal Justice Act* will assist the police in taking a statement in a more efficient manner without the threat of a minor error, such as failing to initial a part of the statement form, derailing the process. However, the court will need to take precautions, particularly in the case of a breach of a young person's rights, to ensure that the error was only a technical irregularity. In *R. v. O.K.*, [2004] B.C.J. No. 1458, 2004 BCPC 210, the British Columbia Youth Court ruled that the young person's statement was inadmissible, since the police officer had informed the young person that he could speak to his lawyer but had not provided the opportunity.

The youth justice court should be convinced that admitting the statement would not bring into disrepute the principle that young persons are entitled to enhanced procedural protection to ensure that they are treated fairly and their rights are protected. This leaves open for debate issues such as who is an appropriate adult, or the police's exclusion of a parent who is the victim, or who is drunk or abusive.

147. (1) *Statements not admissible against young person* **— Subject to subsection (2), if a young person is assessed in accordance with an order made under subsection 34(1) (medical or psychological assessment), no statement or reference to a statement made by the young person during the course and for the purposes of the assessment to the person who conducts the assessment or to anyone acting under that person's direction is admissible in evidence, without the consent of the young person, in any proceeding before a court, tribunal, body or person with jurisdiction to compel the production of evidence.**

(2) *Exceptions* **— A statement referred to in subsection (1) is admissible in evidence for the purposes of**

(*a*) making a decision on an application heard under section 71 (hearing — adult sentences);
(*b*) determining whether the young person is unfit to stand trial;
(*c*) determining whether the balance of the mind of the young person was disturbed at the time of commission of the alleged offence, if the young person is a female person charged with an offence arising out of the death of her newly-born child;
(*d*) making or reviewing a sentence in respect of the young person;
(*e*) determining whether the young person was, at the time of the commission of an alleged offence, suffering from automatism or a mental disorder so as to be exempt from criminal responsibility by virtue of subsection 16(1) of the *Criminal Code*, if the accused puts his or her mental capacity for criminal intent into issue, or if the prosecutor raises the issue after verdict;
(*f*) challenging the credibility of a young person in any proceeding if the testimony of the young person is inconsistent in a material particular with a statement referred to in subsection (1) that the young person made previously;
(*g*) establishing the perjury of a young person who is charged with perjury in respect of a statement made in any proceeding;
(*h*) deciding an application for an order under subsection 104(1) (continuation of custody);
(*i*) setting the conditions under subsection 105(1) (conditional supervision);
(*j*) conducting a review under subsection 109(1) (review of decision); or
(*k*) deciding an application for a disclosure order under subsection 127(1) (information about a young person).

COMMENTARY

Legal Implications

This section also applies to statements made by young persons. The general rule, which was contained in section 13.1 of the *Young Offenders Act*, is that any statement made by a young person while being assessed (medically or psychologically) is not admissible without the consent of the young person.

Like any general rule, there are exceptions, which are also set out in this section. The statement made during an assessment is admissible for certain specified purposes, such as an adult sentence hearing or a hearing that relates to the mental state of the young person and his or her fitness to stand trial.

148. (1) *Testimony of a parent* — **In any proceedings under this Act, the testimony of a parent as to the age of a person of whom he or she is a parent is admissible as evidence of the age of that person.**

(2) *Evidence of age by certificate or record* — **In any proceedings under this Act,**

(*a*) a birth or baptismal certificate or a copy of it purporting to be certified under the hand of the person in whose custody those records are held is evidence of the age of the person named in the certificate or copy; and

(*b*) an entry or record of an incorporated society that has had the control or care of the person alleged to have committed the offence in respect of which the proceedings are taken at or about the time the person came to Canada is evidence of the age of that person, if the entry or record was made before the time when the offence is alleged to have been committed.

(3) *Other evidence* — In the absence of any certificate, copy, entry or record mentioned in subsection (2), or in corroboration of that certificate, copy, entry or record, the youth justice court may receive and act on any other information relating to age that it considers reliable.

(4) *When age may be inferred* — In any proceedings under this Act, the youth justice court may draw inferences as to the age of a person from the person's appearance or from statements made by the person in direct examination or cross-examination.

COMMENTARY

Legal Implications

In this section, which replaces section 57 of the *Young Offenders Act*, the youth justice court should be satisfied that a person was 12 to 17 years of age at the time of the offence in order for the youth justice court to have jurisdiction to hear the case (note the exception in section 16). This section provides the rules for proof of age of a young person.

149. (1) *Admissions* — **A party to any proceedings under this Act may admit any relevant fact or matter for the purpose of dispensing with proof of it, including any fact or matter the admissibility of which depends on a ruling of law or of mixed law and fact.**

(2) *Other party may adduce evidence* — **Nothing in this section precludes a party to a proceeding from adducing evidence to prove a fact or matter admitted by another party.**

COMMENTARY

Legal Implications

Courts base their decisions on facts presented before them, usually when evidence is called; however, the parties (usually the lawyers on behalf of their clients) may admit certain facts in order to shorten the proceedings. This section, like section 58 of the *Young Offenders Act*, authorizes the parties to admit facts in order to avoid the necessity of presenting evidence. Evidence may still be presented, but the ability to have facts admitted speeds up the process.

150. *Material evidence* **— Any evidence material to proceedings under this Act that would not but for this section be admissible in evidence may, with the consent of the parties to the proceedings and if the young person is represented by counsel, be given in such proceedings.**

COMMENTARY

Legal Implications

This provision was contained in section 59 of the *Young Offenders Act* and authorizes admitting into evidence, with the consent of a young person, who is represented by counsel, material evidence that would otherwise not be admissible.

Operational Implications

Some evidence is not admissible in court, even though it may be important to the case before the court. This section allows a court to receive important information that the rules would ordinarily not allow to be admitted except with the consent of a young person who has been advised by counsel.

151. *Evidence of a child or young person* **— The evidence of a child or a young person may be taken in proceedings under this Act only after the youth justice court judge or the justice in the proceedings has**

- **(*a*) if the witness is a child, instructed the child as to the duty to speak the truth and the consequences of failing to do so; and**
- **(*b*) if the witness is a young person and the judge or justice considers it necessary, instructed the young person as to the duty to speak the truth and the consequences of failing to do so.**

COMMENTARY

Legal Implications

This section, which was taken from section 60 of the *Young Offenders Act*, allows youth justice courts to be permitted to receive evidence from children under 12 years of age as well as from young persons 12 to 17 years of age, provided special precautions are taken. In the case of a child, the court should inform the child about the duty of telling the truth and the consequences of not doing so. In the case of a young person, it is the discretion of the court.

152. (1) *Proof of service* **— For the purposes of this Act, service of any document may be proved by oral evidence given under oath by, or by the**

affidavit or statutory declaration of, the person claiming to have personally served it or sent it by confirmed delivery service.

(2) *Proof of signature and official character unnecessary* — If proof of service of any document is offered by affidavit or statutory declaration, it is not necessary to prove the signature or official character of the person making or taking the affidavit or declaration, if the official character of that person appears on the face of the affidavit or declaration.

COMMENTARY

Legal Implications

This section, which was section 62 of the *Young Offenders Act*, sets out the rules to prove that a document has been properly served. Service of a document is a formal way of giving a person notice of some event, or some aspect of a case, and may require the person to do something. The concept of confirmed delivery service is newly introduced (see definition in section 2).

153. *Seal not required* — It is not necessary to the validity of any information, indictment, summons, warrant, minute, sentence, conviction, order or other process or document laid, issued, filed or entered in any proceedings under this Act that any seal be attached or affixed to it.

COMMENTARY

Legal Implications

Historically, courts had a court seal, and documents related to the court procedures would carry the seal of the court to confirm their authenticity. This section has not been changed from section 63 of the *Young Offenders Act*, and confirms that the validity of any procedural documents used in the youth justice court cannot be challenged due to the absence of a court seal.

FORMS, REGULATIONS AND RULES OF COURT

154. (1) *Forms* — The forms prescribed under section 155, varied to suit the case, or forms to the like effect, are valid and sufficient in the circumstances for which they are provided.

(2) *If forms not prescribed* — In any case for which forms are not prescribed under section 155, the forms set out in Part XXVIII of the *Criminal Code*, with any modifications that the circumstances require, or other appropriate forms, may be used.

COMMENTARY

Legal Implications

This section, which has not been changed from section 66 of the *Young Offenders Act*, gives validity to forms prescribed, or authorized by regulation under this Act. It also authorizes the use of forms set out in the *Criminal Code* if no form has been prescribed under section 155 of the *Youth Criminal Justice Act*.

155. *Regulations* — **The Governor in Council may make regulations**

(a) **prescribing forms that may be used for the purposes of this Act;**
(b) **establishing uniform rules of court for youth justice courts across Canada, including rules regulating the practice and procedure to be followed by youth justice courts; and**
(c) **generally for carrying out the purposes and provisions of this Act.**

COMMENTARY

Legal Implications

As was the case in section 67 of the *Young Offenders Act*, the Governor in Council may make regulations regarding forms and rules of court, and for the general carrying out of the purposes of the Act. This allows the flexibility of further developing the law once the Act has come into force. The regulation process is less complicated and more flexible than the legislative process required for the passing of the Act.

AGREEMENTS WITH PROVINCES

156. *Agreements with provinces* — **Any minister of the Crown may, with the approval of the Governor in Council, enter into an agreement with the government of any province providing for payments by Canada to the province in respect of costs incurred by the province or a municipality in the province for care of and services provided to young persons dealt with under this Act.**

COMMENTARY

Legal Implications

This section replaces section 70 of the *Young Offenders Act* and authorizes the federal government to sign agreements with the provinces, territories and municipalities for the payment of the costs of care and services provided to young persons dealt with under this Act.

PROGRAMS

157. *Community-based programs* — **The Attorney General of Canada or a minister designated by the lieutenant governor in council of a province may establish the following types of community-based programs:**

(*a*) programs that are an alternative to judicial proceedings, such as victim-offender reconciliation programs, mediation programs and restitution programs;

(*b*) programs that are an alternative to detention before sentencing, such as bail supervision programs; and

(*c*) programs that are an alternative to custody, such as intensive support and supervision programs, and programs to carry out attendance orders.

COMMENTARY

Legal Implications

This section, which is new, authorizes the designation of programs that are alternatives to the court process. Examples of such programs include victim/offender, mediation and restitution programs. This section also authorizes community-based alternatives to custody, both pre-trial and post-sentence.

Operational Implications

The intent of this new section is to promote the objectives of the *Youth Criminal Justice Act* by keeping youths out of the formal justice system and out of custody. The development of these kinds of programs is critical to the successful implementation of this legislation.

PART 8   TRANSITIONAL PROVISIONS

INTRODUCTION

This part and the sections that follow all deal with the transition from the *Young Offenders Act* to the *Youth Criminal Justice Act*, and are critical to the change-over from the application of the old law to the new. These changes in the manner that youth justice is delivered make it necessary to clarify which law applies.

158. *Prohibition on proceedings* — **On and after the coming into force of this section, no proceedings may be commenced under the *Young Offenders Act*, chapter Y-1 of the Revised Statutes of Canada, 1985, in respect of an offence within the meaning of that Act, or under the *Juvenile Delinquents Act*, chapter J-3 of the Revised Statutes of Canada, 1970, in respect of a delinquency within the meaning of that Act.**

COMMENTARY

Legal Implications

Once the *Youth Criminal Justice Act* came into force, no new proceedings were to be commenced under the *Young Offenders Act* or the *Juvenile Delinquents Act*. The *Juvenile Delinquents Act* is included in this section as a precaution should a proceeding commence for an offence that occurred prior to the time the *Young Offenders Act* replaced the *Juvenile Delinquents Act*.

Operational Implications

This section applies to cases where the offence was committed before the new Act came into force but no proceedings had begun.

159. (1) *Proceedings commenced under Young Offenders Act* — Subject to section 161, where, before the coming into force of this section, proceedings are commenced under the *Young Offenders Act*, chapter Y-1 of the Revised Statutes of Canada, 1985, in respect of an offence within the meaning of that Act alleged to have been committed by a person who was at the time of the offence a young person within the meaning of that Act, the proceedings and all related matters shall be dealt with in all respects as if this Act had not come into force.

(2) *Proceedings commenced under Juvenile Delinquents Act* — Subject to section 161, where, before the coming into force of this section, proceedings are commenced under the *Juvenile Delinquents Act*, chapter J-3 of the Revised Statutes of Canada, 1970, in respect of a delinquency within the meaning of that Act alleged to have been committed by a person who was at the time of the delinquency a child as defined in that Act, the proceedings and all related matters shall be dealt with under this Act as if the delinquency were an offence that occurred after the coming into force of this section.

COMMENTARY

Legal Implications

Where proceedings were commenced under the *Young Offenders Act* prior to the *Youth Criminal Justice Act* coming into force and were not completed by the time the Act came into force, then the proceedings are to continue under the *Young Offenders Act*. In other words, if a proceeding is commenced under the *Young Offenders Act* it will be finished under the *Young Offenders Act*. Where sentencing has not occurred by the time the *Youth Criminal Justice Act* came into force, a young person is to be sentenced under the new law, that is, the *Youth Criminal Justice Act*. This rule, however, does not apply to a young person who has been transferred to ordinary court. Special sentencing rules are set out in section 161 of the *Youth Criminal Justice Act*. Where proceedings were commenced under the *Juvenile Delinquents Act*, all matters are to be dealt with under the *Youth Criminal Justice Act*.

160. *Offences committed before this section in force* — **Any person who, before the coming into force of this section, while he or she was a young person, committed an offence in respect of which no proceedings were commenced before the coming into force of this section shall be dealt with under this Act as if the offence occurred after the coming into force of this section, except that**

(*a*) **paragraph 62(*a*) applies only if the offence is one set out in paragraph (*a*) of the definition "presumptive offence" in subsection 2(1) and the young person was at least sixteen years old at the time of its commission;**
(*b*) **paragraph 110(2)(*b*) does not apply in respect of the offence; and**
(*c*) **paragraph 42(2)(*r*) applies in respect of the offence only if the young person consents to its application.**

COMMENTARY

Legal Implications

Where an offence was committed prior to the *Youth Criminal Justice Act* coming into force, but no proceedings were commenced, then all proceedings are to be under the new law as opposed to the *Young Offenders Act*, with the following limitations:

- a young person convicted of a presumptive offence is not presumed to be given an adult sentence unless the young person was at least 16 years old at the time of its commission;
- a young person convicted of a presumptive offence is excluded from section 110(2)(*b*) of this legislation (publication of identity allowed); and
- a sentence under section 42(2)(*r*) of this legislation (intensive rehabilitation custody and supervision) may be imposed only on consent of the young person.

This section may be subject to amendment as a result of the decision of the Quebec Court of Appeal in *Reference re: Bill C-7 Respecting the Criminal Justice System for Young Persons*, [2003] Q.J. No. 2850 (C.A.).

161. (1) *Applicable sentence* — **A person referred to in section 159 who is found guilty of an offence or delinquency, other than a person convicted of an offence in ordinary court, as defined in subsection 2(1) of the *Young Offenders Act*, chapter Y-1 of the Revised Statutes of Canada, 1985, shall be sentenced under this Act, except that**

(*a*) **paragraph 110(2)(*b*) does not apply in respect of the offence or delinquency; and** (*b*) **paragraph 42(2)(*r*) applies in respect of the offence or delinquency only if the young person consents to its application.**

The provisions of this Act applicable to sentences imposed under section 42 apply in respect of the sentence.

(2) *Dispositions under paragraph 20(1)(k) or (k.1) of Young Offenders Act* — **Where a young person is to be sentenced under this Act while subject to a disposition under paragraph 20(1)(*k*) or (*k*.1) of the** *Young Offenders Act*, **chapter Y-1 of the Revised Statutes of Canada, 1985, on the application of the Attorney General or the young person, a youth justice court shall, unless to do so would bring the administration of justice into disrepute, order that the remaining portion of the disposition made under that Act be dealt with, for all purposes under this Act or any other Act of Parliament, as if it had been a sentence imposed under paragraph 42(2)(*n*) or (*q*) of this Act, as the case may be.**

(3) *Review of sentence* — **For greater certainty, for the purpose of determining when the sentence is reviewed under section 94, the relevant date is the one on which the disposition came into force under the** *Young Offenders Act*, **chapter Y-1 of the Revised Statutes of Canada, 1985.**

COMMENTARY

Legal Implications

Where proceedings were commenced under the *Young Offenders Act* and sentencing has not taken place when the *Youth Criminal Justice Act* came into force, then sentencing is to take place under the *Youth Criminal Justice Act*. This rule does not apply when a young person has been transferred to ordinary court under the *Young Offenders Act*.

When sentencing does take place under the *Youth Criminal Justice Act*, as in section 160, two of the new rules for sentencing do not apply. The new intensive rehabilitative custody and supervision sentence (section 42(2)) is not available, and there is no presumption of publication for a young person who receives a youth sentence for the offences of murder, attempted murder, manslaughter, aggravated assault or three serious violent offences. This presumption of publication applies to youth proceedings under the *Youth Criminal Justice Act*, but not to these transitional cases.

This section also provides for the situation where a young person is sentenced under the *Youth Criminal Justice Act* while serving a custody sentence under the *Young Offenders Act*. The Attorney General is authorized to request the court to order that the remaining portion of the *Young Offenders Act* sentence be treated as if it were a sentence imposed under the *Youth Criminal Justice Act*. This allows for better administration of sentences; however, the order will not be granted if to do so would bring the administration of justice into disrepute.

There is also a provision to clarify that when a sentence under the *Youth Criminal Justice Act* and a disposition under the *Young Offenders Act* are combined, the calculation for eligibility of a review of sentence will be from the time the disposition was imposed under the *Young Offenders Act*.

162. *Proceedings commence with information* — For the purposes of sections 158 to 160, proceedings are commenced by the laying of an information or indictment.

COMMENTARY

Legal Implications

This section clarifies that for these transitional sections, the laying of an information, or indictment, commences the proceedings.

Operational Implications

It is important to be able to determine when proceedings commence in order to determine if these transitional sections apply. The laying of an information or indictment is essentially a peace officer swearing under oath that there are reasonable grounds to believe that the young person committed an offence.

163. *Application to delinquency and other offending behaviour* — Sections 114 to 129 apply, with any modifications that the circumstances require, in respect of records relating to the offence of delinquency under the *Juvenile Delinquents Act*, chapter J-3 of the Revised Statutes of Canada, 1970, and in respect of records kept under sections 40 to 43 of the *Young Offenders Act*, chapter Y-1 of the Revised Statutes of Canada, 1985.

COMMENTARY

Legal Implications

This section provides for the new rules to apply to the keeping, sharing and use of these records kept under the *Young Offenders Act* and the *Juvenile Delinquents Act*. This section also provides that new sections apply with any modification that the circumstances require, allowing some latitude for judgment to be exercised when the old and new rules are different.

Operational Implications

Caution needs to be exercised to ensure that a young person's record would not be used under this Act in a manner that would jeopardize the privacy provisions of the old law.

164. *Agreements continue in force* — Any agreement made under the *Young Offenders Act*, chapter Y-1 of the Revised Statutes of Canada, 1985, remains in force until it expires, unless it is amended or a new agreement is made under this Act.

COMMENTARY

Legal Implications

This section, which provided for agreements between governments under the *Young Offenders Act*, ensures that these agreements remain in force until they expire or are replaced by new agreements. Essentially, this is an administrative section that makes it clear that it is business as usual until new agreements are made.

165. (1) *Designation of youth justice court* — Any court established or designated as a youth court for the purposes of the *Young Offenders Act*, chapter Y-1 of the Revised Statutes of Canada, 1985, is deemed, as of the coming into force of this section, to have been established or designated as a youth justice court for the purposes of this Act.

(2) *Designation of youth justice court judges* — Any person appointed to be a judge of the youth court for the purposes of the *Young Offenders Act*, chapter Y-1 of the Revised Statutes of Canada, 1985, is deemed, as of the coming into force of this section, to have been appointed as a judge of the youth justice court for the purposes of this Act.

(3) *Designation of provincial directors and youth workers* — Any person, group or class of persons or body appointed or designated as a provincial director for the purposes of the *Young Offenders Act*, chapter Y-1 of the Revised Statutes of Canada, 1985, and any person appointed or designated as a youth worker for the purposes of that Act is deemed, as of the coming into force of this section, to have been appointed or designated as a provincial director or youth worker, as the case may be, for the purposes of this Act.

(4) *Designation of review boards and youth justice committees* — Any review board established or designated for the purposes of the *Young Offenders Act*, chapter Y-1 of the Revised Statutes of Canada, 1985, and any youth justice committee established for the purposes of that Act is deemed, as of the coming into force of this section, to have been established or designated as a review board or a youth justice committee, as the case may be, for the purposes of this Act.

(5) *Alternative measures continued as extrajudicial sanctions* — Any program of alternative measures authorized for the purposes of the *Young Offenders Act*, chapter Y-1 of the Revised Statutes of Canada, 1985, is deemed, as of the coming into force of this section, to be a program of extrajudicial sanctions authorized for the purposes of this Act.

(6) *Designation of places of temporary detention and youth custody* — Subject to subsection (7), any place that was designated as a place of temporary detention or open custody for the purposes of the *Young Offenders Act*, chapter Y-1 of the Revised Statutes of Canada, 1985, and any place or facility designated as a place of secure custody for the purposes of that Act is deemed, as of the coming into force of this section, to have been designated for the purposes of this Act as

(a) in the case of a place of temporary detention, a place of temporary detention; and

(b) in the case of a place of open custody or secure custody, a youth custody facility.

(7) *Exception* — If the lieutenant governor in council of a province makes an order under section 88 that the power to make determinations of the level of custody for young persons and to review those determinations be exercised in accordance with the *Young Offenders Act*, chapter Y-1 of the Revised Statutes of Canada, 1985, the designation of any place as a place of open custody or secure custody for the purposes of that Act remains in force for the purposes of section 88, subject to revocation or amendment of the designation.

(8) *Designation of other persons* — Any person designated as a clerk of the youth court for the purposes of the *Young Offenders Act*, chapter Y-1 of the Revised Statutes of Canada, 1985, or any person or group of persons who were designated under that Act to carry out specified functions and duties are deemed, as of the coming into force of this section, to have been designated as a clerk of the youth justice court, or to carry out the same functions and duties, as the case may be, under this Act.

COMMENTARY

Legal Implications

This section preserves the key elements of the youth justice system during the transition from the *Young Offenders Act* to the *Youth Criminal Justice Act*. Designations for all of the officials who carry out day-to-day functions under the *Young Offenders Act* are preserved, and are deemed to be designated under the *Youth Criminal Justice Act*. This section also preserves the courts and the judicial appointments established under the *Young Offenders Act*. Below is a list of the aspects of the system preserved by this section:

- youth courts are deemed youth justice courts;
- youth court judges are deemed to be youth justice court judges;
- provincial directors, youth workers, clerks of the youth court, review boards and youth justice committees are all deemed to be designated or established under the *Youth Criminal Justice Act*;
- alternative measures programs established under the *Young Offenders Act* are deemed to be a program of extrajudicial sanctions under the *Youth Criminal Justice Act*; and

- places of temporary detention are deemed to be places of temporary detention, and places of open or secure detention are deemed to be a youth custody facility.

This section contains a specific provision that preserves the designations of open and secure custody if the province makes an order for the judicial determination of level of custody under section 88 of the *Youth Criminal Justice Act*.

PART 9 CONSEQUENTIAL AMENDMENTS, REPEAL AND COMING INTO FORCE

INTRODUCTION

Sections 166 to 198 deal with technical amendments to ancillary legislation linked to the *Young Offenders Act* to assist in the transition from the *Young Offenders Act* to the *Youth Criminal Justice Act*.

CONSEQUENTIAL AMENDMENTS

Canada Evidence Act

166. Subsection 4(2) of the *Canada Evidence Act* is replaced by the following:

(2) *Accused and spouse* — The wife or husband of a person charged with an offence under subsection 136(1) of the *Youth Criminal Justice Act* or with an offence under any of sections 151, 152, 153, 155 or 159, subsection 160(2) or (3), or sections 170 to 173, 179, 212, 215, 218, 271 to 273, 280 to 283, 291 to 294 or 329 of the *Criminal Code*, or an attempt to commit any such offence, is a competent and compellable witness for the prosecution without the consent of the person charged.

COMMENTARY

Legal Implications

Section 4(2) of the *Canada Evidence Act* is amended to provide for the change of name of the *Young Offenders Act* to the *Youth Criminal Justice Act*.

Contraventions Act

167. (1) The definition "youth court" in section 2 of the English version of the *Contraventions Act* is repealed.

(2) The definition "tribunal pour adolescents" in section 2 of the French version of the Act is replaced by the following:

«tribunal pour adolescents» — « tribunal pour adolescents» À l'égard d'une contravention qui aurait été commise par un adolescent sur le territoire, ou dans le ressort des tribunaux, d'une province, le tribunal établi ou désigné sous le régime d'une loi provinciale, ou encore désigné par le gouverneur en conseil ou par le lieutenant-gouverneur en conseil, afin d'exercer les attributions du tribunal pour adolescents dans le cadre de la *Loi sur le système de justice pénale pour les adolescents*.

(3) Section 2 of the English version of the Act is amended by adding the following in alphabetical order:

"youth justice court" — "youth justice court" means, in respect of a contravention alleged to have been committed by a young person in, or otherwise within the territorial jurisdiction of the courts of, a province, the court established or designated by or under an Act of the legislature of the province, or designated by the Governor in Council or lieutenant governor in council of the province, as the youth justice court for the purposes of the *Youth Criminal Justice Act*.

COMMENTARY

Legal Implications

Section 2 of the *Contraventions Act* is amended to provide for the change from youth court as defined in the *Young Offenders Act* to youth justice court as defined and used in the *Youth Criminal Justice Act*.

168. Section 5 of the Act is replaced by the following:

5. *Relationship with Criminal Code and Youth Criminal Justice Act* — The provisions of the *Criminal Code* relating to summary conviction offences and the provisions of the *Youth Criminal Justice Act* apply to proceedings in respect of contraventions that are commenced under this Act, except to the extent that this Act, the regulations or the rules of court provide otherwise.

169. Subsection 17(2) of the Act is replaced by the following:

(2) *Jurisdiction of adult courts over young persons* — Notwithstanding the *Youth Criminal Justice Act*, a contraventions court or a justice of the peace has jurisdiction, to the exclusion of that of the youth justice court, in respect of any contravention alleged to have been committed by a young person in, or otherwise within the territorial jurisdiction of the courts of, a province the lieutenant governor in council of which has ordered that any such contravention be dealt with in ordinary court.

Part 9 Consequential Amendments, Repeal and Coming into Force   S. 172

170. Paragraph 62(2)(*a*) of the Act is replaced by the following:

(*a*) **for the committal of the offender to custody under the** *Youth Criminal Justice Act*, **for one day, if the offender is a young person; or**

COMMENTARY

Legal Implications

These sections make amendments to the *Contraventions Act* to reflect the change of name from the *Young Offenders Act* to the *Youth Criminal Justice Act*.

Corrections and Conditional Release Act

171. The definition "sentence" in subsection 2(1) of the *Corrections and Conditional Release Act* is replaced by the following:

"sentence" — "sentence" means a sentence of imprisonment and includes a youth sentence imposed under the *Youth Criminal Justice Act* and a sentence imposed by a court of a foreign state on a Canadian offender who has been transferred to Canada pursuant to the *Transfer of Offenders Act*;

COMMENTARY

Legal Implications

Section 2(1) of the *Corrections and Conditional Release Act* is amended by replacing the definition of sentence so that it provides for a sentence imposed under the *Youth Criminal Justice Act*.

172. Subsection 15(1) of the Act is replaced by the following:

15. (1) *Newfoundland* — **Notwithstanding any requirement in the *Criminal Code* or under the *Youth Criminal Justice Act* that a person be sentenced, committed or transferred to penitentiary, such a person in the Province of Newfoundland shall not be received in a penitentiary without the approval of an officer designated by the Lieutenant Governor of Newfoundland.**

COMMENTARY

Legal Implications

This provision applies specifically to the Province of Newfoundland and places a limitation on persons being sent to a penitentiary within the province.

173. The definition "offender" in subsection 99(1) of the Act is replaced by the following:

"offender" — "offender" means
  (a) a person, other than a young person within the meaning of the *Youth Criminal Justice Act*, who is under a sentence imposed before or after the coming into force of this section
     (i) pursuant to an Act of Parliament or, to the extent that this Part applies, pursuant to a provincial Act, or
     (ii) on conviction for criminal or civil contempt of court if the sentence does not include a requirement that the offender return to that court, or
  (b) a young person within the meaning of the *Youth Criminal Justice Act* with respect to whom an order, committal or direction under section 76, 89, 92 or 93 of that Act has been made,

but does not include a person whose only sentence is a sentence being served intermittently pursuant to section 732 of the *Criminal Code*;

COMMENTARY

Legal Implications

The definition of offender is replaced to coincide with the new *Youth Criminal Justice Act*.

174. The Act is amended by adding the following after section 99.1:

99.2 *Young persons* — In this Part, a young person within the meaning of the *Youth Criminal Justice Act* with respect to whom a committal or direction under section 89, 92 or 93 of that Act has been made begins to serve his or her sentence on the day on which the sentence comes into force in accordance with subsection 42(12) of that Act.

COMMENTARY

Legal Implications

This section addresses the question of when a youth serving his or her sentence in an adult facility commences that sentence, and confirms that it will be in accordance with section 42(12) of the *Youth Criminal Justice Act*.

Criminal Code

175. The definitions "adult", "provincial court judge" and "young person" in section 487.04 of the *Criminal Code* are replaced by the following:

"adult" — "adult" has the meaning assigned by subsection 2(1) of the *Youth Criminal Justice Act*;

"provincial court judge" — "provincial court judge", in relation to a young person, includes a youth justice court judge within the meaning of subsection 2(1) of the *Youth Criminal Justice Act*;

"young person" — "young person" has the meaning assigned by subsection 2(1) of the *Youth Criminal Justice Act*.

COMMENTARY

Legal Implications

The definitions for adult, provincial court judge and young person are replaced to coincide with the new *Youth Criminal Justice Act*.

176. The portion of subsection 487.051(1) of the Act before paragraph (*a*), as enacted by section 17 of the *DNA Identification Act*, is replaced by the following:

487.051 (1) *Order* — Subject to section 487.053, if a person is convicted, discharged under section 730 or, in the case of a young person, found guilty under the *Young Offenders Act*, chapter Y-1 of the Revised Statutes of Canada, 1985, or the *Youth Criminal Justice Act* of a designated offence, the court

177. Subsection 487.052(1) of the Act, as enacted by section 17 of the *DNA Identification Act*, is replaced by the following:

487.052 (1) *Offences committed before DNA Identification Act in force* — Subject to section 487.053, if a person is convicted, discharged under section 730 or, in the case of a young person, found guilty under the *Young Offenders Act*, chapter Y-1 of the Revised Statutes of Canada, 1985, or the *Youth Criminal Justice Act*, of a designated offence committed before the coming into force of subsection 5(1) of the *DNA Identification Act*, the court may, on application by the prosecutor, make an order in Form 5.04 authorizing the taking, from that person or young person, for the purpose of forensic DNA analysis, of any number of samples of one or more bodily substances that is reasonably required for that purpose, by means of the investigative procedures described in subsection 487.06(1), if the court is satisfied that it is in the best interests of the administration of justice to do so.

178. Paragraph 487.053(*b*) of the English version of the Act, as enacted by section 17 of the *DNA Identification Act*, is replaced by the following:

(*b*) by the person or young person, that they consent to the entry, in the convicted offenders index of the national DNA data bank established under that Act, of the results of DNA analysis of bodily substances that were provided voluntarily in the course of the investigation of, or taken from them in execution of a warrant that was issued under section 487.05 in respect of, the designated offence of which the person has been convicted, discharged under section 730 or, in the case of a young person, found guilty under the *Young Offenders Act*, chapter Y-1 of the Revised Statutes of Canada, 1985, or the *Youth Criminal Justice Act*, or another designated offence in respect of the same transaction.

179. Subsection 487.056(1) of the English version of the Act, as enacted by section 17 of the *DNA Identification Act*, is replaced by the following:

487.056 (1) *When collection to take place* — Samples of bodily substances referred to in sections 487.051 and 487.052 shall be taken at the time the person is convicted, discharged under section 730 or, in the case of a young person, found guilty under the *Young Offenders Act*, chapter Y-1 of the Revised Statutes of Canada, 1985, or the *Youth Criminal Justice Act*, or as soon as is feasible afterwards, even though an appeal may have been taken.

180. Paragraphs 487.071(1)(a) and (b) of the Act, as enacted by section 20 of the *DNA Identification Act*, are replaced by the following:

(a) provided voluntarily in the course of an investigation of a designated offence by any person who is later convicted, discharged under section 730 or, in the case of a young person, found guilty under the *Young Offenders Act*, chapter Y-1 of the Revised Statutes of Canada, 1985, or the *Youth Criminal Justice Act* of the designated offence or another designated offence in respect of the same transaction and who, having been so convicted, discharged or found guilty, consents to having the results entered in the convicted offenders index;

(b) taken in execution of a warrant under section 487.05 from a person who is later convicted, discharged under section 730 or, in the case of a young person, found guilty under the *Young Offenders Act*, chapter Y-1 of the Revised Statutes of Canada, 1985, or the *Youth Criminal Justice Act* of the designated offence in respect of which the warrant was issued or another designated offence in respect of the same transaction and who, having been so convicted, discharged or found guilty, consents to having the results entered in the convicted offenders index;

COMMENTARY

Legal Implications

Sections 487.051(1), 487.052(1), 487.053(b), 487.056(1), and 487.071(1) of the *Criminal Code*, relating to DNA identification, are amended to account for the change from the *Young Offenders Act* to the *Youth Criminal Justice Act*.

181. The portion of subsection 667(1) of the Act before paragraph (*b*) is replaced by the following:

667. (1) *Proof of previous conviction* — In any proceedings,

(*a*) a certificate setting out with reasonable particularity the conviction or discharge under section 730, the finding of guilt under the *Young Offenders Act*, chapter Y-1 of the Revised Statutes of Canada, 1985, the finding of guilt under the *Youth Criminal Justice Act*, or the judicial determination under subsection 42(9) of that Act, or the conviction and sentence or finding of guilt and sentence in Canada of an offender, signed by
  (i) the person who made the conviction, order for the discharge, finding of guilt or judicial determination,
  (ii) the clerk of the court in which the conviction, order for the discharge, finding of guilt or judicial determination was made, or
  (iii) a fingerprint examiner,
is, on proof that the accused or defendant is the offender referred to in the certificate, evidence that the accused or defendant was so convicted, so discharged or so convicted and sentenced or found guilty and sentenced, or that a judicial determination was made against the accused or defendant, without proof of the signature or the official character of the person appearing to have signed the certificate;

COMMENTARY

Legal Implications

This section amends section 667 of the *Criminal Code*, which provides for the proof of previous convictions and has been specifically incorporated into the adult sentence provisions of this Act (section 68(3)). In order for section 667 of the *Criminal Code* to accomplish its purpose for the adult sentence provisions, it was necessary to make this amendment to make reference to previous findings of guilt under the *Young Offenders Act* and the *Youth Criminal Justice Act*.

182. Subsection 718.3(4) of the Act is replaced by the following:

(4) *Cumulative punishments* — The court or youth justice court that sentences an accused may direct that the terms of imprisonment that are imposed by the court or the youth justice court or that result from the operation of subsection 734(4) or 743.5(1) or (2) shall be served consecutively, when

(*a*) the accused is sentenced while under sentence for an offence, and a term of imprisonment, whether in default of payment of a fine or otherwise, is imposed;

(b) the accused is found guilty or convicted of an offence punishable with both a fine and imprisonment and both are imposed;
(c) the accused is found guilty or convicted of more than one offence, and
   (i) more than one fine is imposed,
   (ii) terms of imprisonment for the respective offences are imposed, or
   (iii) a term of imprisonment is imposed in respect of one offence and a fine is imposed in respect of another offence; or
(d) subsection 743.5(1) or (2) applies.

COMMENTARY

Legal Implications

Section 718.3(4) of the *Criminal Code* is amended for the consecutive sentencing provision of the *Criminal Code* to apply to sentences by the youth justice court.

183. Paragraph 721(3)(b) of the Act is replaced by the following:

(b) subject to subsection 119(2) of the *Youth Criminal Justice Act*, the history of previous dispositions under the *Young Offenders Act*, chapter Y-1 of the Revised Statutes of Canada, 1985, the history of previous sentences under the *Youth Criminal Justice Act*, and of previous findings of guilt under this Act and any other Act of Parliament;

COMMENTARY

Legal Implications

Section 721(3)(b) of the *Criminal Code,* dealing with reports by a probation officer, is amended to make reference to the *Youth Criminal Justice Act,* including a reference to the limitation on access to youth records.

184. Sections 743.4 and 743.5 of the Act are replaced by the following:

743.5 (1) *Transfer of jurisdiction when person already sentenced under Youth Criminal Justice Act* — **If a young person or an adult is or has been sentenced to a term of imprisonment for an offence while subject to a disposition made under paragraph 20(1)(k) or (k.1) of the *Young Offenders Act*, chapter Y-1 of the Revised Statutes of Canada, 1985, or a youth sentence imposed under paragraph 42(2)(n), (o), (q) or (r) of the *Youth Criminal Justice Act*, the disposition or youth sentence shall be dealt with, for all purposes under this Act or any other Act of Parliament, as if it had been a sentence imposed under this Act.**

(2) Transfer of jurisdiction when youth sentence imposed under Youth Criminal Justice Act — If a disposition is made under paragraph 20(1)(*k*) or (*k*.1) of the *Young Offenders Act*, chapter Y-1 of the Revised Statutes of Canada, 1985, with respect to a person or a youth sentence is imposed on a person under paragraph 42(2)(*n*), (*o*), (*q*) or (*r*) of the *Youth Criminal Justice Act* while the young person or adult is under sentence of imprisonment imposed under an Act of Parliament other than the *Youth Criminal Justice Act*, the disposition or youth sentence shall be dealt with, for all purposes under this Act or any other Act of Parliament, as if it had been a sentence imposed under this Act.

(3) Sentences deemed to constitute one sentence – section 743.1 — For greater certainty, the dispositions and sentences referred to in subsections (1) and (2) are, for the purpose of section 139 of the *Corrections and Conditional Release Act*, deemed to constitute one sentence of imprisonment.

COMMENTARY

Legal Implications

A new section 743.5 replaces sections 743.4 and 743.5 of the *Criminal Code*. The purpose of the new section is to deal with a combination of sentences imposed under the *Criminal Code* and either the *Young Offenders Act* or the *Youth Criminal Justice Act*. It is possible to have a disposition under the *Young Offenders Act*, or a sentence under the *Youth Criminal Justice Act*, and then a sentence under the *Criminal Code*, or the reverse. The point of this section is to make it clear when there is a combination of youth and adult sentences, the youth sentence will be treated as if it had been imposed under the *Criminal Code*.

185. The first paragraph of Form 5.03 of the Act, as enacted by section 24 of the *DNA Identification Act*, is replaced by the following:

Whereas (*name of offender*) has been convicted, discharged under section 730 of the *Criminal Code* or, in the case of a young person, found guilty under the *Young Offenders Act*, chapter Y-1 of the Revised Statutes of Canada, 1985, or the *Youth Criminal Justice Act* of (*offence*), an offence that is a primary designated offence within the meaning of section 487.04 of the *Criminal Code*;

186. The portion of the first paragraph of Form 5.04 of the Act before paragraph (*a*), as enacted by section 24 of the *DNA Identification Act*, is replaced by the following:

Whereas (*name of offender*), in this order called the "offender", has been convicted, discharged under section 730 of the *Criminal Code* or, in the case of a young person, found guilty under the *Young Offenders Act*, chapter Y-1 of the Revised Statutes of Canada, 1985, or the *Youth Criminal Justice Act* of (*offence*), an offence that is

COMMENTARY

Legal Implications

These sections amend Forms 5.03 and 5.04 of the *Criminal Code,* which are both Orders Authorizing the Taking of Bodily Substances for Forensic DNA Analysis, and replace the *Young Offenders Act* with the *Youth Criminal Justice Act.*

DNA Identification Act

187. The definition "young person" in section 2 of the *DNA Identification Act* is replaced by the following:

"young person" — "young person" has the meaning assigned by subsection 2(1) of the *Youth Criminal Justice Act*.

COMMENTARY

Legal Implications

Section 187 is an amendment to the definition of "young person" to coincide with the change in name from the *Young Offenders Act* to the *Youth Criminal Justice Act.*

188. (1) The portion of paragraph 9(2)(*c*) of the Act before subparagraph (i) is replaced by the following:

(*c*) in the case of information in relation to a young person who has been found guilty under the *Young Offenders Act*, chapter Y-1 of the Revised Statutes of Canada, 1985, or the *Youth Criminal Justice Act* of any of the following offences, the expiry of ten years after the sentence or all dispositions made in respect of the offence have been completed, namely,

(2) Paragraphs 9(2)(*d*) and (*e*) of the Act are replaced by the following:

(*d*) in the case of information in relation to a young person who has been found guilty under the *Young Offenders Act*, chapter Y-1 of the Revised Statutes of Canada, 1985, or the *Youth Criminal Justice Act* of a designated offence, other than an offence referred to in any of subparagraphs (*c*)(i) to (iii) and sections 235 (first degree murder or second degree murder), 236 (manslaughter), 239 (attempt to commit murder) and 273 (aggravated sexual assault) of the *Criminal Code*, the expiry of five years after the sentence or all dispositions made in respect of the offence have been completed; and

(e) in the case of information in relation to a young person who has been found guilty under the *Young Offenders Act*, chapter Y-1 of the Revised Statutes of Canada, 1985, or the *Youth Criminal Justice Act* of a designated offence that is a summary conviction offence, the expiry of three years after the sentence or all dispositions made in respect of the offence have been completed.

189. (1) The portion of paragraph 10(7)(c) of the Act before subparagraph (i) is replaced by the following:

(c) if the person is a young person who has been found guilty under the *Young Offenders Act*, chapter Y-1 of the Revised Statutes of Canada, 1985, or the *Youth Criminal Justice Act* of any of the following offences, after the expiry of ten years after the sentence or all dispositions made in respect of the offence have been completed, namely,

(2) Paragraphs 10(7)(d) and (e) of the Act are replaced by the following:

(d) if the person is a young person who has been found guilty under the *Young Offenders Act*, chapter Y-1 of the Revised Statutes of Canada, 1985, or the *Youth Criminal Justice Act* of a designated offence, other than an offence referred to in any of subparagraphs (c)(i) to (iii) and sections 235 (first degree murder or second degree murder), 236 (manslaughter), 239 (attempt to commit murder) and 273 (aggravated sexual assault) of the *Criminal Code*, after the expiry of five years after the sentence or all dispositions made in respect of the offence have been completed; and

(e) if the person is a young person who has been found guilty under the *Young Offenders Act*, chapter Y-1 of the Revised Statutes of Canada, 1985, or the *Youth Criminal Justice Act* of a designated offence that is a summary conviction offence, after the expiry of three years after the sentence or all dispositions made in respect of the offence have been completed.

COMMENTARY

Legal Implications

These two sections add a reference to the citation for the *Young Offenders Act* and where to find this reference in the statutes of Canada: Chapter Y-1 of the Revised Statutes of Canada, 1985.

The word "sentence" is added to the reference to disposition in order to provide for the fact that under the *Young Offenders Act*, a disposition is imposed, whereas under the *Youth Criminal Justice Act*, the young person is sentenced.

These two sections set out the details and time periods for the inaccessibility of records of convictions and findings of guilt, and for the destruction of bodily substances.

Note that *An Act to Amend the National Defence Act, the DNA Identification Act and the Criminal Code*, S.C. 2000, c. 10, sections 8(2) and 10(2) repealed sections 9(2)(*c*)-(*e*) and 10(7)(*c*)-(*e*) of the *DNA Identification Act*. Sections 188 and 189 of the *Youth Criminal Justice Act* must be read in light of S.C. 2000, c. 10, as well as the *Interpretation Act* and the *DNA Identification Act*.

Extradition Act

190. Paragraph 47(*c*) of the *Extradition Act* is replaced by the following:

(*c*) the person was less than eighteen years old at the time of the offence and the law that applies to them in the territory over which the extradition partner has jurisdiction is not consistent with the fundamental principles governing the *Youth Criminal Justice Act*;

COMMENTARY

Legal Implications

A reference to the *Youth Criminal Justice Act* is added to the *Extradition Act*.

191. Paragraphs 77(*a*) and (*b*) of the Act are replaced by the following:

(*a*) in respect of a prosecution or imposition of a sentence — or of a disposition under the *Young Offenders Act*, chapter Y-1 of the Revised Statutes of Canada, 1985 — the Attorney General, or the Attorney General of a province who is responsible for the prosecution of the case; and

(*b*) in respect of the enforcement of a sentence or a disposition under the *Young Offenders Act*, chapter Y-1 of the Revised Statutes of Canada, 1985,
  (i) the Solicitor General of Canada, if the person would serve the sentence in a penitentiary, or
  (ii) the appropriate provincial minister responsible for corrections, in any other case.

192. Subsection 78(1) of the Act is replaced by the following:

78. (1) *Request by Canada for extradition* — The Minister, at the request of a competent authority, may make a request to a State or entity for the extradition of a person for the purpose of prosecuting the person for — or imposing or enforcing a sentence, or making or enforcing a disposition under the *Young Offenders Act*, chapter Y-1 of the Revised Statutes of Canada, 1985, in respect of — an offence over which Canada has jurisdiction.

193. The portion of paragraph 80(*a*) of the Act before subparagraph (i) is replaced by the following:

(*a*) be detained or prosecuted, or have a sentence imposed or executed, or a disposition made or executed under the *Young Offenders Act*, chapter Y-1 of the Revised Statutes of Canada, 1985, in Canada in respect of an offence that is alleged to have been committed, or was committed, before surrender other than

194. (1) Subsection 83(1) of the Act is replaced by the following:

83. (1) *Commencement of sentence* — Subject to subsection (3), the sentence or disposition of a person who has been temporarily surrendered and who has been convicted and sentenced, or found guilty and sentenced, in Canada, or in respect of whom a disposition has been made under the *Young Offenders Act*, chapter Y-1 of the Revised Statutes of Canada, 1985, does not commence until their final extradition to Canada.

(2) Subsection 83(3) of the Act is replaced by the following:

(3) *If concurrent sentences ordered* — The sentencing judge may order that the person's sentence, or the disposition under the *Young Offenders Act*, chapter Y-1 of the Revised Statutes of Canada, 1985, be executed concurrently with the sentence they are serving in the requested State or entity, in which case the warrant of committal or order of disposition shall state that the person is to be committed to custody under subsection (2) only for any portion of the sentence or disposition remaining at the time of their final extradition to Canada.

COMMENTARY

Legal Implications

These sections of the *Extradition Act* are amended to include the *Youth Criminal Justice Act* and to add the reference of where to find the *Young Offenders Act* in the statutes of Canada: Chapter Y-1 of the Revised Statutes of Canada, 1985.

Mutual Legal Assistance in Criminal Matters Act

195. Section 29 of the *Mutual Legal Assistance in Criminal Matters Act* is replaced by the following:

29. *Exception for young persons* — Sections 24 to 28 do not apply in respect of a person who, at the time the request mentioned in subsection 24(1) is presented, is a young person within the meaning of the *Youth Criminal Justice Act*.

COMMENTARY

Legal Implications

The *Mutual Legal Assistance Act* is changed to add a reference to the *Youth Criminal Justice Act*.

Prisons and Reformatories Act

196. (1) Paragraph (*b*) of the definition "prisoner" in subsection 2(1) of the *Prisons and Reformatories Act* is replaced by the following:

> (*b*) **a young person within the meaning of the *Youth Criminal Justice Act* with respect to whom no order, committal or direction has been made under paragraph 76(1)(*a*) or section 89, 92 or 93 of that Act,**

(2) Subsection 2(1) of the Act is amended by adding the following in alphabetical order:

"sentence" — "sentence" **includes a youth sentence imposed under the *Youth Criminal Justice Act*;**

COMMENTARY

Legal Implications

This section makes two amendments to the *Prisons and Reformatories Act*, both of which provide for a reference to the *Youth Criminal Justice Act*. One of the amendments adds a definition of "sentence" as one imposed under the *Youth Criminal Justice Act*.

197. Section 6 of the Act is amended by adding the following after subsection (7):

(*7.1*) *Transfer or committal to prison* — **When a prisoner is transferred from a youth custody facility to a prison under section 89, 92 or 93 of the *Youth Criminal Justice Act* or as the result of the application of section 743.5 of the *Criminal Code*, the prisoner is credited with full remission under this section for the portion of the sentence that the offender served in the youth custody facility as if that portion of the sentence had been served in a prison.**

(*7.2*) *Exceptional date of release* — **When a prisoner who was sentenced to custody under paragraph 42(2)(*o*), (*q*) or (*r*) of the *Youth Criminal Justice Act* is transferred from a youth custody facility to a prison under section 92 or 93 of that Act, or is committed to imprisonment in a prison under section 89 of that Act, the prisoner is entitled to be released on the earlier of** (*a*) the date on which the prisoner is entitled to be released from imprisonment in accordance with subsection (5) of this section, and

(*b*) the date on which the custody portion of his or her youth sentence under paragraph 42(2)(*o*), (*q*) or (*r*) of the *Youth Criminal Justice Act* expires.

(7.3) *Effect of release* — When a prisoner is committed or transferred in accordance with section 89, 92 or 93 of the *Youth Criminal Justice Act* and, in accordance with subsection (7.1) or (7.2) of this section, is entitled to be released,

(*a*) if the sentence was imposed under paragraph 42(2)(*n*) of that Act, sections 97 to 103 of that Act apply, with any modifications that the circumstances require, with respect to the remainder of his or her sentence; and

(*b*) if the sentence was imposed under paragraph 42(2)(*o*), (*q*) or (*r*) of that Act, sections 104 to 109 of that Act apply, with any modifications that the circumstances require, with respect to the remainder of his or her sentence.

COMMENTARY

Legal Implications

This section adds three new subsections to the *Prisons and Reformatories Act*: section 6(7.1), (7.2), and (7.3), all of which take into account the new provisions in the *Youth Criminal Justice Act* for committal to custody, transfer and release. These provisions are essential to ensure that the custody regime set out in the *Youth Criminal Justice Act* is carried out in a manner consistent with the *Youth Criminal Justice Act*.

Transfer of Offenders Act

198. The portion of section 17 of the *Transfer of Offenders Act* after paragraph (*a*) is replaced by the following:

(*b*) was, at the time of the commission of the offence of which he or she was convicted, a young person within the meaning of the *Youth Criminal Justice Act*,

an official designated for the purpose by the lieutenant governor in council of the province where the offender is detained may transfer the offender to a youth custody facility within the meaning of subsection 2(1) of the *Youth Criminal Justice Act*, but no person so transferred shall be detained by reason only of the sentence imposed by the foreign court beyond the date on which that sentence would terminate.

COMMENTARY

Legal Implications

This section amends the *Transfer of Offenders Act* to take into account the change in the name of the legislation from the *Young Offenders Act* to the *Youth Criminal Justice Act*, and also for the change in the manner in which youth custody facilities will be designated.

REPEAL

199. Repeal of R.S., c. Y-1 — The *Young Offenders Act* is repealed.

COMMENTARY

Legal Implications

This section repeals the *Young Offenders Act*.

COMING INTO FORCE

200. *Coming into force* — The provisions of this Act come into force on a day or days to be fixed by order of the Governor in Council.

COMMENTARY

Legal Implications

This last section of the Act provides for the Act coming into force on a date set by an order made by the Governor in Council.

By Order in Council on May 29, 2002, the *Youth Criminal Justice Act* came into effect on April 1, 2003.

SCHEDULE

(SUBSECTIONS 120(1), (4) AND (6))

1. An offence under any of the following provisions of the *Criminal Code*:

   (*a*) paragraph 81(2)(*a*) (using explosives);
   (*b*) subsection 85(1) (using firearm in commission of offence);
   (*c*) section 151 (sexual interference);
   (*d*) section 152 (invitation to sexual touching);
   (*e*) section 153 (sexual exploitation);
   (*f*) section 155 (incest);
   (*g*) section 159 (anal intercourse);

Schedule **Sch.**

(*h*) section 170 (parent or guardian procuring sexual activity by child);
(*i*) subsection 212(2) (living off the avails of prostitution by a child);
(*j*) subsection 212(4) (obtaining sexual services of a child);
(*k*) section 231 or 235 (first degree murder or second degree murder within the meaning of section 231);
(*l*) section 232, 234 or 236 (manslaughter);
(*m*) section 239 (attempt to commit murder);
(*n*) section 267 (assault with a weapon or causing bodily harm);
(*o*) section 268 (aggravated assault);
(*p*) section 269 (unlawfully causing bodily harm);
(*q*) section 271 (sexual assault);
(*r*) section 272 (sexual assault with a weapon, threats to a third party or causing bodily harm);
(*s*) section 273 (aggravated sexual assault);
(*t*) section 279 (kidnapping);
(*u*) section 344 (robbery);
(*v*) section 433 (arson — disregard for human life);
(*w*) section 434.1 (arson — own property);
(*x*) section 436 (arson by negligence); and
(*y*) paragraph 465(1)(*a*) (conspiracy to commit murder).

2. An offence under any of the following provisions of the *Criminal Code*, as they read immediately before July 1, 1990:

(*a*) section 433 (arson);
(*b*) section 434 (setting fire to other substance); and
(*c*) section 436 (setting fire by negligence).

3. An offence under any of the following provisions of the *Criminal Code*, chapter C-34 of the Revised Statutes of Canada, 1970, as they read immediately before January 4, 1983:

(*a*) section 144 (rape);
(*b*) section 145 (attempt to commit rape);
(*c*) section 149 (indecent assault on female);
(*d*) section 156 (indecent assault on male); and
(*e*) section 246 (assault with intent).

4. An offence under any of the following provisions of the *Controlled Drugs and Substances Act*:

(*a*) section 5 (trafficking);
(*b*) section 6 (importing and exporting); and
(*c*) section 7 (production of substance).

APPENDICES

(Reproduced from the Department of Justice's Resource Manual for Police)

	Page
Checklist for Police Officers: Police Options (section 6)	233
Checklist for Police, Crown Prosecutors and Officials: Extrajudicial Sanctions (section 10)	235
Extrajudicial Measures: Duty of Police Officer	238
Extrajudicial Measures: YCJA Sections 4-12 Key Points	239
Form 1.1 (Sections 6 and 7) Police Caution to a Young Person	241
Form 1.2 (Section 8) Crown Caution to a Young Person	242
Form 1.3 (Section 8) Notice to the Parent that a Young Person has been given a Crown Caution	243
Form 1.4 (Sections 10 and 11) Notice to Parent of Extrajudicial Sanction	244
Form 5.5 (Criminal Code Sections 499 and 503) Undertaking given to a Peace Officer or an Officer in Charge	245
Form 9.1 (Section 146) Statement of a Young Person	246

Appendices

Checklist for Police Officers: Police Options
(section 6)

1. Do you have *reasonable grounds to believe* that the youth has committed an offence?

    - If you do not, then you should not continue with this checklist.
    - If yes, then you may continue with this checklist.

Note: You should ensure that you have advised the youth of his or her right to counsel and afforded him or her access to counsel wherever that is required during any exercise of police procedures or powers with respect to this incident. See the module on Right to Counsel.

> **Before starting judicial proceedings or considering an extrajudicial sanction**, a police officer must consider whether it would be sufficient to administer one of the measures listed in *YCJA*, section 6: take no further action, warn, caution, or refer the young person.

Note: You should be aware that you may use a conference where you think it might assist you in decision-making in this part of the process. See the module on Conferences.

2. An extrajudicial measure is often the most appropriate, effective and timely response to criminal conduct by youth.

    - In this instance, you should consider using one of the measures listed in section 6 (take no further action, warn, caution, or referral), unless there are *clear indications* that these measures would not be adequate to hold the youth accountable for his or her conduct.

3. If this is a non-violent, first offence by this youth, an extrajudicial measure is presumed to be adequate to hold the youth accountable for his or her conduct.

    - Do you believe that the youth has committed a non-violent offence and has not previously been found guilty of an offence? If so, you must consider using one of the measures listed in section 6 unless there are *exceptional circumstances* that indicate it would not be adequate to hold the youth accountable for his or her conduct.

4. You may choose between one of four measures in order to hold the youth accountable for his or her offence. You may choose

    - to take no further action against the youth,
    - to give the youth a warning,
    - to issue a caution to the youth or

- to refer the young person, with his or her consent, to a program or agency in the community that may assist him or her not to commit offences.

The measure that you use should be applied fairly and be proportionate to the offence. You should use the least restrictive measure that will hold the youth accountable, ensuring the minimum intervention warranted to respond to the conduct. The measure should always be less than one a court would impose for this conduct, should the youth have been tried and found guilty of the offence.

Within the limits of fair and proportionate accountability, the measure should be designed and applied with the following principles and objectives in mind:

- emphasize timeliness (ensuring the measure is applied with as close a link to the conduct as possible, to help the youth understand the relationship between action and consequences);
- be an effective intervention;
- promote the rehabilitation of the youth;
- offer meaningful consequences to the youth;
- encourage the youth to acknowledge harm he or she may have caused;
- encourage the youth to repair harm he or she may have caused;
- involve the family of the youth;
- respect the youth's rights, and especially any special protections or guarantees of rights applying to youth.

Note: For further details and information on the considerations you should bear in mind when deciding which measure to use, see Principles and Objectives in the current module.

Appendices

Checklist for Police, Crown Prosecutors and Officials: Extrajudicial Sanctions (section 10)

1. Do you have *reasonable grounds to believe* that the youth has committed an offence?

    - If you do not, then you should not continue with this checklist.
    - If yes, then you may continue with this checklist.

Note: You should ensure that you have advised the youth of his or her right to counsel and afforded him or her access to counsel wherever that is required in your dealings with the youth in relation to this incident. See the module on Right to Counsel.

2. Have you advised the youth of his or her right to counsel and afforded him or her access to counsel wherever that is required in your dealings with the youth in relation to this incident? See the module on Right to Counsel. In particular, have you addressed the following specific protections set out in *YCJA*, subsection 10(2) and section 25?

> **Before starting or continuing judicial proceedings**, a police officer, the crown prosecutor or other designated official should consider whether an extrajudicial sanction would be adequate to hold the young person accountable.

Note: You should be aware that you may use a conference where you think it might assist you in decision-making in this part of the process. See the module on Conferences.

3. Have you or any other qualified official been satisfied that (a) taking no action, issuing a warning or caution, or making a referral under section 6 or (b) issuing a caution under section 8 would *not* be adequate to hold the young person accountable for this offence?

    - If no such determination has been made, you should not continue with this checklist.
    - If you have made this determination, or accept a determination made by another official, you may continue with this checklist.

4. An extrajudicial measure is often the most appropriate, effective and timely response to criminal conduct by youth.

    - In this instance, you should consider using an extrajudicial sanction, unless there are *clear indications* that this would not be adequate to hold the youth accountable for his or her conduct.

5. If this is a non-violent, first offence by this youth, an extrajudicial measure is presumed to be adequate to hold the youth accountable for his or her conduct.

   - Do you believe that the youth has committed a non-violent offence and has not previously been found guilty of an offence? If so, you must consider applying an extrajudicial sanction unless there are *exceptional circumstances* that indicate it would not be adequate to hold the youth accountable for his or her conduct.

6. Before you may proceed to apply an extrajudicial sanction in this case, you must ensure that several pre-conditions have been met:

   - the young person has been informed of the extrajudicial sanction and consents to it;
   - the young person has been advised of the right to counsel *and* has been given a reasonable opportunity to consult with counsel;
   - the young person accepts responsibility for the offence;
   - there is sufficient evidence to proceed with prosecution of the offence; and
   - the prosecution of the offence is not in any way barred at law.

   As well, you may not proceed with an extrajudicial sanction if:

   - the young person denies participation or involvement in the commission of the offence, or
   - the young person expresses a wish to have the charge dealt with by a youth justice court.

7. In deciding which sanction to apply and how to proceed, you should ensure that it is applied fairly and is proportionate to the offence. You should use the least restrictive measure that will hold the youth accountable, ensuring the minimum intervention warranted to respond to the conduct. The measure should always be less than one a court would impose for this conduct, should the youth have been tried and found guilty of the offence.

   Within the limits of fair and proportionate accountability, the measure should be designed and applied with the following principles and objectives in mind

   - emphasize timeliness (ensuring the measure is applied with as close a link to the conduct as possible, to help the youth understand the relationship between action and consequences);
   - be an effective intervention;
   - promote the rehabilitation of the youth;
   - offer meaningful consequences to the youth;
   - encourage the youth to acknowledge harm he or she may have caused;
   - encourage the youth to repair harm he or she may have caused;
   - involve the family of the youth; and

- respect the youth's rights, and especially any special protections or guarantees of rights applying to youth.

Note: For further details and information on the considerations you should bear in mind when deciding which measure to use, see Principles and Objectives in the current module.

8. Have you, or the responsible official, informed the youth's parent of the sanction?

9. Has a victim requested information about the case? If so, you may inform him or her of the identity of the youth and how the offence has been dealt with.

Extrajudicial Measures

Duty of Police Officer

Section 6 of the *YCJA* requires a police officer, before charging a young person, to take account of the principles in section 4 and consider whether it would be sufficient to:

- Take no further action;
- Warn the young person;
- Give the young person a formal caution; or
- With the consent of the young person, refer the young person to a community program or agency that may assist the young person not to commit offences.

These various extrajudicial measures are discussed below.

The police officer must consider these options in all cases in which a charge could be laid. The police officer must believe on reasonable grounds that the young person has committed an offence. Extrajudicial measures are intended as an alternative to proceeding with charges. If the grounds for a charge are not present, the police officer should not use a warning, caution or referral as a means of dealing with the matter.

Key provisions in section 4 that the police officer must take into account include the principle that extrajudicial measures rather than court proceedings should be used if they would be adequate to hold the young person accountable; the presumption that non-violent first offenders should be dealt with by extrajudicial measures; and the principle that young persons can be dealt with by extrajudicial measures even though they have previously committed offences.

Subsection 6(2) provides that the failure of a police officer to carry out his or [*sic*] duty to consider these non-court options before charging a young person does not invalidate the charge.

Appendices

Extrajudicial Measures
YCJA sections 4-12
Key Points

Before considering a response under the *Youth Criminal Justice Act* (*YCJA*) to alleged criminal conduct by a young person, a police officer must have reasonable grounds to believe that the youth has committed an offence.

Before starting a judicial proceeding or applying an extrajudicial sanction, police must consider whether it would be sufficient, given the principles set out in section 4, to apply one of the options listed in section 6 of the *YCJA*:

- take no further action against the young person;
- warn the young person;
- caution the young person, subject to the existence of a cautioning program in the jurisdiction; or
- refer a young person, with his or her consent, to a community program or agency that may help him/her to not commit offences.

In determining the appropriate response to an incident of youth crime, a police officer should consider the principles and objectives set out in sections 3, 4 & 5 of the *YCJA*, which state that an extrajudicial measure is:

- often the most appropriate, effective, and timely response to youth crime, and
- presumed adequate to hold a young person accountable for his/her conduct, if the offence is a first-time, non-violent offence, and may also be adequate to deal with subsequent offences

The police officer must apply the chosen measure in a manner that

- is fair and in proportionate to the offence
- is the least restrictive measure that will hold the youth accountable
- will ensure the intervention is the minimum the conduct warrants; and
- will ensure the measure is less than what a court would impose, had the youth been tried and a finding of guilt made

Within the limits of fair and proportionate accountability, the extrajudicial measure should:

- be timely (link the measure to the offence as closely as possible, to help the youth understand the relationship between action and consequence);
- be effective;
- promote the young person's rehabilitation;
- offer meaningful consequences to the young person;
- encourage the youth to acknowledge & repair harm caused;
- involve the youth's family; and

- respect the youth's rights, especially special protections or guarantees applicable to youth.

If none of the options listed in section 6 *YCJA* is adequate to hold the youth accountable, police officers should next consider applying an extrajudicial sanction under section 10 *YCJA*. They may do so if conditions set out in subsections 10(2) and 10(3) are met.

If an officer needs help with any of these decisions, a conference may be convened.

Form 1.1
Sections 6 and 7

Youth Criminal Justice Act

Police Caution to a Young Person

To: {name of young person}

When I have reasonable grounds to believe that you have committed a criminal offence, the *Youth Criminal Justice Act* requires me, before starting judicial proceedings, to consider taking measures other than going to court.

Since I have reasonable grounds to believe you have committed a criminal offence, under section 6 of the *Youth Criminal Justice Act* I am giving you a formal caution.

If you break the law in the future there may be more serious consequences, including charges, going to court and the possibility of serious penalties.

{date}
{place}
{name of police officer}
{police department}
Contact # for further information_____

Form 1.2
Section 8

Youth Criminal Justice Act

Crown Caution to a Young Person

To: {name of young person}

The Crown Attorney's office has received a report from {police agency}. In this report police officers inform me that they have reasonable grounds to believe that you have broken the law by:

{set out offence(s)}.

While there is sufficient information to proceed with a prosecution the Crown has decided, under section 8 of the *Youth Criminal Justice Act*, to issue a formal caution to you rather than proceeding with charges for this offence.

If you break the law in the future, more serious consequences, including charges, going to court and possible serious penalties, may follow.

{date}
{place}
{name of person signing on behalf of the Attorney General}
Contact # for further information_____

Form 1.3
Section 8

Youth Criminal Justice Act

Notice to the Parent that a Young Person has been given a Crown Caution

To: {name of parent, guardian or adult with legal responsibility for young person}

This is about {name of young person}.

The Crown Attorney's office has received a report from {police agency}. In this report police officers inform me that they have reasonable grounds to believe that {name of young person} has broken the law by:

{set out offence(s)}

While there is sufficient information to proceed with a prosecution the Crown has decided, under section 8 of the *Youth Criminal Justice Act*, to issue a formal caution to {the young person} rather than proceeding with charges for this offence.

Please understand that if this young person breaks the law in the future, there may be more serious consequences, including charges, going to court, and possible serious penalties.

{date}
{place}
{name of person signing on behalf of the Attorney General}
Contact # for further information_____

Form 1.4
Sections 10 and 11

Youth Criminal Justice Act

Notice to Parent of Extrajudicial Sanction

To: {name of parent, guardian or adult with legal responsibility for young person}

This is about {name of young person}.

I have received a report from {police agency}. In this report police officers inform me that they have reasonable grounds to believe that {name of young person} has broken the law by:

{set out offence(s)}

The following are the criteria that must be met before proceeding to extrajudicial sanctions:
(a) the program must be one that is properly authorized by the Attorney General or other designated government official,
(b) extrajudicial sanctions must be considered appropriate having regard to the needs of the young person and the interests of society,
(c) consent of the young person,
(d) the young person has been advised of the right to legal counsel (a lawyer),
(e) the young person accepts responsibility for the offence(s) alleged to have been committed,
(f) there is sufficient evidence to proceed with a prosecution, and
(g) a prosecution is not barred in law.

These pre-conditions have been met in this case. {The young person} has accepted responsibility for the offence(s) alleged to have been committed and has agreed to participate in a program of extrajudicial sanctions.

Given that these are effective and timely measures that will hold him or her accountable, and {name of young person} has consented to participate in {extrajudicial sanction}, on {date} at {time} at {place}, the following extrajudicial sanction was agreed to:

{describe extrajudicial sanction used}

{date}
{place}
{name of Program Administrator}
{title of Program Administrator}

Contact # for further information_____

Form 5.5

Criminal Code
Sections 499, 503

In the Youth Justice Court for {district}

Undertaking given to a Peace Officer or an Officer in Charge

Canada
{province / territory, district}

> **A young person's right to legal counsel** The young person has the right to have a lawyer provided to advise and represent him/her. The young person can hire their own lawyer, can ask Legal Aid for a lawyer, or can ask a Judge in the Youth Justice Court to appoint a lawyer for him/her.

I, {name of young person, address, date of birth}, understand that a peace officer has stated that he/she has reasonable grounds to believe that I committed the following offence(s):

{set out offence(s)}

I promise to obey any condition or conditions set by a peace officer or by an officer in charge:

- {List condition(s), if any}
-

I understand that I do not have to sign this undertaking. I understand further that if I do not sign this undertaking, I may be kept in custody. Then, I would be brought in front of a justice pursuant to section 503 who can determine whether there should be conditions attached to my release from custody. I understand that, if I sign this undertaking, it will be in effect until a justice ends it or changes it. I understand that I can apply to a justice at any time to ask to change this undertaking.

I also understand that, unless I have a lawful reason, it is a criminal offence under subsection 145(5.1) of the *Criminal Code* not to comply with this under-taking

{date}
{place}
{name of peace officer / officer in charge}
{title of peace officer / officer in charge}

{signature of the young person}

Form 9.1
Section 146

Statement of a Young Person

> **Note to police: If you videotape or audiotape a statement**
> When you videotape or audiotape a statement, you must advise the young person and anyone else present of this before proceeding. The best practice is to have the young person sign the waivers in this form, if applicable, and sign the statement, if one is made, even though the tape also serves as a record of the young person's words.

Time: {time}

Date: {d/m/y}

Place: {town/village/country/province}

Officer(s)taking the statement {name(s) of officer(s)}

Name of young person:
Address: Telephone:
Date of birth: {d/m/y}
Name of parent(s):
Address of parent(s):   Telephone:

We are investigating the offence(s) of:

{set out offence(s)}

and

☐ you have been charged
☐ you may be charged

The law requires that you be told about your rights before I can ask you if you want to make a statement. That is what is going to happen now. I will explain your rights to you and ask to make sure you understand what I have said.

Appendices

> **Note to police: Assess understanding**
> The young person must understand all the warnings, cautions and rights that are set out in this statement form. Be prepared to show the court that the young person understood what you said. Asking questions, such as "Could you explain what I have just said in your own words?" or "What does this mean to you?" can help you to assess understanding, if necessary.

A. If you do not understand a word or something that I have said, tell me and I will explain it to you. It is important that you understand what I am saying. If you do not understand something, stop me at any time and ask.

   Do you understand? Answer_____

B. You do not have to make a statement. This means that you do not have to say anything to me. But, if you make a statement, anything that you say, write or do can be used against you as evidence in court or in other proceedings.

   Do you understand? Answer_____

C. Even if you have already talked to the police or someone else, you do not have to make a statement now.

   Do you understand? Answer_____

D. You should not make a statement because of a favour given or a promise made to you. You should not make a statement because you hope for something in return.

   Do you understand? Answer_____

E. You should not make a statement because you feel threatened or afraid that someone will hurt you or anyone else.

> **Note to police: Warning of possible adult sentence**
> You must give the appropriate warning about the possibility of an adult sentence, if the situation falls into either one of two following categories:

F. **Warning # 1**

> **Presumptive offences-definition-paragraph 2(1)(a)**
> If the young person was 14 to 17 (or the age established under section 61 by the Lieutenant Governor in Council) at the time of the alleged commission of one or more of the following offences: murder, manslaughter, attempted murder, or aggravated sexual assault, you must give this warning:

1. Warning to be given to young person

I must warn you that if you are found guilty, you will receive an adult sentence, unless you or your lawyer can convince the court that you should receive a youth sentence. The most severe adult sentence is life in prison.

Do you understand? Answer_____

☐   warning given
☐   warning not applicable

Warning # 2

---
the Attorney general-crown prosecutor may seek an adult sentence If the young person was 14 - 17 at the time of the alleged commission of an offence for which an adult is liable to imprisonment for a term of more than two years, you must give this warning.

---

2. Warning to be given to young person

I must warn you that if you are found guilty, you could receive an adult sentence. The most severe adult sentence is life in prison.

Do you understand? Answer_____

☐   warning given
☐   warning not applicable

G. You have the right to retain and instruct counsel in private, without delay. This means that you can talk to and get advice from a lawyer now without the police present. A lawyer's job includes telling you what your rights are and giving you advice about whether you should answer my questions or sign this form.

Do you understand? Answer_____

H. You have the right to consult your parent, an adult relative or another appropriate adult in private, without delay. This means that you can talk to and get advice from that person now without the police present. If you decide to talk to a lawyer and parent or another adult, you can choose the order in which you contact them.

Do you understand? Answer_____

Appendices

I. You have the right to have a lawyer and the adult with whom you consult here with you. This means that you can ask a lawyer or an adult or both of them to be here with you while we are talking to you and to be with you if we take a statement from you.

   Do you understand? Answer_____

J. You may consult any lawyer you want for immediate legal advice. You can also ask a lawyer to be here with you. I can give you a telephone book or a list of lawyers to call. Or, I can help you to reach a free lawyer, through legal aid or duty counsel. I can help you to reach a lawyer now. Once you do, police will leave. Your conversation with the lawyer is private.

   Do you understand? Answer_____

> **Note:** *Certain jurisdictions may decide, under subsection 25(10), to put in place a program that would authorize the recovery of the cost of legal counsel. If this is such a jurisdiction, include the following advice in this form.*
>
> You should be aware that the crown may seek from you or your parents costs associated with providing you with access to free legal advice. You should ask your lawyer about how this may affect you or your parents.

K. Do you want to talk to a lawyer in private now?
   Answer _____

If yes:	If yes, but:	If no:
☐ lawyer contacted Additional information, if known: Time: Do you want to have a lawyer here with you? Answer_____	☐ lawyer not contacted {give reason} Time: If the young person was unable to reach a lawyer, do not go to section N or begin to take a statement until the young person has contacted a lawyer.	You have decided not to talk to a lawyer now. If at any time you change your mind, tell me. I will stop asking you questions until you have been able to talk to a lawyer and, if you want, have the lawyer here with you. Do you understand? Answer_____ Time:

If yes: If the young person wants a lawyer present, do not go to section N or begin to take a statement. While you are waiting, you may give the young person the opportunity to exercise the right to contact a parent or other adult (L and M), if this has not yet occurred. If no: You have decided not to have a lawyer here with you. If at any time you change your mind, tell me. I will stop asking you questions until you have a lawyer here with you. Do you understand? Answer_____	While you are waiting, you may give the young person the opportunity to exercise the right to contact a parent or other adult (L and M), if this has not yet occurred.	

Notes:

Note to police: Right to consult parent. Two options Read either column A or column B, as appropriate:

Appendices

L.

If the young person does not want to contact a lawyer or has contacted a lawyer but does not want a lawyer present:	If the young person is waiting to contact a lawyer or waiting for a lawyer to arrive:
☐ You may consult your parent, an adult relative, or another appropriate adult, in private now. You can also ask that person to be here with you. I can help you to reach the person now. Once you do, police will leave. Your conversation is private. Do you understand? Answer_____	☐ While you are waiting for a lawyer, you may consult your parent, an adult relative, or another appropriate adult, in private now. You can also ask that person to be here with you. I can help you to reach the person now. Once you do, police will leave. Your conversation is private. Do you understand? Answer_____

M. Do you want to talk to your parent or another adult in private now?
Answer_____

If yes,	If yes, but	If no:
☐ parent/adult contacted Time: If information known: ☐ person contacted {specify} _____ ☐ relationship to young person _____ Do you want to have your parent or another adult here with you? Answer_____	☐ parent/adult not contacted {give reason} Time: If the young person was unable to reach a parent or other adult, do not go to section N or begin to take a statement until the young person has contacted the parent or other adult.	You have decided not to talk to your parent or another adult now. If at any time you change your mind, tell me. I will stop asking you questions until you have been able to talk to an adult and, if you want, have that person here with you. Do you understand? Answer _____ Time:

If yes: do not go to section N or begin to take a statement until the adult arrives. If no: You have decided not to have an adult here with you. If at any time you change your mind, tell me. I will stop asking you questions until you have that person here with you. Do you understand? Answer _____		

NOTE TO POLICE: STOP

You must stop now and not go on to take a statement:

- ☐ if the young person wants to talk to a lawyer and has not been able to do so
- ☐ if the young person wants to have a lawyer present and the lawyer has not arrived
- ☐ if the young person wants to talk to his/her parent or another adult and has not been able to do so, or
- ☐ if the young person wants to have his/her parent or another adult and the person has not arrived.

If the young person does not want to exercise these rights or has exercised one or more of them but does not want to exercise the others, go on to N.

N. Do you want to make a statement now?

    Answer_____

    If yes: Have waivers signed, as appropriate.
    If no: Stop here

> **Note to police: Waivers**
> The young person must either exercise or clearly waive his/her rights to consult a lawyer; to consult an adult; to have a lawyer present; and to have an adult present.

Waiver of rights

My rights have been explained to me.

_____ [initial] I do not want to talk to a lawyer now. I know I have the right to talk to and get advice from a lawyer now, without the police present.

_____ [initial] I do not want to have a lawyer here with me. I know [*sic*] have the right to have a lawyer here with me.

_____ [initial] I do not want to talk to my parent or another adult now.

I know I have the right to talk to and get advice from my parent, another adult relative or another appropriate adult now without the police present.

_____ [initial] I do not want to have my parent or another adult here with me. I know I have the right to have my parent, another adult relative or another appropriate adult here with me.

[signature of young person]

O. I want to remind you that if you decide to make a statement and say, write or do anything now you can stop at any time. The police will stop asking you questions. You can also, at any time, talk to a lawyer and have a lawyer here with you and talk to a parent or other adult and have that person here with you.

Do you understand? Answer_____

Do you have any questions? Answer_____

> **Note to police: Check waivers**
> If a young person has said that he or she wants to contact a lawyer or to contact an adult or to have a lawyer or adult present and then changes his or her mind, you must go back and ensure the young person has initialed the applicable waiver(s), before you go on.

As I told you at the beginning we are investigating the offence(s) of: *{set out the offence(s)}*

Time:
_____

I am making this statement freely. This is my statement.

I have been given the chance of reviewing my statement.

☐ My statement has been read to me.

☐ I have read my statement over.

☐ I have listened to the audiotape.

☐ I have watched the videotape.

☐ I have _____ [other review of statement].

It is an accurate record of what I told the police.

☐ I do not want to review my statement.

[name and signature of young person]
[name and signature of witness]
[name of other person(s) present]

Time statement concluded

INDEX

References are to sections of the *Youth Criminal Justice Act*.

A

Aboriginal young person
- application of *Criminal Code*, s. 50
- declaration of principle, s. 3
- sentencing, ss. 38, 50

Absolute discharge
- effect of, s. 82
- sentencing option, as, s. 42(2)

Access to records
- adult sentence, s. 117
- application for, s. 123
- application of usual rules, s. 119(9)
- assessment records, s. 119(6)
- authorization required, s. 118
- disclosure for research or statistical purposes, s. 119(8), s. 120(5), s. 123(6)
- DNA analysis, s. 119(6)
- effect of end of access periods, s. 128(1)
- employee exception, s. 118(2)
- exception, s. 119(5)
- extrajudicial measures, s. 119(4)
- introduction of record into evidence, s. 119(7)
- no subsequent disclosure, s. 129
- notice, s. 123(3)
- notice, when not required, s. 123(4)
- period of access, s. 119(2)
- permitted persons, s. 119(1)
- RCMP records, s. 120
- subsequent offences as adult, s. 120(6)
- subsequent offences as young person, s. 120(4)
- time limit, s. 125(8)
- use of record, s. 123(5)
- young person, by, s. 124

Additional youth sentence
- custodial portion, s. 44
- deemed commencement and expiry, s. 43
- supervision when additional to supervision, s. 45(3)
- supervision when custody extended, s. 45(1)
- supervision when custody not extended, s. 45(2)

Adjudication
- guilty plea, s. 36(1)
- not guilty plea, s. 36(2)

Admissions
- condition of extrajudicial measures, as, s. 10(4)
- evidence, of, s. 149

Adult
- defined, s. 2(1)

Adult facility
- placement in, s. 80

Adult sentence
- *see also* **Presumptive offence**
- access to records, s. 117
- appeals, s. 72(5)
- application by Attorney General, s. 64
- application by young person, s. 63
- application of *Criminal Code,* s. 74(1)
- combined with youth sentence, s. 92(4), s. 92(5), s. 184
- conviction under another Act, effect of, s. 79
- defined, s. 2(1)
- election, s. 67
- factors to be considered, s. 72(1)
- finding of guilt becomes conviction, s. 74(2)
- fitness to stand trial, s. 141
- hearing, s. 71
- imposition of, s. 62, s. 73(1)
- included offences, s. 64(3)
- onus, s. 72(2)
- parole board, obligation to inform, s. 77
- placement, s. 76
- pre-sentence reports, s. 72(3)
- reasons, s. 72(4)
- release entitlement, s. 78
- time of commencement, s. 74(3)
- unopposed by young person, s. 64(5)

Age, evidence of, s. 148

Agreements with provinces, s. 156

Alternative measures. *See* **Extrajudicial measures**

Appeals
- adult sentence, s. 72(5)
- contempt of court, s. 37(2), s. 37(3)
- continuation of custody, s. 101
- deemed election, s. 37(7)

Appeals — *cont'd.*
- heard together, s. 37(4)
- jointly-tried offences, s. 37(6)
- no transfer outside province before completion of, s. 57(2)
- Nunavut, s. 37(9)
- placement of adult sentence, s. 76(5)
- publication ban, s. 75(4)
- right to, s. 37(1)
- serious violent offence
- • determination of, s. 42(10)
- summary conviction offences, s. 37(5)
- superior court, s. 37(8)
- Supreme Court of Canada, to, s. 37(10)

Appearance
- compelling, s. 59(6)
- continuation of custody, s. 104(4)
- before judge or justice, s. 32(1)
- not represented by counsel, s. 32(3)
- notice to appear, s. 56(7)
- review, for, s. 94(8)
- waiver, s. 32(2)
- warrant in default of appearance, s. 56(8)

Archivists' records, s. 126

Assessment
- access to records, s. 119(6)
- application to vary, s. 34(6)
- cross-examination, s. 34(8)
- custodial remand
- • presumption against, s. 34(4)
- custody for, s. 34(3)
- disclosure, s. 34(7), s. 34(11)
- hospital order assessments prohibited, s. 141(5)
- inadmissibility of statements, s. 147
- non-disclosure, s. 34(9), s. 34(10)
- part of record, s. 34(12)
- purpose of, s. 34(2)
- qualified person
- • disclosure by, s. 34(13)
- report in writing, s. 34(5)
- youth justice court may require, s. 34(1)

Attendance orders, s. 42(2)

Attorney General
- cautions, s. 8
- consent to private prosecutions, s. 24
- defined, s. 2(1)
- disclosure of information in record, s. 125(2)
- trial by jury, s. 67(6)

B

Bail. *See* **Judicial interim release**

Breach of conditions
- generally, s. 102
- review, s. 103

C

Canada Evidence Act
- consequential amendment of, s. 166

Cautions
- Crown, s. 8
- inadmissibility, s. 9
- police, s. 6, s. 7

Child
- defined, s. 2(1)
- evidence of, s. 151

Child welfare agency
- referral to, s. 35

Clerks of the court, s. 21, s. 165(8)

Coming into force, s. 200

Community-based programs, s. 157

Community service order, s. 42(2), s. 54(9)

Compensation order, s. 42(2)

Conditional discharge, s. 42(2)

Conditional supervision
- conditions of, s. 105
- conditions set at first opportunity, s. 105(6)
- recommendation, s. 96
- report, s. 105(7)
- temporary conditions, s. 105(5)

Conditional supervision suspension
- apprehension after, s. 107
- generally, s. 106
- release or remand into custody, s. 107(5)
- requirement to bring before provincial director, s. 107(4)
- review by provincial director, s. 108
- review by youth justice court, s. 109

Conferences
- convened, s. 19(1)
- defined, s. 2(1)
- generally, s. 41
- mandate, s. 19(2)
- rules, s. 19(3), s. 19(4)

Index

Confirmed delivery service
- defined, s. 2(1)

Consecutive sentences, s. 42(13)

Consent
- physical or mental health treatment, to, s. 42(8)
- prosecute, to, s. 23

Consequential amendments
- *Canada Evidence Act,* s. 166
- *Contraventions Act,* s. 167–s. 170
- *Corrections and Conditional Release Act,* s. 171–s. 174
- *Criminal Code,* s. 175–s. 186
- *DNA Identification Act,* s. 187–s. 189
- *Extradition Act,* s. 190–s. 194
- *Mutual Legal Assistance in Criminal Matters Act,* s. 195
- *Prisons and Reformatories Act,* s. 196, s. 197
- *Transfer of Offenders Act,* s. 198

Contempt
- adults, s. 15
- appeals, s. 37(2), s. 37(3)
- youth justice court, against, s. 15(1)
- youth sentence, s. 15(4)

Continuation
- custody, of, s. 98, s. 99, s. 100, s. 104
- proceedings, of, s. 14(4)

Contraventions Act
- consequential amendments, s. 167–s. 170
- parent's attendance, s. 27(2)
- ticket, notice of, s. 26(3), s. 26(7)

Conviction
- another Act, under, s. 79
- effect of finding of guilt, s. 82(4)

Corrections and Conditional Release Act
- application of, s. 78(2), s. 89(3), s. 92(3), s. 93(3)
- consequential amendments, s. 171–s. 174

Costs
- *Criminal Code* provisions
- • applicability of, s. 142(5)
- recovery of, s. 25(10)

Counsel
- copies to, s. 141(2)
- independent of parents, s. 25(8)
- nonrepresentation by. *See* **Non-representation by counsel**
- notice to, s. 141(2)
- right to. *See* **Right to counsel**

Counts charged in information, s. 143

Court of appeal
- interim release, s. 33(9)
- superior court as youth justice court, s. 37(8)

Court of record, s. 13(4)

Criminal Code
- application of, s. 140
- combination of adult and youth sentences, s. 184
- consecutive sentencing provisions
- • amendment of, s. 182
- copies to counsel and parents, s. 141(2)
- costs provisions, s. 142(5)
- dangerous and long-term offender provisions
- • application of, s. 74(1)
- DNA identification provisions
- • amendment of, s. 176–s. 180
- firearm prohibition orders, s. 51(7), s. 51(8)
- hospital order assessments prohibited, s. 141(5)
- limitation period, s. 142(4)
- mental disorder provisions
- • application of, s. 141
- notice to counsel and parents, s. 141(2)
- probation officer report provisions
- • amendment of, s. 183
- proof of previous convictions
- • amendment of, s. 181
- recognizance provisions
- • nonapplicability of, s. 135(6)
- sections applicable, s. 141(2)
- sentencing provisions
- • application of, s. 50, s. 74(1)
- summary conviction provisions
- • application of, s. 142
- words and expressions in, s. 2(2)
- writ provisions
- • application of, s. 135(7)

Cross-examination
- assessment, s. 34(8)
- pre-sentence report, s. 40(6)

Crown. *See* **Attorney General**

Custodial portion
- defined, s. 2(1)
- if additional youth sentence, s. 44
- maximum total, s. 46

Custodial remand
- presumption against, s. 34(4)

Custody
- alternatives to, s. 39(2)
- application for detention in custody, s. 33
- assessment, for, s. 34(3)
- committal deemed continuous, s. 47(1)
- committal to, s. 39
- continuation of, s. 98
- effect of sentencing order, s. 56(6)
- factors to be considered, s. 39(3)
- intermittent, s. 47(2), s. 47(3)
- length of, s. 39(8)
- levels of, s. 85(1)
- place of, designation, s. 165(6)
- pre-sentence report
- • requirement of, s. 39(6)
- reasons for, s. 39(9)
- social measure, as
- • prohibited, s. 39(5)
- transfer, during, s. 49(2)
- warrant of committal, s. 49(1)

Custody and supervision order, s. 42(2), s. 42(4), s. 97, s. 109(3)

Custody and supervision system
- annual review, s. 94
- breach of conditions, s. 102, s. 103
- conditional supervision. *See* **Conditional supervision**
- conditions, s. 97
- continuation of custody, s. 98, s. 99, s. 100, s. 104
- due process safeguards, s. 86
- factors, s. 85(5)
- functions exercised by youth justice court, s. 88
- levels of custody, s. 85(1)
- optional review, s. 94(3), s. 94(4)
- placement separate from adults, s. 84
- principles, s. 83(2)
- purpose, s. 83(1)
- reintegration leave, s. 91
- youth custody facility
- • designation of, s. 85(2)
- youth worker, s. 90

D

Declaration of principle. *See* **Principles**

Deferred custody and supervision order, s. 42(2), s. 42(5), s. 42(6)

Definitions, s. 2

Descriptive cross-references, s. 2(3)

Destroy
- defined, s. 128(7)

Detention
- application for detention in custody, s. 33
- authorization of provincial authority, s. 30(8)
- presumed unnecessary, s. 29(2)
- separate from adults, s. 30(3)
- social measure, as
- • prohibited, s. 29(1)
- temporary, s. 165(6)
- • *see also* **Judicial interim release**
- transfer by provincial director, s. 30(6)
- transfer to adult facility, s. 30(4)

Disclosure
- assessment, s. 34(9), s. 34(10), s. 34(11)
- assessment, of, s. 34(7)
- copies of record, of, s. 122
- court order, with, s. 127
- defined, s. 2(1)
- foreign state, to, s. 125(3)
- information, of, s. 122
- information in record, s. 125
- information to be kept separate, s. 125(7)
- insurance company, to, s. 125(4)
- no subsequent disclosure, s. 129
- pre-sentence report, s. 40(7), s. 40(8), s. 40(9)
- qualified person, by, s. 34(13)
- research or statistical purposes, for, s. 119(8), s. 120(5), s. 123(6)
- schools, to, s. 125(6)
- time limit, s. 125(8)

Disqualification of judge, s. 130

DNA analysis,
- access to, s. 119(6)

DNA Identification Act, s. 176–s. 180, s. 187–s. 189

Due process safeguards, s. 86

E

Election
- adult sentence, s. 67
- mode of trial where co-accused are young persons, s. 67(5)
- Nunavut, s. 67(3)
- summary conviction, deemed, s. 121

Index

Employment applications, s. 82(3)

Evidence
- admissibility of statements, s. 146
- admissions, s. 149
- admissions as condition of extrajudicial measures, s. 10(4)
- age, of, s. 148
- child or young person, of, s. 151
- extrajudicial measures, s. 9
- material evidence, s. 150
- parent
- • testimony of, s. 148(1)
- record
- • introduction of, s. 119(7)
- transcript of evidence already given, s. 131(2)

Exclusion from hearing, s. 132

Extradition Act
- consequential amendments to, s. 190–s. 194

Extrajudicial measures
- access to records, s. 119(4)
- accountability, s. 4
- admissions as condition, s. 10(4)
- alternative measures continued, s. 165(5)
- cautions, s. 6–s. 8
- continuation of, s. 14(4)
- defined, s. 2(1)
- inadmissibility as evidence, s. 9
- key factors, s. 4
- limitation periods, s. 14(3)
- objectives, s. 5
- principles, s. 4
- referrals, s. 6
- warnings, s. 6

Extrajudicial sanction
- admissions not admissible in evidence, s. 10(4)
- application at pre-charge or post-charge stage, s. 10
- conditions, s. 10(2)
- defined, s. 2(1)
- lay of information, s. 10(6)
- no bar to judicial proceedings, s. 10(5)
- notice to parent, s. 11
- option, as, s. 10
- restriction on use, s. 10(3)
- victim's right to information, s. 12

F

Failure to comply with sentence or disposition, s. 137

Family
- participation of, s. 5

Fines
- conditions, s. 54(7)
- consent of person to be compensated, s. 54(6)
- crediting, s. 54(3)
- discharge of, s. 54(2)
- funding for victims, s. 53(1)
- means to pay, s. 54(1)
- representations, s. 54(4)
- sentencing option, as, s. 42(2)

Fingerprints, s. 113

Firearm prohibition orders, s. 51(7), s. 51(8)

First-degree murder
- election, s. 66
- sentence, s. 42(2)

Fitness to stand trial, s. 141

Foreign state
- disclosure to, s. 125(3)

Forfeiture of recognizance. *See* **Recognizance**

Forms, s. 154

G

Government records, s. 116(1)

Guilty finding not previous conviction, s. 82(4)

Guilty pleas, s. 36(1)

H

Harm
- acknowledgement of harm done, s. 5
- repairing harm, s. 5

Hearing
- exclusion from, s. 132

Hospital order assessments prohibited, s. 141(5)

Index

I

Identification of Criminals Act
- application of, s. 113

Included offences, s. 69

Indictable offences, s. 142(2)

Inducing young person re compliance with sentence or disposition, s. 136(1)

Information
- counts charged in, s. 143
- proceedings commence with, s. 162

Insurance company
- disclosure to, s. 125(4)

Intensive rehabilitative custody and supervision orders, s. 42(2), s. 42(7)

Intensive support and supervision (ISSP), s. 42(2)

Intermittent custody, s. 47(2), s. 47(3)

Interpretation, s. 2

Interprovincial arrangements, s. 58

J

Jointly-tried offences, s. 37(6)

Judge. *See* **Youth justice court judge**

Judgment debtors of Crown, s. 135(3)

Judicial interim release
- application for, s. 33
- application of *Criminal Code,* s. 28
- authorization of provincial authority, s. 30(8)
- court of appeal, s. 33(9)
- designated place of temporary detention, s. 30
- detention as social measure
- • prohibited, s. 29(1)
- detention presumed unnecessary, s. 29(2)
- detention separate from adults, s. 49(3)
- determination of place of detention, s. 30(9)
- exception, s. 30(7)
- notice to prosecutor, s. 33(2)
- Nunavut, s. 33(6)
- persons 20 years or older, s. 30(5)
- placement in responsible person's care, s. 31
- review application, s. 33(5)
- transfer by provincial director, s. 30(6)
- transfer to adult facility, s. 30(4)
- youth justice court judge only, by, s. 33(8)

Judicial measures
- consent to prosecute, s. 23
- private prosecutions, s. 24
- right to counsel, s. 25

Judicial proceedings
- continuation of, s. 14(4)
- limitation periods, s. 14(3)

Jurisdiction
- concurrent, s. 15(3)
- inducing to unlawfully leave custody, s. 136(2)
- records-related offences, s. 138(2)
- transfer of charges, s. 133
- waiver of, s. 58(3)
- youth justice court, s. 15(2)

Justices of the peace
- orders, s. 20(2)
- proceedings before, s. 20(1)

Juvenile Delinquents Act
- proceedings commenced under, s. 159(2)
- prohibition on proceedings, s. 158
- records, s. 163

L

Liberal construction, s. 3(2)

Librarian and Archivist of Canada, s. 126, s. 128(6)

Limitation periods
- *Criminal Code* provision
- • applicability of, s. 142(4)
- prosecution prohibited, s. 14(3)

M

Mandatory prohibition orders, s. 51(1)

Material evidence, s. 150

Medical assessment. *See* **Assessment**

Index

Mental disorder provisions of *Criminal Code*, s. 141

Misrepresentation of age, s. 146(8)

Mode of trial where co-accused are young persons, s. 67(5)

Mutual Legal Assistance in Criminal Matters Act
- consequential amendments to, s. 195

N

Newfoundland, s. 172

Non-custodial sentences
- alternatives to custody, s. 39(2)
- factors to be considered, s. 39(3)
- imposition of same sentence, s. 39(4)
- progress report, s. 59(3)
- review, s. 59, s. 60

Non-representation by counsel
- assistance of adult, s. 25(7)
- direction by court, s. 32(4), s. 32(5)
- pleas and, s. 32(3)
- understanding of charge, s. 32(4), s. 32(5)

Not guilty pleas, s. 36(2)

Notice
- access to records, s. 123(3)
- appear, to, s. 56(7)
- contents of, s. 26(6)
- continuation of custody, s. 99(4), s. 99(6)
- direction of youth justice court judge, on, s. 26(5)
- failure to give notice, s. 26(9), s. 26(10), s. 141(3), s. 141(4)
- intention to establish serious violent offence, s. 64(4)
- nonservice of, s. 26(11)
- parent, to. *See* **Notice to parents**
- proof of
  - serious violent offence, in, s. 68(1)
- prosecutor, to, s. 33(2)
- relative or other adult, to, s. 26(4)
- restitution order, of, s. 54(5)
- review, of, s. 94(13), s. 94(14)
- review of placement of adult sentence, s. 76(8)
- service, s. 94(16)
- specification of custody level, s. 85(7)
- waiver, s. 33(4), s. 94(17)

Notice to parents
- arrest or detention, s. 26(1)
- contents of, s. 26(6)
- *Criminal Code* mental disorder provisions, s. 141(2)
- extrajudicial sanction, of, s. 11
- failure to give notice, s. 26(9), s. 26(10)
- nonservice of, s. 26(11)
- other cases, in, s. 26(2)
- persons over 20 years of age, s. 26(12)
- service, s. 26(8)
- ticket under *Contraventions Act*, s. 26(3), s. 26(7)

Nunavut
- appeals, s. 37(9)
- application for release from or detention in custody, s. 33(6)
- election re adult sentence, s. 67(3)

O

Objectives
- declaration, s. 3(1)
- extrajudicial measures, s. 5

Offences
- committed before Act coming into force, s. 160
- defined, s. 2(1)
- failure to comply with sentence or disposition, s. 137
- inducing young person re compliance with sentence or disposition, s. 136(1)
- records-related, s. 138
- responsible person
  - violation of undertaking, s. 139

Oral statements, s. 146(3)

Orders
- attendance, s. 42(2)
- community service, s. 42(2)
- compensation, s. 42(2)
- custody and supervision, s. 42(2), s. 42(4)
- deemed youth sentences, s. 95
- deferred custody and supervision, s. 42(2), s. 42(5), s. 42(6)
- forfeiture of recognizance, for, s. 135(2)
- intensive rehabilitative custody and supervision, s. 42(2), s. 42(7)
- intensive support and supervision (ISSP), s. 42(2)
- jurisdiction of youth justice court, s. 14(2)
- justices of the peace, s. 20(2)
- parent's attendance, s. 27
- personal service, s. 42(2)

Index

Orders — *cont'd.*
- probation, s. 42(2)
- prohibition, s. 42(2)
- restitution, s. 42(2)
- sentencing. *See* **Sentencing order**

Over 20 years of age. *See* **Young person aged 20 or older**

P

Palmprints, s. 113

Parent
- copies to, s. 141(2)
- counsel independent of, s. 25(8)
- defined, s. 2(1)
- failure to attend, s. 27(4)
- not person in authority, s. 146(9)
- notice to. *See* **Notice to parents**
- order requiring attendance, s. 27
- participation of, s. 5
- sentencing order
- • copy of, s. 56(2)
- testimony of, s. 148(1)
- warrant to arrest, s. 27(5)

Parole board
- obligation to inform, s. 77

Peace Officer. *See* **Police**

Personal service order
- duration, s. 54(8)
- sentencing option, as, s. 42(2)

Persons in authority, s. 146(9)

Photographs, s. 113

Placement
- adult facility, in, s. 80
- adult sentence, s. 76
- age limit, s. 76(9)
- conviction under another Act, s. 79
- responsible person's care, s. 31
- separate from adults, s. 84
- when adult and youth sentences, s. 92(4)
- young person aged 20 or older, s. 89

Pleas
- guilty, s. 36(1)
- non-representation by counsel, and, s. 32(3)
- not guilty, s. 36(2)

Police
- arrest without warrant, s. 107(3)
- cautions, s. 6, s. 7
- disclosure of information in record, s. 125(1)
- option to warn, caution or refer, s. 6
- records, s. 115
- right to counsel
- • • need to advise of, s. 25(2)

Police caution program, s. 7

Pre-charge screening, s. 23(1)

Pre-charge screening program, s. 23(2)

Pre-sentence report
- adult sentence, s. 72(3)
- contents of, s. 40(2)
- copies of, s. 40(5)
- cross-examination, s. 40(6)
- defined, s. 2(1)
- disclosure, s. 40(7), s. 40(8), s. 40(9)
- dispensing with, s. 39(7)
- generally, s. 40(1)
- inadmissibility of statements, s. 40(10)
- oral report with leave, s. 40(3)
- part of record, s. 40(4)
- requirement of, s. 39(6)
- withholding from private prosecutor, s. 40(7)

Preliminary inquiry, s. 67(7), s. 67(8)

Presumptive offence
- *see also* **Adult sentence**
- age for purpose of, s. 61
- application by Attorney General, s. 64
- application by young person, s. 63
- custody and supervision order, s. 42(2)
- defined, s. 2(1)
- fitness to stand trial, s. 141
- included offences, s. 69
- publication ban, s. 75
- when not applicable, s. 65

Principles
- custody and supervision system, s. 83(2)
- declaration of, s. 3
- extrajudicial measures, s. 4
- sentencing, s. 38(2)

Prisons and Reformatories Act
- application of, s. 78(1), s. 89(3), s. 92(3), s. 93(3)
- consequential amendments, s. 196, s. 197

Index

Privacy protection
- application for leave to publish, s. 110(5)
- *ex parte* application for leave to publish, s. 110(4)
- exception, s. 110(3)
- limitation, s. 110(2)
- non-application, s. 112
- offender identity not to be published, s. 110(1)
- victim or witness identity not to be published, s. 111

Private prosecutions
- consent required, s. 24
- pre-sentence report
- • withholding of, s. 40(7)

Probation orders
- firearm prohibition orders
- • application of, s. 51(7)
- review of, s. 52
- sentencing option, as, s. 42(2)

Procedure
- counts charged in information, s. 143
- subpoenas, s. 144
- warrant
- • execution of, s. 145

Progress report, s. 59(3), s. 94(9), s. 94(10), s. 94(11), s. 94(12)

Prohibition orders
- discretionary, s. 51(3)
- duration, s. 51(2), s. 51(4)
- mandatory, s. 51(1)
- period of access
- • determination of, s. 119(3)
- reasons for, s. 51(5)
- records resulting in, s. 119(10)
- sentencing option, as, s. 42(2)

Proportionality
- principle of, s. 3(1)

Prosecutions
- consent to prosecute, s. 23
- private. *See* **Private prosecutions**

Provincial authority
- authorization of detention, s. 30(8)
- determination of place of detention, s. 30(9)

Provincial correctional facility, s. 89, s. 92(2), s. 93

Provincial director
- agreement as to sentence, s. 42(3)
- conditional supervision recommendation, s. 96
- defined, s. 2(1)
- designation of, s. 165(3)
- disclosure of pre-sentence report, s. 40(9)
- duties, s. 22
- functions, s. 22
- parole board
- • obligation to inform, s. 77
- powers, s. 22
- review after suspension of conditional supervision, s. 108
- specification of custody level, s. 85(3), s. 85(4)
- transfer by, s. 30(6)
- withholding of information, s. 86(2)

Psychological assessment. *See* **Assessment**

Publication
- application for leave to publish, s. 110(5), s. 111(3)
- ban, s. 75
- defined, s. 2(1)
- *ex parte* application for leave to publish, s. 110(4)
- prohibition on, s. 110, s. 111

Punishment
- employment application, s. 139(3)
- inducing young person re compliance with sentence or disposition, s. 136
- responsible person
- • violation of undertaking, s. 139

Q

Qualified person
- defined, s. 34(14)
- disclosure by, s. 34(13)

R

Reasons
- adult sentence, s. 72(4)
- custody, s. 39(9)
- prohibition orders, s. 51(5), s. 51(6)
- youth sentence, s. 48

Recognizance
- *Criminal Code* provisions applicable, s. 135(7)
- *Criminal Code* provisions not applicable, s. 135(6)

Recognizance — *cont'd.*
- deposit made, s. 135(5)
- filing of order, s. 135(4)
- forfeiture of, s. 134
- judgment debtors of Crown, s. 135(3)
- justices of the peace
  - orders of, s. 20(2)
- order for forfeiture of recognizance, s. 135(2)
- proceedings in case of default, s. 135

Records
- access to. *See* **Access to records**
- assessment as part of record, s. 34(12)
- custody of archivists, in, s. 126
- defined, s. 2(1)
- destroy
  - defined, s. 128(7)
- disclosure of copies, s. 122
- disclosure of information in, s. 125
- disclosure with court order, s. 127
- disposal of, s. 128(2)
- effect of end of access periods, s. 128(1)
- government, s. 116(1)
- kept by youth justice court
  - review board and other courts, s. 114
- other records, s. 116(2)
- police, s. 115
- pre-sentence report as part of, s. 40(4)
- previous acts, under, s. 163
- RCMP, of, s. 115(3), s. 120, s. 124(5), s. 128(3), s. 128(4)
- related offences, s. 138
- resulting in prohibition orders, s. 119(10)

Referrals
- child welfare agency, to, s. 35
- generally, s. 6

Regulations, s. 155

Rehabilitation
- principle of, s. 3(1)

Reintegration
- leave, s. 91
- principle of, s. 3(1)

Release hearing, s. 25(6)
- *see also* **Judicial interim release**

Repeat offenders
- sentencing, s. 38

Reports
- conditional supervision, s. 105(7)
- conditional supervision suspension, s. 109(6)
- continuation of custody, s. 98
- disclosure of information in record, s. 125(5)
- medical or physical assessment. *See* **Assessment**
- pre-sentence. *See* **Pre-sentence report**
- preparation of, s. 125(5)
- progress. *See* **Progress report**

Reprimand, s. 42(2)

Responsible person
- condition of placement, s. 31(3)
- inquiry as to availability, s. 31(2)
- placement in care of, s. 31(1)
- removal from care, s. 31(4), s. 31(5), s. 31(6)
- violation of undertaking, s. 139

Restitution order
- conditions, s. 54(7)
- consent of person to be compensated, s. 54(6)
- means to pay, s. 54(1)
- notice of order, s. 54(5)
- representations representing orders, s. 54(4)
- sentencing option, as, s. 42(2)

Restitution to purchaser of property, s. 42(2)

Review
- annual review of custody, s. 94
- application for, s. 87(1)
- breach of conditions, s. 103
- conditional supervision suspension, s. 109
- exclusion during, s. 132(3)
- factors, s. 87(4)
- final decision, s. 87(5)
- if appeal pending, s. 94(7)
- non-custodial sentences, s. 59, s. 60
- notice of, s. 94(13), s. 94(14)
- optional review of custody, s. 94(3), s. 94(4)
- order of appearance, s. 94(8)
- orders deemed youth sentences, s. 95
- placement of adult sentence, s. 76(6)
- probation order, s. 52
- procedural safeguards, s. 87(2)
- progress report, s. 59(3), s. 94(9), s. 94(10), s. 94(11), s. 94(12)
- sentence, of, s. 59, s. 60, s. 94, s. 161(3)
- where notice not given, s. 94(18)
- youth sentence, s. 94

Review board
- defined, s. 2(1), s. 141(12)
- designation of, s. 165(4)
- permitted records, s. 114

Index

Review board — *cont'd*
- right to counsel
- • need to advise of, s. 25(3)
- withholding of information, s. 87(3)

Right to counsel
- appointment of counsel, s. 25(5)
- arresting officer to advise of, s. 25(2)
- assistance of adult, s. 25(7)
- costs
- • recovery of, s. 25(10)
- counsel independent of parents, s. 25(8)
- described, s. 25
- justice to advice of right, s. 25(3)
- persons over 20 years of age, s. 25(11)
- release hearing, s. 25(6)
- review board to advise of right, s. 25(3)
- statement of right, s. 25(9), s. 94(15), s. 99(5)
- trial, hearing or review, at, s. 25(4)
- youth justice court to advise of right, s. 25(3)

Royal Canadian Mounted Police
- records of, s. 115(3), s. 120, s. 124(5), s. 128(3), s. 128(4)

Rules of court, s. 17

S

Schools
- disclosure to, s. 125(6)

Seal not required, s. 153

Second-degree murder
- election, s. 66
- sentence, s. 42(2)

Sentencing
- *see also* **Custody**; **Youth sentence**
- adult sentences. *See* **Adult sentence**
- alternatives to custody, s. 39(2)
- application of *Criminal Code,* s. 50
- committal to custody, s. 39
- conferences' recommendations, s. 41
- considerations, s. 42(1)
- custodial sentences, s. 39
- custody as social measure
- • prohibited, s. 39(5)
- factors to be considered, s. 38(3), s. 39(3)
- first-degree murder, s. 42(2)
- imposition of same sentence, s. 39(4)
- maximum duration of custodial portion, s. 46
- principles, s. 38(2)
- purpose, s. 38(1)
- repeat offenders, s. 38
- second-degree murder, s. 42(2)

Sentencing order
- commencement, s. 56(5)
- communication of order, s. 56
- effect
- • case of custody, in, s. 56(6)
- endorsement by young person, s. 56(3)
- notice to appear, s. 56(7)
- required conditions, s. 55
- validity, s. 56(4)
- warrant in default of appearance, s. 56(8)
- where payment required, s. 54

Serious violent offence
- appeal of determination, s. 42(10)
- defined, s. 2(1)
- determination of, s. 42(9), s. 68(2), s. 68(4), s. 68(5)
- inquiry by court, s. 68(3)
- inquiry by court to young person, s. 70
- notice of intention to establish, s. 64(4)
- proof, s. 68(3)
- proof of notice, s. 68(1)

Service
- nonservice
- • effect of, s. 26(11)
- notice of application for continuation of custody, s. 99(6)
- notice of review, s. 94(16)
- notice to parents, s. 26(8)
- order requiring parent's attendance, s. 27(3)
- proof of, s. 152
- subpoenas, s. 144(2)

Short title, s. 1

Statements
- admissibility of, s. 146
- duress, under, s. 146(7)
- inadmissible, s. 147
- misrepresentation of age, s. 146(8)
- oral, s. 146(3)
- parent not person in authority, s. 146(9)
- pre-sentence reports, s. 40(10)
- right to counsel, of, s. 25(9), s. 94(15), s. 99(5)
- technical irregularities, s. 146(6)
- waiver of right to consult, s. 146(4), s. 146(5)
- youth justice court
- • custody and supervision order, in, s. 42(4)

Subpoenas, s. 144

Substitution of judge, s. 131

Index

Summary conviction offences
- appeals, s. 37(5)
- *Criminal Code* provisions
- • application of, s. 142
- deemed election, s. 121
- • appeal, on, s. 37(7)

Superior court judge
- appeals from, s. 37(8)
- powers of, s. 14(7)

Supreme Court of Canada
- appeals to, s. 37(10)

T

Ticket under *Contraventions Act*, s. 26(3), s. 26(7), s. 27(2)

Timeliness, s. 5

Transfer hearings. *See* **Adult sentence; Presumptive offence**

Transfer of charges, s. 133

Transfer of Offenders Act
- consequential amendments to, s. 198

Transfer to adult facility, s. 30(4), s. 92(1)

Transitional provisions
- agreements continue in force, s. 164
- alternative measures continued, s. 165(5)
- applicable sentence, s. 161
- clerks of the court
- • designation of, s. 165(8)
- offences committed before Act coming into force, s. 160
- place of custody
- • designation of, s. 165(6)
- proceedings commence with information, s. 162
- proceedings under previous Acts, s. 159
- prohibition on proceedings, s. 158
- provincial director
- • designation of, s. 165(3)
- records under previous acts, s. 163
- review board
- • designation of, s. 165(4)
- temporary detention
- • designation of, s. 165(6)
- youth justice committee
- • designation of, s. 165(4)
- youth justice court
- • designation of, s. 165(1)
- youth justice court judge

- • designation of, s. 165(2)
- youth worker
- • designation of, s. 165(3)

U

Uncertain status, s. 16

V

Victim fine surcharge, s. 53(2), s. 54(2)

Victims
- extrajudicial sanction, and, s. 12
- funding for, s. 53(1)
- participation, s. 5
- publication prohibition, s. 111
- right to information, s. 12

W

Waiver of right to consult, s. 146(4), s. 146(5)

Warnings, s. 6

Warrant
- committal, of, s. 49(1)
- default of appearance, in, s. 56(8)
- execution of, s. 145
- suspension of conditional supervision, s. 107(2)

Y

Young Offenders Act
- agreements continue in force, s. 164
- designations, s. 165
- dispositions under, s. 161
- proceedings commenced under, s. 159(1)
- prohibition on proceedings, s. 158
- records, s. 163
- repeal, s. 199
- review of sentence, s. 161(3)

Young person
- access to record, s. 124
- defined, s. 2(1)
- evidence of, s. 151
- notice of application for detention in custody, s. 33(2)
- over 18 years of age, s. 14(5)
- respect for rights of, s. 5
- status uncertain, s. 16
- understanding of charge, s. 32(4), s. 32(5)

Index

Young person aged 20 or older
- judicial interim release, s. 30(5)
- notice to parents, s. 26(12)
- placement, s. 89
- provincial correctional facility, s. 93
- right to counsel, s. 25(11)

Youth criminal justice system, s. 13–s. 17

Youth custody facility
- defined, s. 2(1)
- designation of, s. 85(2)
- limit on age, s. 76(9)

Youth justice committee, s. 18, s. 165(4)

Youth justice court
- concurrent jurisdiction, s. 15(3)
- contempt against, s. 15(1)
- court of record, s. 13(4)
- custody and supervision order, s. 42(4)
- deemed, s. 13(2), s. 13(3)
- defined, s. 2(1)
- designation, s. 13(1), s. 165(1)
- direction for representation by counsel, s. 32(5)
- exclusive jurisdiction, s. 14(1)
- functions exercised by, s. 88
- interprovincial arrangements, s. 58
- jurisdiction, s. 15(2)
- orders, s. 14(2)
- permitted records, s. 114
- right to counsel, need to advise of, s. 25(3)
- rules of court, s. 17
- uncertain status of offender, s. 16

Youth justice court judge
- defined, s. 2(1)
- designation of, s. 165(2)
- direction as to notice, s. 26(5)
- disqualification of, s. 130
- interim release by, s. 33(8)
- powers of, s. 14(6)

- substitution of, s. 131
- superior court judge
  - powers of, s. 14(7)

Youth sentence
- *see also* **Sentencing**; **Sentencing order**
- additional, s. 43–s. 45
- agreement of provincial director, s. 42(3)
- application for further time for completion, s. 54(10)
- combined with adult sentence, s. 92(4), s. 92(5), s. 184
- coming into force, s. 42(12)
- consecutive, s. 42(13)
- consent to physical or mental health treatment, s. 42(8)
- considerations, s. 42(1)
- continuation when adult, s. 42(17)
- defined, s. 2(1)
- duration for different offences, s. 42(15)
- duration for single offence, s. 42(14)
- duration when made at different times, s. 42(16)
- effect of termination, s. 82
- exception when in respect of earlier offence, s. 46
- imposition of, s. 73(2)
- inconsistency, s. 42(11)
- interprovincial arrangements, s. 58
- no appeal when on review, s. 37(11)
- no election, s. 66
- orders deemed youth sentences, s. 95
- provincial correctional facility, in, s. 89
- range of options, s. 42(2)
- reasons for, s. 48
- review, s. 94
- where custody not involved, s. 59, s. 60
- serious violent offence
  - determination of, s. 42(9)
- transfer of, s. 57

Youth worker
- defined, s. 2(1)
- designation, s. 90(1), s. 165(3)
- role of, s. 90(1)